ENTERTAINMENT-EDUCATION

A Communication Strategy
for Social Change

ॐ ✦✦ ॐ

ENTERTAINMENT-EDUCATION

A Communication Strategy for Social Change

ও ✦ ✦ ঙ

Arvind Singhal
Ohio University

Everett M. Rogers
University of New Mexico

LEA LAWRENCE ERLBAUM ASSOCIATES, PUBLISHERS
1999   Mahwah, New Jersey   London

Lawrence Erlbaum Associates, Inc., Publishers
10 Industrial Avenue
Mahwah, New Jersey 07430-2262

Cover design by Kathryn Houghtaling Lacey

Library of Congress Cataloging-in-Publication Data

Singhal, Arvind, 1962–
    Entertainment-education : a communication strategy for
social change / by Arvind Singhal and Everett M. Rogers.
        p. cm.
    Includes bibliographical references and index.
    ISBN 0-8058-3235-1 (cloth : alk. paper). — ISBN
0-8058-3350-1 (pbk. : alk. paper)
    1. Soap operas—Social aspects—Developing countries.
2. Television in education—Developing countries. I. Rogers, Everett M. II. Title.
PN1992.8.S4S49 1999
302.23'45'091724—dc21   99-17956
                                                                      CIP

Books published by Lawrence Erlbaum Associates are printed
on acid-free paper, and their bindings are chosen for strength
and durability

Printed in the United States of America
10 9 8 7 6 5 4

*This book is dedicated to the pioneering spirit of
Miguel Sabido, Elaine Perkins, Garth Japhet,
David Poindexter, and Phyllis Piotrow—innovators
who believed in the potential
of the entertainment–education strategy
and made it happen.*

Contents

Preface

Ev Rogers first heard of an unintended use of the entertainment-education strategy in 1975 when a Mexican television official doing graduate work at Stanford University told him about *Simplemente María,* a 1969 Peruvian television soap opera. In this Cinderella story, María, a household domestic employee, becomes rich and famous through her proficiency with a Singer sewing machine. This *telenovela* (television novel) was extremely popular in Peru and throughout Latin America when it was broadcast in other Spanish-speaking nations. The resulting rapid increase in the sales of Singer sewing machines was totally unexpected. Viewers of *Simplemente María* identified with María as a role model for their behavior. They also enrolled in sewing classes and in adult literacy classes, as María had done in the television series.

Such were the early beginnings, 30 years ago, of the entertainment-education strategy in television soap operas, which was then formulated by Miguel Sabido of Mexico's television network as a formal, reproducible set of design and production techniques for the construction of persuasive messages. This promising technology consequently spread to India in 1984 (with the broadcast of the television soap opera, *Hum Log*), to Kenya in 1988 and Tanzania in 1993, and back to India in 1996 (when the radio soap opera *Tinka Tinka Sukh* was broadcast). This international diffusion was facilitated by the efforts of David Poindexter, then president of Population Communications International (PCI), in New York, with considerable assistance from Miguel Sabido. Dr. Phyllis T. Piotrow and her staff in Population Communication Services at Johns Hopkins University adapted Sabido's strategy in family planning communication messages, ranging from popular songs in Mexico, the Philippines, and Nigeria, to radio and television soap operas in Nigeria, Turkey, The Gambia, Pakistan, and other nations. To date, the entertainment-education strategy has spread to projects in 75 countries, utilized in the United States, Europe, and, especially, in the developing nations of Latin America, Africa, and Asia. Entertainment-education has promoted family planning, adult literacy, HIV/AIDS prevention, sexual abstinence for adolescents, gender equality, preservation of the environment, and responsible parenthood.

Entertainment-education is the process of purposely designing and implementing a media message to both entertain and educate, in order to increase audience knowledge about an educational issue, create favorable attitudes, and change overt behavior. This strategy uses the universal appeal of entertainment to show individuals how they can live safer, healthier, and happier lives. The idea of combining entertainment with education is not new. For thousands of years, entertainment media traditions in music, drama, and print have been utilized for education, information, and instruction. However, the conscious use of the entertainment-education strategy in mass communication (especially in television, radio, and film) is a recent phenomenon. Entertainment formats such as soap operas, rock music, feature films, talk shows, cartoons, comics, and theater are used in various countries to promote messages about educational issues.

The entertainment-education strategy questions the needless dichotomy that is made in almost all mass media content: that mass media programs must either be entertaining or educational. Often the profit motive of the commercial media undermines their educational potential. For example, in order to gain higher ratings, commercial television usually broadcasts sensational programs containing sex and violence. Such programs may have harmful effects, such as encouraging children's aggressive behavior. At best they serve little positive function in society. Audiences infer meanings from every program, such as what it is like to witness a murder or to hear a New York accent. The entertainment-education strategy has the potential to create a situation in which the educator's goals and those of the commercial media institutions can both be realized in a win–win situation.

The general purpose of entertainment-education programs is to contribute to *social change*, defined as the process in which an alteration occurs in the structure and function of a social system (Singhal & Rogers, 1994). Social change can happen at the level of the individual, community, an organization, or a society. Entertainment-education by itself sometimes brings about social change. And, under certain conditions (in combination with other influences), entertainment-education creates a climate for social change. The entertainment-education strategy is not free of problems. Here we present a balanced picture of the entertainment-education strategy, identifying ethical and other problems that accompany efforts to bring about social change.

We thank the many individuals who helped us write this book and who supported our research projects on the effects of entertainment-education, including the Rockefeller Foundation, David and Lucile Packard Foundation, Ford Foundation, Lang Charitable Trust, Weyerhaeuser Family Foundation, and the United Nations Population Fund (UNFPA). We acknowledge Dr. William J. Brown, professor and dean of the College of Communication and the Arts at Regent University, who read the book, and who has collaborated with us since the *Hum Log* project in India in the mid-1980s. Dr. Thomas W. Valente, associate professor in the Johns Hopkins University School of Hygiene and Public Health, an important scholar of entertainment-education, also read the manuscript, as did Dr. Srinivas Melkote, associate dean of the Graduate School and Professor of Telecommunications at Bowling Green State University.

We also thank Dr. Peter Vaughan of the Department of Communication and Journalism at the University of New Mexico, a colleague in our Tanzania and India projects, who also commented extensively on the manuscript; David Poindexter, former president, and Bill Ryerson, former executive vice president, Population Communications International, New York; Miguel and Irene Sabido, the creators of the Mexican entertainment-education *telenovelas*; Manohar Shyam Joshi, the scriptwriter of *Hum Log*; Usha Bhasin, former director of programmes, All India Radio and executive producer and director of the radio soap opera *Tinka Tinka Sukh*; Dr. N. Bhaskara Rao, chairman of the Centre for Media Studies, New Delhi, and his staff, especially P.N. Vasanti and Mumtaz Ahmed, who collaborated with us in evaluating the effects of *Tinka Tinka Sukh* in India; Ramadhan M.A. Swalehe, Verhan Bakari, and the staff at Population Family Life Education Programme (POFLEP), who collaborated with us in evaluating *Twende na Wakati* in Tanzania; Dr. Phyllis T. Piotrow, Patrick L. Coleman, and the staff of Population Communication Services, Center for Communication Programs, Johns Hopkins University, Baltimore; Professor Nora Mazziotti, a leading scholar of *telenovelas* in Argentina and Dr. Martine Bouman, a noted European scholar of entertainment-education at the Wageningen Agricultural University and founder of the Netherlands Entertainment-Education Foundation; our colleagues Dr. Shaheed Mohammed, Suruchi Sood (now at Johns Hopkins University), Dr. Peer J. Svenkerud (now with Burson-Marsteller, Norway), Krista Alford, and Corinne Shefner-Rogers at the University of New Mexico and Dr. Vibert C. Cambridge, Dr. Nagesh Rao, Dr. Michael J. Papa, Sweety Law, Li Ren, Jianying Zhang, Saumya Pant, and Krishna Kandath at Ohio University, who collaborated with us on various research projects on entertainment-education in Tanzania, India, and China. We especially thank Peggy Sattler and Lars Lutton at Ohio University for preparing the artwork and photos, and to Mahendra, Shashi, Anuja, Aaryaman, and Anshuman Singhal for supporting our journey. Finally, we thank the thousands of respondents in our research in India and Tanzania, who helped us understand the effects of entertainment-education.

This present discussion of the entertainment-education strategy illustrates the main events as the entertainment-education strategy evolved, but is not exhaustive of all entertainment-education projects. We focus on those salient events where the practice of entertainment-education gained prominence, by design or through serendipity, accident, or intuition. The story of entertainment-education is told here as it happened, complete with paradoxes, occasional self-denials, and other complexities. The history of this important strategy is still being created as we write this book. We hope that the present book will serve as a launching pad for future research and theorizing about entertainment-education, an important tool for improving the world.

—*Arvind Singhal*
—*Everett M. Rogers*

Entertainment-Education

For the past ten years I had lost my way but Tinka Tinka Sukh *showed me a new path of life. . . . I used to be delinquent, aimless, and a bully. I harassed girls . . . one girl reported me to the police and I was sent to prison. I came home unreformed. One day I heard a program on radio. . . . After listening to the drama, my life underwent a change. . . . I started to listen regularly to All India Radio [AIR]. . . . One day I learned that* Tinka Tinka Sukh, *a radio soap opera, will be broadcast from AIR, Delhi. I waited expectantly. Once I started listening to the radio program, all my other drawbacks and negative values were transformed.*
—Birendra Singh Khushwaha
(a tailor in the Indian village of Lutsaan)

In December 1996, a colorful 21 × 27 inch poster–letter–manifesto, initiated by a village tailor (quoted above) with the signatures and thumbprints of 184 villagers, was mailed to All India Radio (AIR) in New Delhi, then broadcasting an entertainment-education soap opera *Tinka Tinka Sukh* (Happiness Lies in Small Things). The poster-letter came from a village named Lutsaan in India's Uttar Pradesh State. It stated: "Listening to *Tinka Tinka Sukh* has benefited all listeners of our village, especially the women. . . . Listeners of our village now actively oppose the practice of dowry—they neither give nor receive dowry." This unusual letter was forwarded to us by Usha Bhasin, the radio program's director and executive producer at AIR.

We were intrigued and visited the village. The poster-letter suggested that strong effects of *Tinka Tinka Sukh* had occurred in this village (see Photos 1.1, 1.2, and 1.3). We wondered whether the villagers had been able to actually change dowry behavior, a practice deeply ingrained in Indian cul-

1

Photo 1.2. Birendra Singh Khushwaha, the tailor in Village Lutsaan who initiated the poster-letter. (*Source:* Personal files of the authors.)

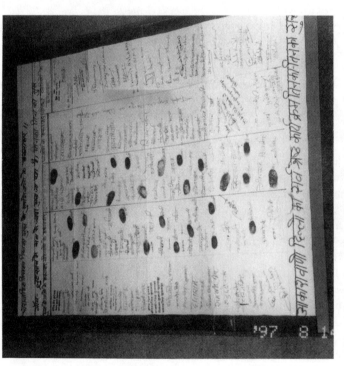

Photo 1.1. The poster-letter from Lutsaan, including the signatures and thumbprints of 184 community members, pledging not to give or accept dowry. (*Source:* Personal files of the authors.)

Photo 1.3. A hand-painted sign in Village Lutsaan in July 1998 promoting *Yeh Kahan Aa Gaye Hum* (Where Have We Arrived?), the successor radio soap opera about the environment following *Tinka Tinka Sukh*. The sign lists some members of the newly formed radio listeners' club, established since the first visit of our research team to Lutsaan in August 1997. (*Source:* Personal files of the authors.)

ture. We thought that the study of these effects in Lutsaan might enhance understanding of the process through which entertainment can change audience behavior. Some months later, in August 1997, when we approached Lutsaan on the road from Aligarh, the nearest city, we noticed that the village rises some 90 feet above the surrounding Gangetic Plain. Most of the village's approximately 1,000 homes are located on the sides of a small hillock, topped by an ancient fort. The adobe homes neighbor in a dense manner. The population of Lutsaan is about 6,000. A few homes, including those of the *pradhan* (village chief) and the tailor, are located on the main road, a short distance from the village center. Numerous narrow paths meander among the mud houses. Buffalo are everywhere, and the smell of dung pervades the village. Fertile, flat fields surround Lutsaan, and its farmers travel out to work on them each day.

On arriving in the village, we met first with the *pradhan*, who described the village as relatively well-off, with 60 radios, 5 television sets, and 10 tractors. Nearly every household owns a bicycle and 25 households possess a motorcycle. Lutsaan has two village schools that offer 8 years of education. The ratio of boys to girls in these schools was 90:10, but changed to about 60:40 in the past year, in part due to the effects of *Tinka Tinka Sukh*.

The village has a Shyam Club (named after the Hindu God Krishna) with about 50 active members. It carries out various self-development activities, including village clean-up, fixing broken waterpumps, and reducing religious and caste tensions in the village. The village postmaster, Om Prakash Sharma (called *Bapu*, or respected father, by the villagers) is chair of the Club. He told us that when an interpersonal conflict occurred recently, members of the Shyam Club met with the disputants until a solution was mediated. In 1996–1997, stimulated by *Tinka Tinka Sukh*, the Shyam Club devoted its attention to such gender equality issues as encouraging female children to attend school and opposing child marriage and dowry.

The plot of *Tinka Tinka Sukh* centered around the daily lives of a dozen main characters in *Navgaon* (New Village), who provided positive and negative role models to audience individuals for the educational issues of family planning, female equality, and HIV prevention. Shyam Club members reported that the Navgaon village in *Tinka Tinka Sukh* was much like their own village, progressive yet traditional, and with a cast of characters much like the ones portrayed in the radio soap opera.

Listeners to the program in Lutsaan said they were "emotionally stirred" by Poonam's character in *Tinka Tinka Sukh*. Poonam, a young bride, is beaten and verbally abused by her husband and in-laws for not providing an adequate dowry, the payment by a bride's parents to the groom's parents, in whose home she lives after marriage. In recent decades, dowry payments in India became exorbitant, usually including cash or gold, a television set, or a refrigerator. If dowry payments are inadequate, the bride may by mistreated by the husband's family. In extreme cases, the bride is burned to death in a kitchen accident, called a *dowry death*. In the radio soap opera, Poonam was humiliated and sent back to her parents after incorrectly being accused by her in-laws of infidelity to her husband. In desperation, she commits suicide. Lutsaan's poster-letter noted:

> It is a curse that for the sake of dowry, innocent women are compelled to commit suicide. Worse still. . . . women are murdered for not bringing dowry. The education we got from *Tinka Tinka Sukh*, particularly on dowry is significant. . . . People who think differently about dowry will be reformed; those who practice dowry will see the right way and why they must change.

Tinka Tinka Sukh also opposed child marriage. In the soap opera, Kusum is married before the legal age of 18, impregnated, and dies in childbirth. Although child marriage is illegal, it is common in Indian villages. Equal opportunity for girls is stressed in the radio soap opera. The poster-letter stated:

> In comparison with boys, education of girls is given less importance. Even if some girls wish to develop themselves through their own efforts and assert their individuality, their family is not supportive. . . . Whenever girls were given equal opportunities for educating themselves, they have done as well as the boys.

Family planning/population size issues were stressed in *Tinka Tinka Sukh*. The poster-letter stated: "Our society has to take a new turn in their thinking concerning family size. As the cost of living rises, having more children than one can afford is inviting trouble. . . . This message of *Tinka Tinka Sukh* comes across very clearly."

Both individual and collective efficacy were emphasized in the radio soap opera. After being left by her husband, a young bride, Sushma, takes charge of her life by starting a sewing school. She is rewarded in the storyline for this efficacious behavior. Efficacy is also demonstrated by Sunder, a drug abuser, who gets clean and then obtains a job. Ramlal, a pampered son and male chauvinist, represented a negative role model in the early episodes of *Tinka Tinka Sukh*. Later, he becomes a development officer, leading Navgaon village in a variety of progressive activities. The tailor in Lutsaan identified with this transitional role model, as he stated in the poster-letter: "I saw myself, in fact many of my antisocial ways, reflected in Ramlal who is also reformed." Such parasocial involvement with a transitional role model is one way in which entertainment-education affects behavior change.

Collective efficacy is also stressed in *Tinka Tinka Sukh*, as Navgaon village displays collaborative spirit in solving its problems. For example, villagers construct a new hospital, reject government assistance, and raise the needed funding themselves. As the poster-letter stated: "The problems of the village are tackled collectively, and in the event of any major problem, the matter is put before the *panchayat* [village council] for resolution."

THE TAILOR AND THE POSTMASTER

One reason for the relatively strong effects of *Tinka Tinka Sukh* in Village Lutsaan was traced to two villagers, the tailor, Birendra Singh Khushwaha, and the postmaster, *Bapu*. Although they are a generation apart in age, and belong to different castes, they have much in common. Both are in occupations that bring them in contact with many villagers on a daily basis. Both are sparkplugs for social change in Lutsaan.

The tailor is a hyperactive fan of AIR, listening for 8 to 10 hours a day, and writing to AIR an average of five letters per day! He keeps a stack of postcards at hand in his tailor shop so he can jot down a comment to a radio program on the spur of the moment. He has 20 different name stamps that he uses to address the letters to his favorite AIR program or to sign his name on the postcards (he stamped the 1996 poster-letter about dowry with three different stamps). He says that he has written 12,000 postcards and letters to AIR since the early 1990s. In the poster-letter, he told how he became a fan of AIR (explained at the opening of this chapter). The tailor had personally experienced certain of the educational issues discussed in the radio soap opera and related to the characters, especially Ramlal who changes his stripes from being a vicious village bully to become a development change agent. The tailor's shop is located centrally in the village, and its door is always open, with the radio on. Several people are usually in the tailor shop, gossiping, listening to AIR, and discussing the program. The traffic through the tailor's shop provided a convenient way for the tailor to obtain signatures and thumbprints on the poster-letter.

Om Prakash Sharma (*Bapu*), the 55-year-old postmaster of Lutsaan, has a home-cum-office. The post office is located in one room of his home. He is a Brahmin, one of the few high-caste individuals in Village Lutsaan, which is dominated by the Jat farmer caste. He has the only telephone in the village, which he allows others to use. *Bapu* is known for his altruism. He has a small buffalo corral in the courtyard of his home and this is where villagers bring their sick buffalo for treatment. *Bapu* barters the cost of the drugs in exchange for milk. Like the tailor, *Bapu* was a devoted fan of *Tinka Tinka Sukh*, often delaying his evening meal in order to listen. He says that: "Six months later, we still talk about *Tinka Tinka Sukh*." Often, *Bapu* listened to the radio soap opera and then discussed the episode with his friends. He knows the names of each character and can describe what they are like. *Bapu*'s son, Prem Shankar, aged 30, was married one month before our visit to Lutsaan. *Bapu* would not accept dowry from the bride's parents. Prem volunteers his time as secretary at the all-women dairy cooperative in Lutsaan, maintaining their financial ledgers. He told us that his inspiration is Suraj, a positive role model in *Tinka Tinka Sukh*, who volunteers his time for community development activities.

One week before our visit to Lutsaan, a 14-year-old girl was married, suggesting that *Tinka Tinka Sukh* was not completely effective in changing the village norms. This child marriage meant that she had to drop out of school. Her father, a low-caste community member, told us that he knew that child marriage and paying dowry were illegal in India, but he did not expect the police to interfere. Bapu, the postmaster, although visibly angered by this recent marriage, shrugged it off as being a problem with the lower caste. This child marriage in Lutsaan suggests that an entertainment-education program can only do so much.

Why was *Tinka Tinka Sukh* so effective in stimulating social changes in Lutsaan? Exposure to the radio soap opera was higher in Lutsaan than elsewhere in North India. Prior conditions in the village helped magnify the effects of this entertainment-education radio program: a hyperactive radio listener (the tailor), a highly respected village leader in the postmaster, group-listening to the radio episodes, and the activities of a village self-help group.

Our experience in Village Lutsaan, during hot summer days in India in 1997, enriched our understanding of the potential and the limitations of entertainment-education.[1]

ENTERTAINMENT'S UNREALIZED
EDUCATIONAL POTENTIAL

This chapter investigates the basic tenets of the entertainment-education communication strategy, including its historical roots and recent applications in the United States and in developing countries. Entertainment, whether via a nation's airwaves, popular magazines, or newspapers, is the most pervasive mass media genre; it tells us how to dress, speak, think, and behave (Browne,

---

[1]Some members of our research team (Saumya Pant and Mumtaz Ahmed) revisited Lutsaan in July 1998, a year later. The effects of the radio soap opera continued and were perhaps magnified by the impact of our previous visit. Radio listening clubs had been organized for a follow-up entertainment-education program, *Yeh Kahan Aa Gaye Hum* (Where Have We Arrived?), about preserving the environment. Several large hand-painted signs appeared in the village, stating "After *Tinka Tinka Sukh* listen now to *Yeh Kahan Aa Gaye Hum*, broadcast from All India Radio." Members of the listening club donate $1 a month toward the cost of radio batteries, for paint and poster supplies, and to purchase tree seedlings (the radio program promotes reforestation). The tailor continued flooding AIR with letters, many now containing the conclusion of listening club discussions. *Bapu* was arranging the marriage of his second son, refusing to accept dowry. We again visited Lutsaan in January, 1999, when we observed further social changes, including formation of an all-women radio listening club. Enrollment in the village school was about 40% girls and 60% boys.

1983; Piotrow, 1990). Thus, we are "educated" by the entertainment media, even if unintended by the source and unnoticed by the audience (Barnouw & Kirkland, 1989; Bineham, 1988; Chaffee, 1988; Cooper-Chen, 1994; Fischer & Melnik, 1979; Piotrow, Kincaid, Rimon, & Rinehart, 1997; Postman, 1985; Rogers, Aikat, Chang, Poppe, & Sopory, 1989; Rogers & Singhal, 1989, 1990; Singhal & Brown, 1996; Vink, 1988; Wang & Singhal, 1992). Often, such education can have negative influence on people's lives.

The entertainment media have a high potential to educate the public about various social problems, for instance, about HIV prevention, family planning, maternal and child health, a more equal status for women, and child development (Johns Hopkins University, 1998; Bouman, 1998). However, little of this potential has been tapped to date. For at least three compelling reasons, national policymakers, media practitioners, and international donor agencies in both developed and developing countries should more seriously consider the educational potential of entertainment media. These reasons are discussed here:

1. Development problems loom large all over the world (including the United States): ethnic conflicts, environmental catastrophes, infectious diseases, hunger and famine, and unsupported population growth. Resources to tackle these problems are scarce. To address such problems, pragmatic media strategies are needed that appeal to the audience members, are commercially viable, and are socially responsible. Using the entertainment media for educational purposes provides an unusual opportunity to achieve these objectives.

2. Leisure and entertainment represent one of the most important megatrends of recent decades (Bernstein, 1990). Entertainment media, spurred by advances in such new communication technologies as satellite and cable television, VCRs, and multimedia; and by economic progress, reach expanding audiences worldwide. The hard-to-reach rural poor are increasingly accessible through the mass media, and at a relatively low cost.

3. The entertainment media needlessly suffer from the stigma of being a "mindless" genre. Audience research shows that carefully designed entertainment media messages can help educate audiences, promote prosocial behavior, and be economically profitable. Furthermore, research in many countries shows that consumers prefer socially responsible and wholesome entertainment, when available.

THE ENTERTAINMENT-EDUCATION STRATEGY

A needless dichotomy exists in almost all mass media content: Mass media programs must either be entertaining or educational (Fischer & Melnik, 1979; Singhal, 1990; Singhal & Rogers, 1989a). The entertainment-education strategy abrogates this arbitrary dichotomy. *Entertainment-education* is the process of purposely designing and implementing a media message both to entertain and educate, in order to increase audience members' knowledge about an educational issue, create favorable attitudes, and change overt behavior. Entertainment-education seeks to capitalize on the appeal of popular media to show individuals how they can live safer, healthier, and happier lives (Piotrow et al., 1997; Piotrow, Meyer, & Zulu, 1992; Singhal & Brown, 1996).

If implemented correctly, this strategy can offer advantages to development officials of governments, broadcasting networks, educators, commercial sponsors, and audiences. National governments in many developing countries feel obligated to produce educational broadcasts. Such programs usually require a heavy investment, are perceived by audiences as dull, and attract sparse attention. Educational programs are usually not popular with commercial advertisers. On the other hand, entertainment programs generally obtain high ratings and are popular with sponsors. The entertainment-education strategy thus provides an opportunity for an instructional message to pay for itself and fulfill commercial and social interests (Brown, 1991; Piotrow, 1990; Singhal & Rogers, 1989b).

The purpose of entertainment-education programming is to contribute to directed *social change*, defined as the process by which an alteration occurs in the structure and function of a social system (Singhal & Rogers, 1994). This change can occur at the level of individual, community, or some other system. The strategy contributes to social change in two ways. First, it can influence audience awareness, attitudes, and behaviors toward a socially desirable end. Here, the anticipated effects are located in the individual audience members. An illustration is provided by a radio soap opera, *Twende na Wakati*, in Tanzania, which convinced several hundred thousand sexually active adults to adopt HIV prevention behaviors (like using condoms and reducing their number of sexual partners).

Second, it can influence the audiences' external environment to help create the necessary conditions for social change at the group or system level. Here, the major effects are located in the sociopolitical sphere of the audiences' external environment. The entertainment-education media can serve as an advocate or agenda-setter, influencing public and policy initiatives in a socially desirable direction (Wallack, 1990). The case of Lutsaan, the Indian village that rejected dowry, illustrates the system-level social changes resulting from entertainment-education.

Definitions

Entertainment-education has many labels: *enter-educate, edutainment,* and *infotainment.* Everyone agrees, however, that the key idea is to combine entertainment and education to obtain certain advantages from each (Singhal

& Rogers, 1989b). For this reason, in this volume, we generally use the term *entertainment-education*, which emerged as the terminology of choice in the 1990s.

Scholars have used more than 28 definitions of the concept of entertainment (e.g., as an activity that provides fun, amusement, arousal, pleasure, and so on; Tannenbaum, 1980). We define *entertainment* as a performance or spectacle that captures the interest or attention of individuals, giving them pleasure and/or amusement (Singhal, 1990). Scholars have also conceptualized education in various ways: formal versus nonformal education, classroom versus distance education, individual awareness versus public consciousness, and so on. We define *education* as either a formal or informal program of instruction and training that has the potential to develop an individual's skill to achieve a particular end by boosting his or her mental, moral, or physical powers (Singhal, 1990).

Entertainment: Overcoming a Negative Image

For several decades, the popular culture carried by entertainment media were subject to a condescending appraisal by the elite guardians of high culture (Gans, 1975). Why is entertainment perceived negatively? Sources of this view include the following (Mendelsohn, 1966; Singhal & Brown, 1996):

1. The Hebraic–Christian concept of sin placing entertainment and enjoyment in opposition with moral teachings.
2. The concept of the Protestant Work Ethic positioning entertainment as a waste of time, equating its consumption with laziness.
3. The rise of secular-royalism casting disdain on the entertainment products of the public.
4. The rise of reform movements and liberalism attacking social institutions (including the media) for corrupting the public.
5. The rise of ideological Marxism attacking entertainment as a source of false consciousness.
6. The rise of Freudian psychoanalytic theory raising fears about fantasy gratification.

Several scholars have defended the legitimacy of mass popular culture, arguing that it provides recreation and escape from hard work (Bettelheim, 1977; Denisoff, 1983; Fischer & Melnik, 1979; Huizinga, 1950; Katz, Blumler, & Gurevitch, 1974; Katz, Gurevitch, & Haas, 1973; Mendelsohn, 1966; Mendelsohn & Spetnagel, 1980; Stephenson, 1967, 1988; Tannenbaum, 1980). Mendelsohn (1966) formulated a "First Law of Mass Entertainment": "When most people are confronted with a choice between deriving pleasure from serious non-entertainment fare or from non-serious entertainment fare, they will choose the latter in much greater proportion than the former" (pp. 143–144).[2]

Surprisingly, despite the importance of entertainment in our lives, research on the entertainment functions of the mass media is limited (Fischer & Melnik, 1979; Tannenbaum, 1980). Existing studies include (a) content analyses describing "fun" themes and characters, (b) "effects" studies primarily investigating benefits or harm, (c) uses-and-gratifications studies, and (d) critical cultural studies emphasizing the importance of considering the "context" when interpreting the "text": audiences, technologies, effects, and institutional aspects of entertainment (Himmelweit, Swift, & Jaeger, 1980, Modleski, 1986; Williams, cited in Heath & Skirrow, 1986). Katz et al. (1974) said it best: "The choice to study mass media as agents of persuasion, rather than as agents of entertainment, is highly intriguing" (p. 20). Over the years, we have encountered colleagues who question our study of entertainment-education because they cannot understand how we could be serious about studying such a frivolous topic as soap operas.

A Promising Alternative

The entertainment-education strategy grew out of a recognition of, and as a counter to, at least two undesirable trends in contemporary mass media programming: entertainment-degradation programs, and boredom-education programs (Fig. 1.1).

Entertainment-Degradation Programs. A growing trend is to degrade a message in order to increase its entertainment attractiveness. The increasing use of sex and violence in U.S. entertainment television represents one example of degrading a message to achieve higher audience ratings and greater profits. Concern about the harmful, antisocial effects of entertainment media, especially of television, goes back several decades. In 1952, the U.S. Congress held its first hearing on the harmful effects of television violence, and in 1972 the U.S. Surgeon General's Office published a five-volume report linking exposure to television violence and aggressive behavior. Since the 1970s, several thousand studies have been conducted on the antisocial effects of television content, focusing on issues such as the following:[3]

1. The harmful effects of television violence (see, e.g., Andison, 1980; Bryant & Zillmann, 1986, 1994; Comstock, 1977; Donnerstein, 1980, 1983;

---

[2]While Mendelsohn was revisiting the role of popular entertainment, Stephenson (1967, 1988) presented his play theory of mass communication, which further reinforced the useful role that entertainment media can play in the lives of individuals.

[3]Several of these studies are cited in Brown (1991).

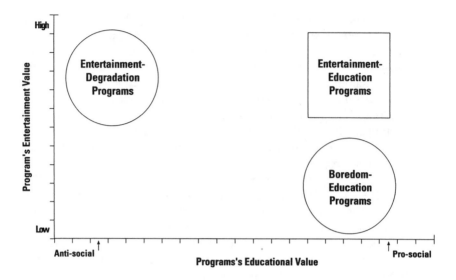

FIG. 1.1. Many mass media programs are either entertainment-degradation or boredom-education programs. Entertainment-education programs represent a relatively unique genre in mass media programming that is prosocial and high in entertainment value.

Federman, 1998; Harrison, 1981; Phillips, 1982; Tannenbaum & Zillmann, 1975; Zillmann & Bryant, 1982).

2. The harmful effects of inaccurate health-related information on television (see, e.g., Backer & Rogers, 1993; Barnum, 1975; Cassata, Skill, & Boadu, 1979; Long, 1978; Lowry & Towles, 1989; Resnick, 1990; Smith 1972; Tan & Tan, 1986).

3. The portrayal of inaccurate and negative images of women and children on television (see, e.g., Cassata & Skill, 1983; Downing, 1974; Goldsten, 1975; Liebert, Neale, & Davidson, 1973; Noble, 1975; Tuchman, Daniels, & Benet, 1978).

4. The unrealistic depiction of interpersonal and social relationships on television (see, e.g., Alexander, 1985; Buerkel-Rothfuss & Mayes, 1981; Estep & MacDonald, 1985; Greenberg, Abelman, & Neuendorf, 1981; Greenberg & D'Alessio, 1985; Lowry, Love, & Kirby, 1981; Sutherland & Siniawsky, 1982). For instance, the afternoon soap operas on U.S. television show several sexual acts per hour but ignore the consequences of unprotected sex (Greenberg & Busselle, 1996; Kunkel, Cope, & Colvin, 1998).

Each year, U.S. prime-time television portrays approximately 20,000 scenes of suggested sexual intercourse and sexual innuendo (Sprafkin & Silverman, 1981). For every sexual act that is depicted between spouses, soap operas show six extramarital sexual encounters. Some 94% of sexual encounters on soap operas are between unmarried people (Greenberg et al., 1981). Although there is an abundance of sexually explicit and implicit material on U.S. television, little media content deals with the consequences of sex, pregnancy, family planning, and sexually transmitted diseases (Greenberg & Busselle, 1996; Kunkel et al., 1998). The scorecard of U.S. entertainment television in depicting violence, alcoholism, and racial equality is equally dismal (Medved, 1992; O'Connor, 1990).

In contrast to the vast literature on the antisocial effects of television, a relatively small percentage of media studies have focused on the prosocial effects of entertainment television.[4] One purpose of creating more prosocial entertainment-education programs is to counter the "entertainment-degradation" trend in television programming in many countries.

Boredom-Education Programs. With this type of educational programming the educational content is often emphasized to the point that audience members are put off. Audience members also tune out because of the slow-paced, nonengaging presentational style of such programs. Certain broadcast channels become branded by audiences as educational and then have difficulty attracting large audiences.

Entertainment-education programs provide an opportunity to overcome the limitations of entertainment-degradation and boredom-education programs and, conversely, to be socially responsible and commercially profitable. But entertainment-education is not a panacea. A 1976 experience in Mexico (see chap. 3, this volume) showed that entertainment-education may not be able to teach mathematics or literacy to adult populations, but it was able to motivate hundreds of thousands of Mexicans to enroll in adult literacy classes, where they learned numeracy and literacy.

THE RISE OF ENTERTAINMENT-EDUCATION

The idea of combining entertainment with education is not new: It goes as far back in human history as the timeless art of storytelling. In countries where a rich oral tradition persists, folktales with morals and larger-than-life heroes are an integral part of a child's nonformal education (Griswold, 1918; Ryder, 1949). For instance, two well-known epic poems in India, Maharishi Valmiki's *Ramayana* and Ved Vyas's *Mahabharata*, written several thousand years ago, are examples of combining the art of storytelling with a social

---

[4]Examples are Amato and Malatesta (1987); Ball-Rokeach, Rokeach, and Grube (1984); Bryan and Walbek (1970); Collins and Getz (1976); Gunther (1984); Hurr and Robinson (1978); Leifer, Gordon, and Graves, (1974); Lovelace and Huston (1982); Rushton (1982); and Wander (1977).

and moral commentary. In the past decade, both epics were broadcast as television programs in India and earned record ratings (Bhargava, 1987; Bhatia, 1988). Children in many other lands are told Aesop's fables, each with an educational lesson. Similarly, for thousands of years, music, drama, dance, and various folk media have been used in many countries for recreation, devotion, reformation, and instructional purposes (Murdock, 1980; Parmar, 1975; Thomas, 1993).

Although combining entertainment with education is not new, entertainment-education is a relatively new concept. Its use in radio, television, comic books, and rock music, at least when designed according to communication and social psychological theories, is a matter of the past 25 years. In radio, the first well-known illustration of the education strategy occurred in 1951, when the British Broadcasting Corporation (BBC) began broadcasting *The Archers*, a radio soap opera that carried educational messages about agricultural development (see chap. 6, this volume). In the late 1950s, Elaine Perkins, a writer-producer on Jamaican radio (trained at the BBC), also began experimenting with the entertainment-education strategy in radio serials to promote family planning and other development issues (see chap. 6, this volume).

The entertainment-education strategy in television was discovered more-or-less by accident in Peru in 1969, when the *telenovela* (literally "television novel" or soap opera) *Simplemente María* was broadcast (see chap. 2, this volume). The main character, María, a migrant to the capital city, faced tragic setbacks, like becoming a single mother. María worked during the day and enrolled in adult literacy classes in the evening. She then climbed the socioeconomic ladder of success through her hard work, strong motivation, and her skills with a Singer sewing machine. *Simplemente María* attracted very high audience ratings, and the sale of Singer sewing machines boomed in Peru, as did the number of young girls enrolling in adult literacy and sewing classes. When *Simplemente María* was broadcast in other Latin American nations, similar effects were recorded. Audience identification with María was very strong, especially among poor, working-class women: She represented a role model for upward social mobility.

Inspired by the audience success and the (unintended) educational effects of *Simplemente María*, Miguel Sabido, a television writer-producer-director in Mexico, developed a methodology for entertainment-education soap operas (see chap. 3, this volume). This strategy, with certain modifications, is dominant in most entertainment-education projects throughout the world. Between 1975 and 1982, Sabido produced seven entertainment-education soap operas (one each year), which spurred enrollment in adult literacy classes, encouraged the adoption of family planning, promoted gender equality, and so forth (Nariman, 1993). Sabido's soap operas were also commercial hits for Televisa, the Mexican television network, demonstrating that educational messages do not limit the popularity of entertainment programs.

Through these events of the past several decades, the idea of combining education with entertainment in the mass media was born and has since spread to many countries, spurred by the efforts of institutions like Population Communications International (PCI), a nongovernmental organization headquartered in New York City. Led by David Poindexter, its former president, PCI helped transfer the entertainment-education soap opera strategy from Mexico to (a) India, where two television soap operas, *Hum Log* (We People) in 1984–1985 (see chap. 4, this volume) and *Hum Raahi* (Co-Travelers) in 1992–1993, and the radio soap opera, *Tinka Tinka Sukh* (Happiness Lies in Small Things), in 1996–1997 (see chap. 6, this volume), were broadcast; (b) Kenya, where a television soap opera, *Tushauriane* (*Let's Discuss*), and a radio soap opera, *Ushikwapo Shikimana* (When Given Advice, Take It), were broadcast from 1987 to 1989; and (c) Tanzania, where a family planning/AIDS radio soap opera, *Twende na Wakati* (Let's Go With the Times) was broadcast from 1993 to 1998. This technology transfer process is complex and time-consuming, and the results have been mixed. However, important lessons about creating, implementing, and maintaining the entertainment-education strategy have been learned (see chap. 9, this volume). These lessons inform our understanding of the promises and problems of the entertainment-education strategy.

Patrick L. Coleman, deputy director of Johns Hopkins University's Center for Communication Programs (JHU/CCP), while working in El Salvador as a Peace Corps volunteer in the early 1970s, viewed a Sabido soap opera and observed its effects. He invited Sabido to teach his strategy at a conference sponsored by JHU in Quito, Ecuador in 1983. Since this turning point, Coleman and his colleagues at JHU have pioneered the utilization of the entertainment-education approach in rock music for promoting sexual responsibility among adolescents in Latin American countries and the Philippines, for promoting responsible parenthood in Nigeria, and in more than 60 other entertainment-education media projects in more than 30 countries (see chap. 5, this volume).

The entertainment-education strategy has been widely invented and re-created by pioneering and creative media professionals in television, radio, films, print, and theater. For example, Dr. Garth Japhet in South Africa developed the long-running "Soul City" mass media campaign, providing a model approach to health promotion that is advocated by the European Union and United Nations agencies like UNICEF and UNAIDS. John Riber in India, Bangladesh, and Zimbabwe, and professionals in other countries have produced films with social messages (Hill, 1993; Smith, 1989; Wray, 1991). Dr. Seuss in the United States and professionals in other countries have produced books, comics, and cartoons to educate children and adults about social issues (Barron, 1993; Lent, 1995; Maggs, 1990; Monaghan, 1991). Groups like *Shatavdi, Jagran,* and *Nalamdana* in India, and other groups in other countries have used street theater and pantomime to promote educational messages (Bakshi, 1989; Boal, 1985; Menon, 1993; Valente & Bharath, in press; Valente, Poppe, Alva, Briceño, & Cases, 1995; Van Erwen, 1987, 1989).

The social problems of the developing countries of Latin America, Africa, and Asia are especially grave. Thus, it is not surprising that many entertainment-education projects in recent decades were implemented in developing nations.[5] The strategy has also been widely used in the United States, although in somewhat different ways.

Entertainment-Education in the United States

The Hollywood film-television-music industry and the Public Broadcasting Service (PBS) in the United States have used the entertainment-education strategy. Hollywood television producer Norman Lear[6] attacked racial and ethnic prejudice in the United States through his popular 1970's CBS series, *All in the Family,* featuring Archie Bunker as a negative role model for bigotry (Tate & Surlin, 1976; Vidmar & Rokeach, 1974; see chap. 7, this volume). Hollywood television programs and films have raised such social issues as drunk driving, gay and lesbian rights, AIDS, child abuse, infant mortality, and drug abuse (Backer & Rogers, 1993; Montgomery, 1989). Often, one of these issues is incorporated in a single episode, or perhaps several episodes, of a prime-time television series through the efforts of what Montgomery (1989) called "Hollywood lobbyists." Notable examples of Hollywood lobbying include "Maude's Dilemma" and the Harvard Alcohol Project. A highly rated television program is viewed by up to 30 million people in the United States, so the impacts can be considerable.

Maude's Dilemma. One of the earliest and most widely known illustrations of a Hollywood advocacy group injecting a social issue into prime-time television occurred in 1972 when Maude,[7] a 47-year-old woman (played

---

[5]The entertainment-education strategy, in this sense, is one of development communication (see Melkote, 1991; Rogers, 1976).

[6]During the mid-1970s, Lear's sitcoms—*All in the Family, Maude, Good Times, The Jeffersons, Sanford and Son, Hot L Baltimore,* and *One Day at a Time*—reached 120 million viewers each week (Batra, 1982). His sitcoms addressed such controversial issues as ethnic and racial prejudice, birth control, abortion, menopause, aging, sodomy, manic depression, and mental retardation. All earned generally high audience ratings, demonstrating that commercial entertainment television need not be at odds with educational television.

[7]Lear, remarkably, drew on his personal life experiences in designing television shows. Maude's character was inspired by his acerbic second wife and Archie Bunker by his irascible father (Wright, 1991). *Maude* was a spin-off from *All in the Family,* and its main character was in opposite polarity to that of Archie Bunker. Maude was as bigoted a liberal as Archie was a stubborn conservative (Batra, 1982).

by Bea Arthur) in Lear's CBS series by the same name, became pregnant. Indecisive for two episodes (called "Maude's Dilemma"), Maude finally decided to obtain an abortion rather than bear an unwanted child. Within minutes, CBS received 373 angry telephone calls and a public controversy erupted (Montgomery, 1989).

Pro-life organizations called for a more balanced treatment of the abortion issue, demanding two sequel episodes of *Maude*, supporting the right-to-life of unborn babies (Montgomery, 1989), which CBS rejected. More controversy erupted when the two episodes were about to be rebroadcast the following season. Fearing customer backlash, several advertisers withdrew their spots from the *Maude* time slot, and one fourth of all CBS affiliates, lacking advertiser support, refused to carry the rebroadcasts. CBS officials debated whether or not to rerun "Maude's Dilemma." PCI's Poindexter, a successful Hollywood lobbyist of the 1970s (and later a promoter of Sabido's entertainment-education soap operas), rallied the network to rebroadcast the two controversial episodes (Montgomery, 1989).

The *Maude* controversy "tested, as never before, the boundaries of acceptability for program content" on prime-time broadcasts (Montgomery, 1989, p. 28). The broadcasts of *Maude* represented an important event in Hollywood's brush with entertainment-education, and demonstrated that situation comedies (sitcoms) need not be looked on as a "mindless genre" (Miller, 1993).

The Harvard Alcohol Project for Designated Drivers. In the 1980s, Mothers Against Drunk Driving (MADD), a very influential lobby group, played a key role in implementing tougher state laws to prevent drunk driving. MADD was founded when the daughter of Candy Lightner of Sacramento, California was killed by a drunk driver. Lightner organized MADD, which grew rapidly into a huge organization with 600 local chapters and a multimillion dollar annual budget (Reinarman, 1988). Inspired by MADD, Harvard University, a prestigious U.S. academic institution, utilized its position to combat drunk driving via prime-time television.

During 1988 and 1989, representatives of the Harvard School of Public Health worked closely with network executives, creative producers, and writers in Hollywood to incorporate messages in prime-time television programs warning against drinking and driving.[8] Dr. Jay Winsten, director of the Harvard Alcohol Project in the Harvard School of Public Health, was inspired by designated-driver behavior in Sweden, in which a group of friends selects one person to abstain from alcohol and be responsible for driving; other group members then have the choice of consuming alcohol (DeJong & Winsten, 1990).

---

[8]See Breed and De Foe (1982) for a discussion of early efforts in Hollywood to lobby against excessive and inappropriate depictions of alcohol.

The Harvard Alcohol Project represents a rare case in which the effects of a Hollywood lobbyist's[9] activities were evaluated. During the 1988 and 1989 television seasons, some 77 prime-time programs promoted the designated-driver concept by including at least a few lines of dialogues: For example, on an episode of *LA Law*, Michael Kuzak (played by Harry Hamlin) asked a bartender to call his girlfriend "and tell the lady I need a ride home" (Finke, 1988; Winsten, 1990). Such episodic dialogues were supplemented by public service announcements (PSAs) encouraging designated-driver behavior. A before–after research design indicated higher levels of awareness among the U.S. television audience about the designated-driver concept and somewhat higher levels of designated-driver behavior (Gelman, 1989; Montgomery, 1993; Winsten, 1990).

What factors contributed to the relative success of the Harvard Alcohol Project? Harvard representatives did not confront the extensive (beer and wine) alcohol advertising on the television networks. Their purpose was to attack drunk driving, not alcoholism. Furthermore, they did not ask network producers for major changes in program content, but rather small adjustments that could be easily incorporated.

In addition to Hollywood lobbyist-initiated prime-time programming, PBS in the United States broadcast some notable entertainment-education programs over recent decades. Notable examples include *Sesame Street, Canción de la Raza,* and *Que Pasa, U.S.A.?*.

"Sesame Street": The Longest Street in the World. One exceptional example of an entertainment-education program in the United States is *Sesame Street.*[10] Created in 1969 by the Children's Television Workshop (CTW) of New York, *Sesame Street* is watched by an estimated 12 million Americans every week, including 6 million preschoolers, about 40% of all U.S. children aged 2 to 5 (CTW, 1987). The television series, which helps prepare preschoolers for classroom learning, has been broadcast in an English-language version in 53 countries. Sixteen foreign language adaptations of *Sesame Street* have been broadcast in 47 countries (CTW, 1988). Reaching audiences in more than 140 countries in six continents, *Sesame Street* is easily "the longest street[11] in the world" (CTW, 1998; Lesser, 1974).

The idea of creating CTW originated in 1966 when Joan Ganz Cooney, then a television producer, and Lloyd Morrisett, an executive at the Carnegie Foundation, decided to explore television's usefulness in teaching young

---

[9]A "Hollywood lobbyist" is a group, usually with an office in Los Angeles, that seeks to persuade scriptwriters and producers of prime-time television shows to include issues like abortion, designated driving, or the environment in television episodes (Montgomery, 1989).

[10]The quality of children's programming is generally quite dismal worldwide (see Palmer, 1988).

[11]In foreign adaptations of *Sesame Street*, the production set of the "street" is replaced by an appropriate cultural space. For instance, in Poland, it is a courtyard; in Mexico, it is a plaza.

children (Palmer, 1988). Start-up funds of $7 million were obtained from government agencies and private foundations to create the CTW, an autonomous, nonprofit organization free from political and economic pressures (Lesser, 1974). Eighteen months of formative evaluation research preceded the first broadcast of *Sesame Street* in 1969. Entertaining formats with strong educational appeals were pretested and often revised many times to obtain the desired effects. Such intense evaluation, which continues in present-day productions, is a major reason for *Sesame Street*'s audience success (Singhal & Rogers, 1994). Entertainment-education represents a delicate balance between entertainment and education and thus requires use of formative evaluation. In fact, CTW pioneered the idea of formative evaluation.

Sesame Street's purpose is to develop the cognitive learning skills of preschool children, teaching them letters, numbers, geometric forms, and such valued prosocial qualities as kindness and cooperation. The program utilizes Piaget's (1952) principle of knowledge acquisition: In order to teach something new, relate it to something that the learner already knows. For instance, to teach the letter "Y," a comparison is made with a forked road and with a slingshot. Each lesson is repeated several times for enhanced learning. Other techniques are employed to make the child an active participant in the learning process, overcoming the one-way nature of most television broadcasting. A variety of entertainment formats are employed to hold children's attention: muppets, music, animation, live-action films, special effects, and celebrity visits (CTW, 1988). Each segment of *Sesame Street* is short (usually less than 3 minutes) and designed to catch and hold the attention of children.

Every year, CTW creates a new series of 130 hour-long *Sesame Street* programs. These 1-hour programs are broadcast by PBS stations every morning and repeated in the afternoon each weekday for 26 weeks. Then the 5-day, 26-week cycle is rebroadcast during the second half of the year. The annual production costs of the 130 hour-long episodes are about $15 million, with each episode costing $115,000.[12] CTW, a nonprofit organization, meets two thirds of the program's total production costs from self-generated revenues (such as the sale of *Sesame Street* books, tee-shirts, toys, and so forth), which makes it the largest single contributor to public television programming in the United States. The other one third of the cost is provided by foundations, corporate grants, and PBS.

Summative evaluations of the U.S. and international productions of *Sesame Street* consistently show that children who have been viewers score

---

[12]The cost of producing an episode of a foreign-language adaptation of *Sesame Street* is also high (as compared to producing, for instance, a *telenovela* episode), one reason why *Sesame Street* has only 16 foreign language adaptations. Most countries, like Australia and Great Britain, prefer to just broadcast the U.S.-made series.

higher than nonviewers in tests of ability in all curriculum areas (Ball & Bogatz, 1970; Bogatz & Ball, 1971; Tan, 1985; CTW, 1988). *Sesame Street's* success comes from combining the technology of television with the art of entertainment and specific educational aims, claimed Morrisett (cited in Lesser, 1974). However, there is evidence that *Sesame Street* might increase the information gap between children that are already better informed and of higher socioeconomic status than their less fortunate counterparts (Cook et al., 1975). That is, the program raises the level of information of all children, but it especially benefits the information-rich, thus widening the information gap (Tichenor, Donohue, & Olien, 1970).

Sesame Street is only one of the several entertainment-education television series created by CTW. Others include *3-2-1 Contact*, a series focusing on science and technology; *The Electric Company*, designed to enhance students' reading skills; and *Square One TV*, geared to enhancing children's mathematical ability. In Jordan, CTW co-produced *Al Manaahil* (*The Sources*), a new Arabic television series designed to enhance language and reading skills among Arab children. The international transfer of the *Sesame Street* (CTW's) methodology is not just one-way: *Rechov Sumsum*, the Israeli version of *Sesame Street* has been adapted into a series of home video programs for consumption in America. Titled *Shalom Sesame*, the purpose of the video series is to motivate (and supplement) the learning of Hebrew as a second language in the United States and to spread awareness among Americans about Israeli people, places, and culture (CTW, 1988).

Several lessons have been learned about the entertainment-education communication strategy from *Sesame Street* (CTW, 1988; Lesser, 1974):

1. *Entertainment television can be used to educate young viewers without making the educational content subtle, and still attract large audiences.* For instance, *Sesame Street* makes little effort to disguise its educational content: "It is an experiment to see how well entertainment could be used in the service of education" (CTW, 1988).

2. *Start-up costs for entertainment-education programs are typically high, and such programs take a relatively longer time to produce than do strictly entertainment programs, in part due to the time and costs of formative evaluation research.* On the other hand, entertainment-education programs have been found to be very efficient in achieving relatively low-cost behavior change.

3. *Formative evaluation research is crucial to the success of entertainment-education.*

4. *A balance between artistic creativity and communication research is needed in producing effective entertainment-education programs.* CTW represented a success story in bringing these two quite different "cultures" together.

5. *The design, production, and evaluation research for an entertainment-education program can be transferred across national and cultural boundaries, with suitable adaptation to local conditions.*

6. *Entertainment-education television programs offer tremendous economies of scale in delivering messages to a target audience. For example, the cost of reaching each preschooler in the United States via Sesame Street is less than 1 cent per child per viewing hour* (Lesser, 1974).

7. *Television content is strongly shaped by economic and political realities.* One disappointment with *Sesame Street* was that it did not inspire commercial television networks to broadcast similar entertainment-education programs.

Canción de la Raza. *Canción de la Raza* (Song of the People), a 65-episode PBS television series broadcast in the late 1960s, was designed to address problems of the Mexican-American ethnic community in Los Angeles.[13] It promoted Mexican-American culture, focusing on such issues as family harmony, literacy, social welfare services, and ethnic prejudice (Mendelsohn, 1971). The story revolved around the lives of the Ramos family, a bilingual, low-income Mexican-American family, who resided in an East Los Angeles *barrio*.

Canción de la Raza relied heavily on formative research for assessing audience needs in the construction of messages. Creative professionals (including the series' producer, director, writers, and others) of Station KCET in Los Angeles, and scholars at the University of Denver's Communications Arts Center, led by its director, Dr. Harold Mendelsohn, collaborated to produce *Canción de la Raza*. The series represented "the most thoroughly researched mass communications effort of its kind," at that time (Mendelsohn, 1969, p. 19).

The show was viewed by 15% of all Mexican-American households in Los Angeles, 250,000 people (Mendelsohn, 1971). Viewers represented all socioeconomic segments, including the most neglected audience groups: the poor, the young, and female viewers. The soap opera (*telenovela*) format was popular with the Hispanic audience. The series content was perceived as relevant and credible by its audience. Some 60% of viewers gained information about how to cope with their problems, 16% reported modifying their complacent attitudes, and 6% asserted they had become involved in a socially ameliorative activity as a consequence of watching the television series. In summary, the program "intervened in a positive way in the Mexican-American community in Los Angeles" (Mendelsohn, 1971, p. 53).

---

[13]This series was based on the prior 1967 experience of *Operation Stop-Gap*, another entertainment-education television series that was targeted to poor ethnic segments in the United States (Mendelsohn, Espic, & Rogers, 1968).

Que Pasa, U.S.A.? *Que Pasa, U.S.A.?* (*What's Happening, U.S.A.?*) was a bilingual sitcom with a social purpose. Set in Little Havana, Miami's Cuban exile community, it depicted the lives of Cuban Americans trying to "make it" in their new homeland (WPBT, 1978). Although the series was primarily designed to help Spanish-speaking immigrants bridge cultural gaps in the United States, it accomplished much more.

The idea of creating a bilingual sitcom was the brain child of Manuel Mendoza, a professor at Miami-Dade Community College in Florida. Surveys that Mendoza conducted for the Community Action and Research Group in Miami found that the isolation of Cuban-American teenagers was an important social problem. Mendoza believed that this problem could be addressed in the classroom, through the use of an entertaining and educational television program. He joined hands with Channel 2 (WPBT) of Miami to secure federal funding for his project. The result was *Que Pasa, U.S.A.?* Eighteen half-hour episodes were created with a budget of $500,000 (U.S.).

Inspired by Norman Lear, Mendoza created a program comparable to *All in the Family* dealing with a typical Cuban-American family of three generations: a pair of teenage children who had been largely assimilated into U.S. life; their parents, who were caught between the two cultures; and their grandparents, who spoke no English and clung to the Cuban culture (Brown, 1978). The father, Pepe Peña, was depicted as a Cuban Archie Bunker: A firm believer in "machismo," he disliked change, although he grudgingly accepted it. He objected to his daughter's social activities. He was parsimonious and highly opinionated but also warm and affectionate toward his family.

Que Pasa, U.S.A.? was originally created by the Miami public television station for local broadcast in the Miami and Tampa areas, where about 500,000 Hispanic audience members, largely of Cuban descent, lived.[14] However, the popularity of the show cut across cultural boundaries. Some 70 public television stations in the United States broadcast the series when it was nationally syndicated (Jory, 1978). The program was watched by an estimated 20 million viewers, 40 times the size of the original target audience.

Social themes promoted on the program included the importance of learning English, the maintenance of Cuban culture and traditions, the importance of family solidarity, intergenerational conflict, ethnic and racial prejudices, and dealing with peer pressure. The show was accompanied by instructor's manuals for classroom use (WPBT, 1978).

Que Pasa, U.S.A.? offered a 50–50 English–Spanish language content (Jory, 1978). Dialogues were carefully constructed, and English and Spanish expressions were mixed line by line. It was hoped that the bilingual nature of

---

[14]Miami, in the late 1990s, is the most culturally diverse major city in the United States, with only 12% of its population composed of White Euro-Americans (Rogers & Steinfatt, 1999).

the series would help Cuban viewers learn English. As an unintended consequence, the show also helped English-speaking individuals learn Spanish.[15]

Entertainment-education has been used extensively in the United States.
Nevertheless, the most spectacular applications of entertainment-education
strategy have been in developing countries, where it has been utilized in a
somewhat different way.

* * *

Readers are invited to journey with us to Peru, Mexico, India, the Philippines, Nigeria, England, Jamaica, Kenya, and Tanzania in the chapters that
follow, as we trace the evolution of entertainment-education and scholarly
research on its process and effects. The modern history of entertainment-
education really begins in Peru, in 1969, with a series of unplanned, unan-
ticipated events.

---

[15]Inspired by the audience popularity of *Que Pasa, U.S.A.?*, media entrepreneurs in the
United States (15 years later in 1993) created another television series called *Destinos*
(*Destination*) to teach Spanish language. Workbooks and audiotapes supplemented the
educational content of this entertaining soap opera.

CHAPTER TWO

Simplemente María[1]

The telenovela *was so popular that the military junta in Peru suspended Cabinet meetings in order to watch* Simplemente María.

—Ricardo Blume (an actor in *Simplemente María*, personal communication, May 18, 1990)

When we got to the Church [to film María's wedding], it was crazy. Everybody in Lima was there. It was impossible to shoot [the television episode]. The Police came to help because people were screaming, fainting. That was unbelievable.

—Mariela Trejos (an actress in *Simplemente María*, personal communication, March 22, 1994)

THE MAID WEDS THE MAESTRO

After a 20-year on-screen romance, will María, the household maid, marry Maestro Esteban, her former literacy teacher? For more than 10 months in 1969–1970, this question was discussed and debated by millions of Peruvians, who tuned their TV sets each evening to watch the hit soap opera *Simple-*

[1]This chapter draws on Singhal, Obregon, and Rogers (1994). The research reported here was supported by grants from Ohio University's Center for International Affairs and its John Houk Fund. We thank Henry Geddes-Gonzales, Dr. Teresa Quiroz, Walter Saba, Moshe Furgang, James Dettlef, Dr. Nora Mazziotti, and other scholars and the producers of Peruvian television for their help in the present research. We acknowledge the helpful comments of Dr. Hugh M. Culbertson and Professor Guido Stempel III, both at the Scripps School of Journalism, Ohio University.

mente María (Simply Mary). When María finally agreed to marry Esteban in episode 225 of the *telenovela* (about halfway through the 21 months of the broadcasts), Peruvians cheered and celebrated. As one respondent recalled: "After all, one of our own—our darling María—was getting married." The wedding was announced on the front page of *El Comercio*, Peru's leading newspaper. "It was the wedding of the century in Peru," according to Mariela Trejos, an actress in *Simplemente María* (personal communication, March 22, 1994).

"The wedding paralyzed Lima" (personal communication, H. Polar, March 23, 1994). A crowd of about 10,000 people gathered in the plaza outside the Church of Santa Teresita del Niño Jesús in Lima, where the wedding sequence was shot (the location of the wedding had been announced in a previous episode). Some 2,000 people were crowded into the church itself, so many that the television actors and camera crew could not enter (Photo 2.1). The assembled people, dressed in their best clothes and carrying bouquets and gifts for María and the Maestro, agreed to move outside when promised there would be a reception line in which they could congratulate the newlyweds after the marriage ceremony. *El Comercio* described this unusual event: "Last Saturday, fiction became reality for many viewers: María wed Maestro Esteban in a real Church, with real people, with guests, with a real priest, with a reception, with champagne, with gifts for the bride and groom. People were dressed in their best outfits; several people fainted, gripped by their emotions. Women cried when María finally said 'yes' to Esteban" (*Simplemente Absurdo*, 1970; Vasquez, 1970).

"The day following the wedding, newspapers pushed the limits of fiction and reality, by covering the marriage of María on their front page [Photo 2.2]. The theatrical marriage, prepared and previewed, was reported like real news," stated *El Comercio* (*Simplemente Absurdo*, 1970). Fiction and fantasy were mixed in the wedding episode of *Simplemente María*. As the soap opera's producer, Vlado Radovich, noted: "There was confusion about who was getting married, whether they were María and the schoolteacher, Maestro Esteban, or Saby Kamalich and Braulio Castillo [the actress and the actor who played these roles]" (personal communication, V. Radovich, March 18, 1994). After the wedding, Peruvian newspapers reported that the newlyweds traveled on their honeymoon to visit Machu Picchu (*Una Novia Radiante*, 1970). To many viewers, María and Esteban were not just television roles played by actors, they represented real people. Viewers perceived their relationship with the characters as real, as if they were in a personal relationship with them, not a mass-mediated one.

In fact, television fantasy directly affected reality in this particular case. The priest at the church, Father Teodoro Piscinelli, initially refused to perform the María and Maestro wedding ceremony; he had been forbidden by his archbishop to marry the television couple (*Simplemente Absurdo*, 1970). The

SIMPLEMENTE ABSURDO

Photo 2.1. Some 10,000 people, dressed in their best outfits and carrying flowers and gifts, showed up for the wedding of María and Maestro Esteban, conducted in a church in Lima, Peru. *El Comercio*, the national newspaper, called this audience response *Simplemente Absurdo* (simply absurd). (*Source:* Personal files of the authors.)

priest relented when the *telenovela*'s executive producer promised that PAN-TEL, the network that broadcast *Simplemente María*, would repair the leaking roof of the church. However, the wedding "was world news and the infor-mation reached the Vatican. The priest was then removed from Lima and assigned to another country" (V. Radovich, personal communication, March 18, 1994). When last heard from, Father Piscinelli was still posted at a small parish in the Amazon River basin.

The wedding was a defining moment in *Simplemente María* and in stimu-lating the entertainment-education strategy.

MARIA SE CASA HOY CON EL "MAESTRO" ESTEBAN

Photo 2.2. A leading Peruvian newspaper, *El Expresso* (1970) printed this headline and picture proclaiming: "Maestro Esteban and the beautiful María Ramos were married this morning in what was considered 'the wedding of the year' in the Church of Santa Teresita del Niño Jesus. . . . The actors that were eternally united before God today are Saby Kamalich ('María Ramos') and Braulio Castillo ('Maestro Esteban Pasciarotti'). They were married, in the television version, after a romance of more than 20 years. Extraordinary interest in the marriage was expressed, especially by the female population" (translated by the authors). (*Source:* Personal files of the authors.)

RETRACING *SIMPLEMENTE MARÍA*

Unfortunately, no scholarly research was conducted on the audience effects of *Simplemente María* when it was broadcast in Peru, in 1969–1971.[2] Only fragmentary and anecdotal evidence was available concerning the *telenovela*'s audience effects. We embarked on a research journey intended to reconstruct the history of *Simplemente María*, to better understand its role in stimulating the entertainment-education strategy, and to find theoretical explanations for its seemingly strong audience effects.

Our repeated efforts during past years to obtain scripts, videotapes, scholarly articles, and newspaper and magazine reports on this *telenovela*, were unsuccessful. Then, in 1990, we were able to interview Saby Kamalich, the actress who played María, in Mexico City where she lived. We also corresponded with Ricardo Blume, another principal actor in *Simplemente María*. In 1992, one of the authors, Arvind Singhal, met Professor Henry Geddes-Gonzalez, a Peruvian scholar of *telenovelas* teaching at the University of Massachusetts in Amherst, who led us to several scholarly articles about Peruvian *telenovelas*.

In 1994, Singhal and a colleague, Rafael Obregon, traveled to Peru to reconstruct the history of *Simplemente María* to understand better the reasons for its appeal. Geddes-Gonzalez recommended several Peruvian scholars at the University of Lima. Walter Saba, program officer at Johns Hopkins University's Center for Communication Programs, and previously an official in the Peruvian Ministry of Health, facilitated contacts with several private television producers in Peru. James Dettlef, a lecturer in communication at the University of Lima, and previously a graduate student at Ohio University, agreed to serve as a research outpost in Peru.

Singhal and Obregon interviewed several actors and actresses and various officials who were involved in *Simplemente María*. The team also obtained 61 newspaper articles published in *El Comercio* during the 21 months the *telenovela* was broadcast, from April 1969 to January 1971, and videotapes of the few surviving episodes of *Simplemente María*.[3]

An in-depth focus-group interview was conducted with four female and two male viewers of *Simplemente María* in Lima. These six individuals reported having viewed almost every episode of the *telenovela* when originally broadcast. Various aided and unaided recall techniques were used to

---

[2]This lack of scholarly research on the effect of *telenovelas* may be explained because communication research was just getting underway at that time in Latin America. The first university-based schools of communication were established in Mexico and Brazil in the late 1960s. Research on *telenovelas* is an important topic of study by communication scholars today in Latin America, but it was relatively unknown in 1969.

[3]The master videotapes of *Simplemente María* were destroyed during the military government's takeover of PANTEL in the 1970s.

reconstruct the history, storyline, and qualitative data about the audience effects of *Simplemente María*. For instance, the focus-group respondents were asked to narrate the most poignant scenes they could remember. They were asked to think of adjectives that best described each of the main characters. The tape-recorded discussion, scheduled for 1 hour, continued for more than 3 hours. Respondents had little difficulty recalling salient details about the *telenovela* they had viewed 25 years previously. In fact, they sang the theme song of *Simplemente María*.

THE *SIMPLEMENTE MARÍA* STORY

Simplemente María was a television soap opera broadcast in black-and-white for 21 months from 1969 to 1971, produced by Panamericana de Televisíon (PANTEL) in Peru (Quiroz & Cano, 1988).[4] The *telenovela* consisted of 448 episodes, each lasting 1 hour, broadcast daily from Monday through Friday (*Simplemente María se acabo*, 1971). *Simplemente María* was the longest running *telenovela* in Latin America. Nearly three decades later, it is still remembered as the most popular *telenovela* ever broadcast in Latin America.

The central character, María Ramos, a rural–urban migrant from the Andes Mountains, arrives in the city in search of a better life (Table 2.1). She is overwhelmed by the tall buildings and the traffic and feels lost in the un-familiar urban setting. She finds work as a maid in the household of a wealthy family. María and her friend Teresa (also a maid) meet Roberto, a rich medical student, and his friend in a park. Roberto is instantly attracted to María. He seduces her in the first episode, gives her the impression that he will marry her, and then deserts her. A pregnant María loses her job as a maid and is forced to move into a lower middle-class immigrant neigh-borhood where she struggles to survive. However, she shows no animosity toward the self-centered Roberto: "After all he was her first love, the father of her son" (M. Trejos, personal communication, March 22, 1994). One focus-group respondent said, "There was an inherent goodness in María, which was intriguing to us."

María works as a maid during the day and in the evening attends adult literacy classes, conducted by "Maestro" Esteban, for neighborhood maids. When María gives birth to Antonio, she is fired by her employers, ending her career as a maid. Esteban's mother, Doña Pierina, teaches María how to sew. María works as a seamstress in a local dress shop where she uses

---

[4]Television soap operas are the dominant television genre in Latin America. They represent 70% of the hours of exported television programs by Latin American nations (Rogers & Antola, 1985). Most television systems in Latin America broadcast a dozen *telenovelas* daily, mostly in prime-time evening hours. *Telenovelas* became so popular in Latin America from 1975 to 1990 that they replaced many of the U.S. television imports that had been broadcast in prime time.

TABLE 2.1
Main Characters of *Simplemente María*

Character	Actor/Actress	Character Description
1. María Ramos, the central character.	Saby Kamalich, a Peruvian actress	The central female character, who migrates to the city to work as a maid. Through hard work, strength of character, and tenacity, she climbs the social ladder of success. She marries Esteban in a later episode.
2. Roberto, Caridi, María's lover, and later in the *telenovela* her son, Antonio.	Ricardo Blume, a Peruvian actor	A medical student who seduces María in the first few episodes and deserts her after making her pregnant.
3. Esteban Pasciarotti, the literacy teacher who eventually weds María.	Braulio Castillo, a Puerto Rican actor	María's teacher, admirer, lover, and later husband. He is righteous, generous, and kind.
4. Doña Pierina de Pasciarotti, Esteban's mother.	Elvira Travesí, a Peruvian actress	Esteban's mother and a supporter of María. She teaches María how to sew and starts her on a highly successful sewing career.
5. Teresa, a maid who befriends María.	Mariela Trejos, a Colombian actress	María's closest friend, who (like María) begins life in the city as a maid and later helps María in her business and household affairs.
6. Antonio Ramos, María's son.	Ricardo Blume, a Peruvian actor	Son of María and Roberto. He is raised by María (in the absence of Roberto), and marries Ita, Roberto's niece, causing some family complications.
7. Ita Ramos, María's daughter-in-law.	Gladys Rodrigues, a Peruvian actress	Wife of Antonio who dies during childbirth.

Source. Based on our personal interviews with the program producers of *Simplemente María*, the focus-group interview, and our analysis of the media coverage of *Simplemente María*.

a Singer sewing machine. She then launches her own fashion business. Soon, María's fame spreads, and she becomes a successful fashion designer, lives in a large mansion, and eventually moves to Paris to direct her fashion empire.

During these years, Maestro Esteban secretly loves María but is too shy to ask her to marry him. María, who was hardened by her first romantic experience with Roberto, is cautious in expressing her love for Maestro Esteban, even though she reciprocates his romantic feelings.

This melodramatic tension involved the audiences in the *telenovela's* plot, as María's life story moved through four decades during the 21 months of the soap opera's broadcasts. The high point of the *telenovela's* storyline occurred when María and Maestro Esteban ended their 20-year courtship and married.

María was depicted in the series as hard working, honest, progressive, and idealistic. She provided a positive role model for upward social mobility. María symbolized the classic Cinderella story, rising from desperate poverty to become the owner of a high-fashion empire. Her upward social mobility resulted from hard work, study, and self-improvement. Her success was earned, rather than resulting from winning the lottery or from inheritance (S. Kamalich, personal communication, April 6, 1990).

The series showed the real-life problems faced by migrants to urban areas. *Simplemente María* boldly addressed many social topics that were considered taboo in Peru at that time: The liberation of migrant women, just treatment of domestic maids, and inter–ethnic romance (Geddes-Gonzalez, 1992; personal communication, P. Poppe, March 3, 1987; Singhal, 1990). Other social themes in the *telenovela* were social class conflict, intergenerational differences, and the value of adult literacy.

Recreating the Archetypical María

At least five versions of *Simplemente María* have been broadcast in almost all countries of Latin America (Garavito, 1989; personal communication, S. Kamalich, April 6, 1990), each version a tremendous audience hit. The Peruvian version of *Simplemente María* in 1969–1971 was an adaptation of an original Argentinean version[5] broadcast in 1967–1968. Venezuela produced a third version in 1972, and Argentina broadcast a color version in the early 1980s. Mexico produced the fifth version of *Simplemente María* in 1989–1990, which was broadcast in Mexico and elsewhere in Latin America and exported for broadcast to Hispanic populations in the United States. It was also dubbed in various languages for broadcast in other non-Spanish-speaking countries.[6] In 1994, this television soap opera earned the highest audience ratings ever achieved in Russia (Stanley, 1994).

---

[5]The original Argentinean television version of *Simplemente María* was adapted from a *radionovela* script written in the early 1960s by scriptwriter Celia Alcántara.

[6]Several other very successful Latin American *telenovelas* have been closely patterned after *Simplemente María*. For example, *Cafe* is a Colombian *telenovela* which tells the story of Gaviota, a poor coffee picker who falls in love with the son of a rich coffee grower and rises socially. *Cafe* revolves around the world of coffee, from its cultivation to the negotiations in London by the International Coffee Association. This *telenovela* earned ratings of 70% in Colombia and was distributed by RCN Television, a Colombian broadcasting company, throughout Latin America (it was broadcast by Telemundo, a Spanish-language television network, in the United States in 1995). Another contemporary *telenovela* similar to *Simplemente María* is *Mari Mar*, produced in Mexico and broadcast (in Tagalog) in the Philippines. The heroine of this extremely popular *telenovela* is brutalized by poverty, rescued by a wealthy boy-husband who then turns on her. She eventually seeks revenge when she becomes wealthy and powerful (Gargan, 1996).

What explains the audience popularity of each of these versions of *Simplemente María?* One explanation may lie in the archetype represented by the central character, María (Lozano, 1992; Svenkerud, Rahoi, & Singhal, 1995). *Archetypes* are forms and images that are part of a universal and collective memory (Lozano & Singhal, 1993). Archetypes exist "independently of mediation in each individual" and comprise "identities of experience" that are common worldwide (Jung, 1958, p. 130). Archetypical figures such as *mother* and *virgin* and heroes such as *the warrior* and *the lover* fascinate audience members worldwide. At least three levels of universally appealing archetypes seem to be operating in *Simplemente María.*[7]

1. María represented the archetype of self-reliance, reflected in her desire for self-belonging and self-determination, while overcoming poverty and tragedy (Singhal & Udornpim, 1997; Svenkerud et al., 1995). The ability of María to endure, a strength derived from her moral superiority to those who inflicted hardship on her made this archetypical dimension especially resonant with audience members.

2. María reflected the archetype of a "disobedient female," where a women reshapes her world and that of others through endurance, determination, and curiosity (Allen, 1979). The archetypical María disobeyed the social restraints that forced her into oppression, creating a better place for herself in society. María's disobedience was universally celebrated, rather than condemned (Singhal & Udornpim, 1997; Svenkerud et al., 1995).

3. María embodied the archetype of the heroic struggle, a powerful role that resonates universally. Her struggle was waged against "human monsters, ill-fortune, and poverty" (Singhal & Udornpim, 1997; Svenkerud et al., 1995). María was a hero in the classical Jungian sense because, in the final reckoning, she did not let the monster devour her. Rather, she subdued it, not once, but many times (Campbell, 1971). María exemplified the counterinterpretation of Foucault's idea "where there is power, there is resistance" into "where there is resistance, there is power" (Svenkerud et al., 1995).

WHY WAS *SIMPLEMENTE MARÍA* SO POPULAR?

When *Simplemente María* was broadcast in Peru during 1969–1971, it achieved average ratings of 85%. Certain episodes had ratings of nearly 100%. When the Peruvian version of *Simplemente María* was exported to other Spanish-speaking nations in Latin America, it also achieved extremely high ratings (personal communication, V. Radovich, March 18, 1994). For

[7]These archetypical dimensions were also dominant in *Oshin*, the popular Japanese television soap opera named after its female protagonist (see Shefner-Rogers, Rogers, & Singhal, 1998; Singhal & Udornpim, 1997; Svenkerud, Rahoi, & Singhal, 1995; Udornpim & Singhal, in press).

example, in Mexico the series earned record-breaking ratings of 56% (at the time, extremely popular Mexican *telenovelas* earned ratings of 35%). Certain episodes, for instance, the much-anticipated broadcast in which María weds Esteban, earned higher audience ratings when broadcast in Mexico than the World Cup Soccer championship games—an impressive accomplishment given Mexico's obsession with televised soccer (personal communication, H. Polar, March 23, 1994). In Chile, when the director of the national penitentiary cut off prisoners' access to the broadcasts of *Simplemente María*, a riot ensued and was resolved only when the broadcasts were resumed (personal communication, M. Trejos, March 22, 1994).

Why was *Simplemente María* such a big hit with the audience?

Timing and Social Changes

The timing of *Simplemente María* coincided with important social changes occurring in Peruvian society:

1. The relative novelty of the *telenovela* genre in Peru, the duration of *Simplemente María's* broadcasts (21 months), its prime-time broadcasting hour, and its indigenous production quality (at a time when most *telenovelas* on Peruvian television were imported from Mexico or Brazil) contributed to its strong audience effects. Peruvian television from 1969 to 1971 broadcast many hours of imported programs from the United States.

2. The television audience in Peru and other Latin American countries was expanding rapidly in 1969–1970 due to increased television set ownership.

3. The conditions portrayed in *Simplemente María*, such as rural-to-urban migration, social class struggle, the welfare of minorities, and so forth, were perceived at that time as salient social changes by the public (Quiroz, 1992). *Simplemente María's* timing also coincided with a military reform movement in Peru that especially focused on the welfare of peasants and rural–urban migrants (P. Poppe, personal communication, March 3, 1987), themes central to the *telenovela's* plot.

4. The moral legitimacy of Peruvian elites, vis-à-vis rural migrants, had begun to erode in Peru during the 1960s, a class struggle that was captured in *Simplemente María* (personal communication, H. Geddes-Gonzalez, March 8, 1994).

5. *Simplemente María* traced one individual's success in moving from a village to the city and, by overcoming numerous difficulties, climbing the social class ladder despite resistance from urban elites—the inspiring story told of a "poor girl of Andean ancestry, who was able like a modern-day

Pygmalion to triumph over discrimination and racism" (Garavito, 1989, p. 8). This upward-mobility theme was inspiring to the *telenovela*'s mass audience, especially the underprivileged.

Ingenious Production of the *Telenovela*

Simplemente María represented a "triumph" in television production, claimed the *telenovela*'s camera director, Barrios Porras (personal communication, March 23, 1994). The best available actors (see Table 2.1) were hired, the production team (Table 2.2) worked ingeniously to solve problems, and production costs were kept at a minimum. The production lacked sophisticated equipment, studio space, and other resources, limitations that were overcome by improvisation. The executive producer requested studio space of 2,000 square meters minimum in which to film, but only 185 square meters was available. "So I had to go from a big living room scene to a

TABLE 2.2
Production Team of *Simplemente María*

Team Member	Role in the Production
1. Genaro Delgado Parker, television entrepreneur.	General manager of PANTEL, the leading Peruvian private channel. Delgado Parker served as the "brain" behind *Simplemente María*'s conception, production, and marketing. He purchased the scripts in Argentina, hand-picked several of the *telenovela*'s actresses, and aggressively marketed *Simplemente María* outside of Peru.
2. Celia Alcántara, scriptwriter.	Famous Argentinean scriptwriter, who wrote the original scripts.
3. Alberto Terry, director of scenery.	Worked closely with Genaro Delgado Parker in the conception and production.
4. Vlado Radovich, executive producer.	Experienced actor, director, and producer of Peruvian *telenovelas*.
5. Carlos Barrios Porras, director of camera.	Used the limited resources (obsolete equipment, cramped studio space, inadequate sets) judiciously.
6. Queca Herreros, Peruvian scriptwriter.	Famous Peruvian scriptwriter who adapted the Argentinean scripts of *Simplemente María* to appeal to the wider Latin American audience.
7. Manal Delgado Parker, radio entrepreneur and brother of Genaro Delgado Parker.	General manager of Radio Perogramas, the leading private radio network in Peru. He coordinated the radio production of *Simplemente María*.
8. Orlando Sacha, radio director.	An actor in the *telenovela* who served as the director of the *Simplemente María radionovela*.

Source. Based on our personal interviews, the focus group interview, and our analysis of the media coverage of *Simplemente María*.

yard and a kitchen all in a very limited space," said Radovich. "To cover the space problem, we had no choice but to shoot close-ups. So we hired the best actors."

Many episodes were produced with just two cameras, although later, a third camera was also used. Each episode was shot in sequence because the production team lacked adequate editing facilities (personal communication, B. Porras, March 23, 1994). One episode was completed each day, Monday through Saturday. This frenetic production pace at PANTEL continued through the 448 episodes of the *telenovela.*

PANTEL had very limited resources. "We began *Simplemente María* with only ten episodes [in the can], covering two weeks," said Radovich. "This was like bread production. You make bread, sell it, and with that money you make more bread. . . . We had great luck in self-financing the *telenovela.*" The salary for all actors and actresses was about $1,200 U.S. per episode, and the cost per episode of *Simplemente María* was only about $2,000 U.S. The outstanding acting ability of the cast helped overcome technical shortcomings.

Outstanding Acting

The television technology of 1969–1971 in Peru consisted of black-and-white, 2-inch videotape (with limited editing capability). Quality actors were sought "to limit the number of retakes during shooting" (B. Porras, personal communication, March 23, 1994). Fortunately, production of *Simplemente María* took place during a golden era for Peruvian actors and actresses coming from theater experience into television (S. Kamalich, personal communication, April 6, 1990). Saby Kamalich and her co-star Ricardo Blume, who played her playboy lover early in the *telenovela* and their son in later episodes, came from stage roles. Even actors and actresses with relatively minor roles in the *telenovela* were carefully selected by the program producers: For instance, Elvira Travesi, a respected actress, played Doña Pierina, mother of Maestro Esteban (B. Porras, personal communication, March 23, 1994; V. Radovich, personal communication, March 18, 1994).

Furthermore, popular actors from other Spanish-speaking Latin American nations were hired to play major roles. The role of Teresa, María's closest friend and eventual business partner was played by Mariela Trejos, an accomplished Colombian actress. The role of Esteban was played by Braulio Castillo, a respected Puerto Rican actor. One reason for the popularity of *Simplemente María* in Central American countries, Mexico, and among the Spanish-speaking audience in the United States was Braulio Castillo, who was already a television celebrity in these countries (B. Porras, personal communication, March 23, 1994; V. Radovich, personal communication, March 18, 1994).

Audience Identification and Parasocial Interaction

Audience identification with *Simplemente María's* characters, especially with María, seems to have been a key reason for the *telenovela's* popularity: "The actors were so human, they were credible," Trejos remembered. Executive Producer Vlado Radovich recalled how the producers sought to foster this audience identification: "Early on, we discovered which characters had most audience penetration, so we gave more participation [airtime] to these characters." For example, María was present in more than 90% of the *telenovela's* episodes.

Bandura's (1977) social learning theory posits that viewers can learn new behaviors by observing role models in the mass media. This modeling effect is enhanced if a high degree of identification occurs between a viewer and the media personality. María mirrored the aspirations of many viewers, especially women and urban migrants, particularly household maids, of which 90,000 were then employed in Lima, a city whose population also included 250,000 former maids (Smith, 1975). María moved up the social class ladder through hard work and persistence, and without compromising her basic principles (Geddes-Gonzalez, 1992). The 1994 focus-group respondents in Lima remembered María as follows:

> She was a tenacious woman. A woman who had a lot of pride. She did not want things to come to her easily. She wanted to achieve everything by herself. These were good values that she personified.

> Even when María broke her leg in the car accident, she didn't stop sewing. She had to pay the rent. . . . that is why, even with a broken leg and a sick child, she continued working.[8]

> María was a very kind person. When she started making money, she sent part of the money to her family in the Andean highlands.

Men especially identified with the character of Maestro Esteban, a kind, gentle person who was first María's teacher, then her business manager, and later her lover and husband.[9] Our focus group remembered the Maestro this way:

---

[8]María's struggle to overcome this car accident constitutes a role model for self-efficacy.

[9]This tendency for audience individuals to identify with same-gender role models in an entertainment-education soap opera has also been reported in later evaluations of this genre's effects (Rogers et al., 1997; Singhal, 1990).

Esteban was righteous, generous, and a dutiful son. He helped everybody, especially María.

Maestro was too shy. He couldn't tell María that he loved her.

The audience, especially men, suffered with Esteban for 20 years in the *telenovela*'s story line, until he finally mustered courage to ask María to marry him, according to one of our focus-group respondents: "The wedding was what everybody was waiting for, and what everybody wanted." The identification of certain viewers with the role of María, and its consequences on behavior change, are illustrated by the following comment of actor Ricardo Blume (1990): "I used to watch the *telenovela* at home with my wife. Our maid watched the *telenovela* with us, and she got very much into the story, to the point where she repeated the words that the school teacher [Maestro Esteban] was teaching to María."

Parasocial interaction is the quasi-interpersonal relationship between an audience member and a media personality, like a television performer (Horton & Wohl, 1956). Some viewers perceive their relationship with the television character as real, as if they were face-to-face. According to our 1994 focus group, audience members regularly talked to the characters during broadcasts of *Simplemente María*: "Yes, we always made comments. When María was being ill-treated, we comforted her. When the bad lady, who was rude to María, came on the scene, we booed her."

Letter Writing. After only a few broadcasts of *Simplemente María*, it was evident that the show was very popular. Radovich was astounded by the spectacular success: "Every time that the actors and actresses appeared in public, they were cheered and blocked by the people. Letters began to come in." Thousands of viewers wrote letters to their favorite characters. This letter writing began in a completely accidental manner. Radovich said, "The curious thing is that the letters were not sent to PANTEL [as the address was not provided in the program credits], . . . but to a barber shop in Lima." The barber shop was unintentionally shown in one of the outdoor scenes and viewers began sending letters to this address. PANTEL agreed to list Barber Shop Yataco in the credits of each episode, including the address. "So people would see the *telenovela*, and know to send their letters to Yataco's place," said Radovich. Thousands of letters were mailed to Mr. Yataco's Barber Shop, not only from Peruvians, but also from individuals in other Spanish-speaking countries when the *telenovela* was broadcast there. "This guy who at that time had a small barber shop, now has a network of barber shops as a result of his popularity through *Simplemente María*," the producer reported (Radovich, 1994).

Viewer letters also provided plot suggestions to scriptwriters, and were a source of feedback about the progress of the storyline.[10] Very few of these messages were simply fan letters.

Mixing Fantasy and Reality. For many viewers, *Simplemente María* blurred the distinction between fantasy and reality, greatly contributing to its popular appeal. The characters seemed real, according to our focus group: "The school teacher was as school teachers are. The maid was as a maid is . . . not with a lot of make-up or elegance."

As with the televised wedding of María and Maestro Esteban, numerous other events merged fantasy with reality. For example, when María's daughter-in-law, Ita, died during childbirth, television viewers grieved. Several thousand Lima residents came to the televising of Ita's funeral, dressed in mourning clothes. According to Radovich, "People cried. Flower shops in Lima ran out of flowers, and pharmacies made brisk sales of valium." One respondent stated: "The screen reflected reality. . . . María was an authentic maid. . . . She was so real that she even had the accent of those people from the [Andes] highlands."

The blending of reality and fantasy in the *Simplemente María* experience became a key element in the entertainment-education strategy derived from this *telenovela. The reality of the educational content is merged with the fantasy of the entertainment context, which increases the educational effects.* Audience members identify with the fictionalized roles depicted in the *telenovela* and translate this fantasy into changes in their behavior.

Group Viewing. Group viewing of *Simplemente María* increased its popularity and its effects. As one focus-group respondent recalled: "I remember that the majority of the people would stop doing whatever they were doing in order to watch *Simplemente María*. The broadcast time of *Simplemente María* was sacred. Many of us watched together with relatives, neighbors, and friends."

Telenovelas are a topic of animated discussion among family members, friends, and others in Latin America (Geddes-Gonzalez, 1992; Quiroz, 1993). People often watch soap operas collectively and discuss them at home, in their neighborhoods, and in the workplace. One respondent stated: "We used to talk about the *telenovela* . . . with our relatives and neighbors. If somebody had not seen the previous episode, we would tell them about the entire episode."

---

[10]Later entertainment-education soap operas in other nations have also elicited a large number of letters from audience members, 400,000 in the case of a 1984–1985 Indian television soap opera, *Hum Log* (Singhal, 1990), and 150,000 letters to a 1996–1997 Indian radio soap opera, *Tinka Tinka Sukh.*

At the time of *Simplemente María's* broadcasts, starting in 1969, the penetration of television sets in Peruvian households was about 25%, which encouraged group viewing. (The *telenovela's* popularity also caused the wider diffusion of television sets in Peru.) One respondent recalled in 1994: "Many people watched *Simplemente María* in shopping centers, where TV sets were on sale." Interpersonal communication among peers about an educational topic, stimulated by exposure to an entertainment-education soap opera, greatly magnifies the effects of the mass media message.[11]

Simplemente María was a family-oriented *telenovela*, and, unlike most previous Peruvian *telenovelas*, attracted a large male viewership. But it was especially popular with domestic maids and rural-to-urban migrants (*Simplemente María* promote, 1969). Often a maid joined the entire family in watching an episode of the *telenovela*. The characters of María and Esteban "who must contend with tragic destiny, were the subject of everyone's sympathy" (Geddes-Gonzalez, 1992). The *telenovela's* popularity overcame social class differences. *Simplemente María* was popular among both rich and poor in Peru, our 1994 focus group noted.

Multimedia Versions

The popularity of *Simplemente María* was boosted by a radio version of the *telenovela*, which began broadcasting on Panamericana-owned radio stations in Peru in January 1970 (9 months after the *telenovela* made its debut; *TV y no TV,* 1970). The radio version featured the same actors as the *telenovela*, thus maintaining the "star" quality of the cast. The *radionovela* is reported to have exerted a multiplier effect on *Simplemente María's* television audience. In 1970, the number of television sets in Peru was one third the number of radio receivers.

A 2-hour feature film called *Simplemente María* was also produced, casting the already famous *telenovela* actors, and distributed widely in Latin America (*Actriz Peruana,* 1970). Newspapers and magazines covered the success of the *telenovela*, the *radionovela*, and the feature film and described the personal lives of the cast. *Simplemente María* "fever" raged in Peru and in other Spanish-speaking Latin American countries in the early 1970s.

A Culturally Shareable Product

The production of *Simplemente María* began in 1969, when PANTEL obtained the rights to the *telenovela* from its Argentinean scriptwriter, Celia Alcántara. The Argentinean soap opera comprised 100 episodes. Queca Her-

---

[11]Evidence for this explanation of the generally strong effects of entertainment-education media messages has been reported by Rogers et al. (1997) for a radio soap opera, *Twende na Wakati,* about family planning and HIV prevention in Tanzania.

reros, a noted Peruvian scriptwriter, rewrote the Argentinean script to create a version that was more appropriate for Peru and other Latin American nations. Because of its popularity and profitability, the *telenovela* in Peru was lengthened to 448 episodes. *Simplemente María* had been a modest hit when the original was broadcast in Argentina. However, Argentinean television was produced in a format different from that used by other Latin American nations. Genero Delgado Parker, the general manager of PANTEL, obtained the rights to *Simplemente María* as part of a larger plan to begin producing Peruvian television soap operas for export to other Spanish-speaking nations.

Simplemente María was designed to be a culturally shareable media product, one that would appeal to audiences in a broader sociocultural context, outside the local or national boundary (Singhal & Svenkerud, 1994). Consequently, there were no direct references in the series to the country of origin (Peru) or to a specific city, Lima (Geddes-Gonzalez, 1992). The language used was deliberately a special version of Peruvian Spanish, perceived as neutral in other countries of Latin America (personal communication, H. Polar, March 23, 1994).

From the beginning, the intended audience was all of Latin America. Accordingly, Radovich explained, PANTEL set out to create "a Latin American María," not "a Peruvian María." In the *telenovela's* first episode, María is shown arriving by train in a large city. She "not only arrives in Lima, but in Bogotá, Caracas, Santiago, and Buenos Aires, through mixed images by editing," said Radovich. "Then, when people [in various nations] watched the *telenovela*, the people felt this María was theirs."

This pan-Latin American strategy was also followed in casting the main characters. The popularity of *Simplemente María* in Spanish–speaking countries outside Peru was due to its universal setting, characters, themes, and plot. The story and the theme of "good triumphs over evil" appealed to audiences in all Latin American countries. Polar (personal communication, March 23, 1994) stated: "When a poor girl struggles and improves her life after going through tough times, everybody likes that."

THE EFFECTS OF *SIMPLEMENTE MARÍA*

What were the intended and unintended effects of *Simplemente María?* The primary intention of the producers was to design a profitable *telenovela* in Peru, which could be marketed in other Spanish-speaking countries. This expectation was fulfilled and surpassed: *Simplemente María* was more than a calculated, planned success. "It was epic," claimed Radovich. Another PANTEL official stated, "*Simplemente María* opened the international market to us" (B. Porras, personal communication, March 23, 1994). The record-breaking ratings of *Simplemente María* in 18 countries earned large profits for PANTEL and established the export of Peruvian television programs to other Latin American countries (*Sera presentada*, 1971). Profits from *Simplemente María* were used to produce other popular Peruvian *telenovelas* like *Natacha*, which had several common elements with the *Simplemente María* story and which also met with commercial success outside of Peru (Quiroz, 1992). PANTEL began to export its *telenovelas* throughout the region when U.S. imports no longer dominated Latin American television, and in the face of increasing popularity of Brazilian and Mexican *telenovelas* (Rogers & Antola, 1985).

   Simplemente María created a *telenovela culture* in Latin America (personal communication, M. Quiroz, March 23, 1994). *Telenovelas* became part of people's daily lives. Each country in Latin America, especially Mexico, Brazil, Venezuela, and Colombia, developed its unique style. But *Simplemente María* helped establish *telenovelas* as the dominant genre of television broadcasting in the region.

Sewing Fever

The most intriguing aspect of the series was its unintended educational effects. In countries in which *Simplemente María* was broadcast, housemaids began to sew.[12] The number of sewing centers increased in Peru and other Latin American countries, and enrollment in sewing classes rose sharply. This effect is striking because the sewing of clothes at home then was being replaced by cheaper manufactured clothing throughout Latin America.

   The sale of Singer sewing machines increased sharply in each Spanish-speaking country where the series was broadcast. María used a Singer machine on television, and Singer purchased advertising in the broadcasts. The company reported "record sales and earnings" in 1969, 8.6% higher than the previous year (Reckert, 1970). Sales in 1973 reached 1 million in the United States, but 2.1 million sewing machines were sold elsewhere (Carberry, 1975). Owing to the popularity of the *telenovela*, Singer earned net profits of more than $20 million in Latin America (Rogers & Antola, 1985). Singer presented Saby Kamalich, who played María, with a small gold sewing machine in gratitude for her role in inadvertently promoting their product (S. Kamalich, personal communication, April 6, 1990).

   As a result of the *telenovela*, many household maids in Lima wanted to purchase a sewing machine, although this acquisition was beyond their economic means (Smith, 1975). Of those who bought sewing machines, many were disappointed that they neither became rich nor famous like María. Out

---

[12]The most popular occupational asspiration for Peruvian maids in the early 1970s, presumably as a result of viewing *Simplemente María*, was dressmaker (Ximena & Chaney, 1985, p. 68).

of the resulting frustration, a group of self-identified radical maids emerged in Lima in 1970, known as *Las Marías*.

Enrollment in Adult Literacy Classes

Maids and other domestic employees began to ask their bosses for time off to participate in evening adult literacy classes, as María did. Our 1994 focus-group respondents recalled:

"Before *Simplemente María*, maids in Peru never went to school. They had no aspirations. No one had primary education."

"*Simplemente María* helped many people who were working as maids. They saw that the only way to improve was by studying. Many women completed primary school and learned how to sew."

Enrollment in adult literacy classes expanded in Peru, Mexico, and other Latin American countries when the soap opera was broadcast there. In Peru, the military government launched a special program of literacy classes for maids. The Mexican government began a nationwide literacy campaign, inspired by the impact of *Simplemente María*. The Mexican campaign in the mid-1970s led Miguel Sabido to produce Mexico's first entertainment-education *telenovela*, *Ven Conmigo*, to promote enrollment in literacy classes (see chap. 3, this volume). *Ven Conmigo* was written at Sabido's request by Celia Alcántara, the Argentinean scriptwriter who wrote the original scripts of *Simplemente María*.

Increased Consideration for Maids

Focus-group respondents in Peru stated that *Simplemente María* was important in influencing the attitudes of elite Peruvians toward their maids: "After watching the *Simplemente María* story, we realized that the treatment of maids was very bad." Maids were stereotyped as illiterate and backward. The series helped viewers understand problems associated with rural–urban migration, the acculturation process of migrants, and the specific problems faced by domestic maids in the city. Many families began to call their maids "María" and to become more interested in their maid's welfare, said one of the *telenovela*'s actors (R. Blume, personal communication, May 18, 1990). One respondent recalled: "Employers became more flexible in allowing maids to go for night classes. They understood that the maids also had rights, the right to education and self-improvement."

Rural–Urban Migration

No precise data exist to indicate a causal relationship between the broadcasting of *Simplemente María* in Peru and rural-to-urban migration. A massive migration certainly took place during the period of the *telenovela*'s broadcasts. Lima's population increased from 2.27 million in 1965, to 2.92 million in 1970, and 3.70 million in 1975 (United Nations, 1987).

This rural–urban migration was caused by several factors, including attractive portrayals of city life by the mass media (Téllez, 1994). The series producers credited *Simplemente María* with speeding the migration of young village women to urban areas. Radovich stated: "Many women from rural areas, under María's influence, came to the city." Broadcasts of the *telenovela*, which depicted urban life as attractive and provided role models for urban migration, occurred contemporaneously with a sharp increase in rural–urban migration in Peru. *Simplemente María* may have contributed to this urbanization, an example of the unintended effects of entertainment-education.

The Actors Become Stars

Simplemente María's success vaulted the actors and actresses of the *telenovela* into celebrity status. Saby Kamalich explained that she initially refused to play the role of María because she was 33 years old in 1969 and did not look like the 17-year-old "little Indian girl" she was asked to portray. Kamalich was also light-skinned, green-eyed, and relatively tall. Furthermore, the idea of playing a low-status maid did not appeal to her. When Kamalich first appeared on the television set, she wore an elegant hairstyle by Yataco, a well–known hair designer in Lima. Radovich told her: "You look like Saby, not like María. Get two ponytails and please learn to speak in a neutral accent." Eventually the actress portrayed the role of a household maid so effectively, the executive producer stated in a 1994 interview, "she became María."

The soap opera made Kamalich a legend in Latin America, "from Tierra del Fuego [in the South] to the Rio Bravo [the Rio Grande River]" (Garavito, 1989). The president of Panama, General Manuel Torrijos, accompanied Kamalich "on a tour of several provinces with the idea of taking a popular person to his people" (personal communication, S. Kamalich, April 6, 1990). Young women knelt and kissed the hem of her skirt, a symbol of great respect bordering on idol worship.

Adulation for Kamalich was so great in Peru that she moved to Mexico City, the center of Spanish-language *telenovela* production in Latin America. Ricardo Blume, who played the roles of her seducer and her son, also moved to Mexico to act in *telenovelas* (R. Blume, personal communication, May 18, 1990). Kamalich later starred in numerous Mexican *telenovelas* following her role in *Simplemente María*, but she said that "there was nothing quite like *Simplemente María*. Nor will there ever be."

Stimulating the Entertainment-Education Strategy

The most important indirect effect of *Simplemente María* occurred in the early 1970s, when Sabido developed the entertainment-education strategy based on his analysis of the audience effects of *Simplemente María* in Mexico (see chap. 3, this volume). Sabido realized the educational potential of *telenovelas* by analyzing the "educational" effects of the Peruvian *telenovela*'s broadcasts he observed in Mexico: Sharp increases in the enrollment in adult literacy and sewing classes, and in the sale of Singer sewing machines. The success of *Simplemente María* indirectly led to implementation of numerous other entertainment-education efforts utilizing television and radio soap operas, popular music, films, comic books, and street theater (see Fig. 3.1)—It was a watershed in the development of the entertainment-education strategy.

ETHICAL PROBLEMS GENERATED BY *SIMPLEMENTE MARÍA*

Simplemente María was not free of limitations; it raised several ethical dilemmas with respect to the entertainment-education strategy.

1. The blurring of fantasy and reality was a mixed blessing. Perhaps *Simplemente María* helped contribute to rural–urban migration in Peru. It could also be argued that the series helped keep people in rural areas. In the *telenovela*, María sends earnings to her family so they could buy land, perhaps inspiring other urban migrants to do the same.

Furthermore, "Many women decided to get their [Singer sewing] machines and imitate María's work and behavior," reported Radovich. "Up to this point, the effects of the *telenovela* were positive. But . . . they could not make the dream a reality, the dream of becoming María Ramos, the dictator of world fashion." The *telenovela* may have frustrated individuals who incorrectly learned from that ability with sewing machinery offered a fast track to higher socioeconomic status. As noted previously, some maids formed a radical group, *Las Marías*, to press for improved pay and working conditions in Peru (Smith, 1975).

2. The strong audience involvement in *Simplemente María* presents certain ethical dilemmas for media producers, policymakers, and audience members. Radovich said: "We have to be very careful about using mass media. They may be used for negative or positive purposes. We should be well prepared to define where fantasy ends, and where reality begins." He went on to say: "I believe that a good educational *telenovela* should show a story where a woman like *Simplemente María* would go back to the highlands and would create development there. That would be great. But to sell Cinderella is fantasy, not reality." A key ethical question arising from the audience success of *Simplemente María* is who is to determine what is right for whom? This issue is involved in the design of any message with intentional effects. But it is especially important in entertainment-education

soap operas, which have been found to have strong effects (Shefner-Rogers & Rogers, 1997).

3. Profits from *Simplemente María* were more important for PANTEL than the *telenovela's* educational usefulness to society. As Radovich (1994) said: "María's story could have easily finished in less than 100 episodes. . . . It was extended due to economic factors. As more episodes were produced, the more money we got." Maintaining a balance between commercial profits and social responsibility may be difficult in the production of entertainment-education programs. No established formula exists for the ideal mix of entertainment and educational content. Commercial interests often dominate social interests, although striking a balance is possible (as suggested by Sabido's experience in Mexico and by the Johns Hopkins University's rock music campaigns in Latin America, the Philippines, and Nigeria).

CONCLUSIONS

Simplemente María represents an intellectually intriguing and pioneering case for examining entertainment-education for several reasons:

1. *Simplemente María* was a highly entertaining *telenovela* that led to unexpected educational effects: It inspired low-status women viewers to enroll in adult literacy classes and sewing classes, raising their perceived self-efficacy. The seemingly "mindless genre" of a *telenovela*, had strong educational effects, a major surprise at the time.

2. *Simplemente María* demonstrated that television programs could be commercially profitable as well as socially responsible. It also demonstrated the limitations and ethical dilemmas associated with entertainment-education.

3. *Simplemente María* directly influenced the formulation of a theoretically based entertainment-education strategy, the idea of consciously combining entertaining and educational media content (although the *telenovela* itself was not theoretically based).

4. *Simplemente María* helped pave the way for scholars of entertainment-education to seek theoretic explanations for its strong audience effects. Audience identification occurred with the *telenovela's* main character, María, leading to social modeling (Bandura, 1977). Furthermore, a high degree of parasocial interaction—a quasi-interpersonal relationship between an audience member and a media personality (Horton & Wohl, 1956)—took place between the viewers and the *telenovela* characters, reflecting high levels of audience involvement. The duration of the *telenovela's* broadcasts—approximately 2 years—provided an opportunity for repeating the motivational

messages, leading to stronger audience effects than occur from most single-shot messages.

5. *Simplemente María* blurred the distinction between fantasy and reality, which was then intentionally created in applications of the entertainment-education strategy by Sabido—a theoretically based approach for creating educational effects widely used in other nations.

Miguel Sabido and the Entertainment-Education Strategy

The worth of a theory is ultimately judged by the power of the change it produces. Psychologists are skillful at developing theories but rather slow in translating them into practice.

Albert Bandura (Stanford University psychologist, cited in Evans, 1980, p. 159)

Soap operas succeed because of three rules. . . . audience members like to interact with their TV sets. . . . much like a Nintendo. . . . Second, audience members like to gossip about what has happened and what will happen with the characters. . . . Third, we are all looking consciously or unconsciously for behavior models.

Miguel Sabido (personal communication, December 13, 1997)

The history of the entertainment-education strategy in television is inextricably linked with the work of Miguel Sabido, a writer-producer-director of theater and television in Mexico.[1] More than any other individual, Sabido helped formulate the intellectual basis for the entertainment-education strategy in television. Sabido's work in Mexico directly inspired other entertainment-education efforts worldwide (see Fig. 3.1), including the Indian tele-

---

[1]This chapter draws upon Nariman (1993), Sabido (1989), Televisa's Institute of Communication Research (1981a, 1981b), and the authors' dozen or so meetings with Sabido over the past 15 years. Author Arvind Singhal attended a 1986 workshop in Mexico City conducted by Sabido on how to create entertainment-education television soap operas. In addition, Singhal interviewed Sabido in Los Angeles in 1987, 1988, and 1989; in Beijing, China in 1993; and in Athens, Ohio and Mexico City in 1997. Author Rogers has known Sabido since 1976.

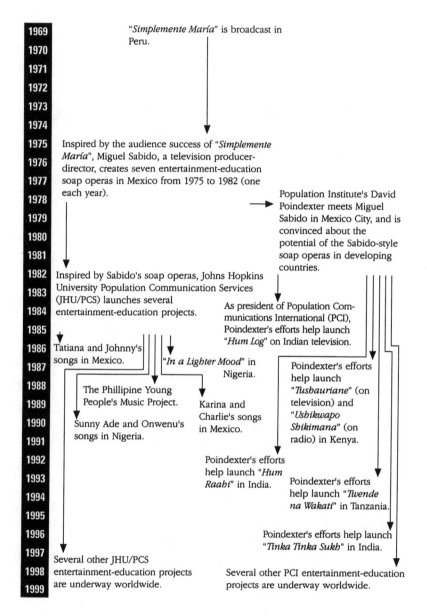

1969	"*Simplemente María*" is broadcast in Peru.
1970	
1971	
1972	
1973	
1974	
1975	Inspired by the audience success of "*Simplemente*
1976	*María*", Miguel Sabido, a television producer-director, creates seven entertainment-education
1977	soap operas in Mexico from 1975 to 1982 (one
1978	each year).
1979	
1980	
1981	
1982	Inspired by Sabido's soap operas, Johns Hopkins
1983	University Population Communication Services (JHU/PCS) launches several
1984	entertainment-education projects.
1985	
1986	
1987	
1988	
1989	
1990	
1991	
1992	
1993	
1994	
1995	
1996	
1997	
1998	
1999	

Population Institute's David Poindexter meets Miguel Sabido in Mexico City, and is convinced about the potential of the Sabido-style soap operas in developing countries.

As president of Population Communications International (PCI), Poindexter's efforts help launch "*Hum Log*" on Indian television.

Tatiana and Johnny's songs in Mexico.

"*In a Lighter Mood*" in Nigeria.

Poindexter's efforts help launch "*Tushauriane*" (on television) and "*Ushikwapo Shikimana*" (on radio) in Kenya.

The Phillipine Young People's Music Project.

Karina and Charlie's songs in Mexico.

Sunny Ade and Onwenu's songs in Nigeria.

Poindexter's efforts help launch "*Hum Raahi*" in India.

Poindexter's efforts help launch "*Twende na Wakati*" in Tanzania.

Poindexter's efforts help launch "*Tinka Tinka Sukh*" in India.

Several other JHU/PCS entertainment-education projects are underway worldwide.

Several other PCI entertainment-education projects are underway worldwide.

FIG. 3.1. A family tree of entertainment-education projects worldwide showing how each was influenced by its predecessors. (*Source:* Singhal, 1990).

vision soap operas, *Hum Log* (We People; see Chap. 4, this volume) and
Hum Raahi (Co-Travelers); the Tanzanian radio soap opera *Twende na
Wakati* (Let's Go with the Times) and the Indian radio soap opera *Tinka
Tinka Sukh* (Happiness Lies in Small Things; see Chap. 6, this volume).
Sabido's work also inspired Johns Hopkins University's Population Communication Services (JHU/PCS) to re-invent the entertainment-education strategy in rock music campaigns promoting sexual responsibility among teenagers in Latin America, the Philippines, and Nigeria (see Chap. 5, this
volume), and to implement other entertainment-education projects.

MIGUEL SABIDO

Miguel Sabido's television soap operas are almost unknown among communication scholars, although these programs represent one of the most
notable illustrations of the entertainment-education communication strategy.
Research on Sabido's work in Mexico was limited to local evaluations not
found in the mainstream literature of communication study. These studies
were conducted by Sabido's research institute. Even though Sabido's first
telenovela was broadcast 30 years ago, the literature consists of (a) a paper
presented by Sabido at the 1981 International Institute of Communication
conference in Strasbourg, France (Televisa's Institute for Communication
Research, 1981a; 1981b), (b) a master's thesis by Sabido protégé Carmen
Galindo Burrueta (1986) at Universidad Iberoamericano in Mexico, and (c)
a book by Heidi Nariman (1993), a U.S. communication scholar who resides
in Mexico City. Nariman's book represents the first comprehensive account
of Sabido's methodology for designing and producing entertainment-education soap operas, including an analysis of the aggregate effects of Sabido's
programs in Mexico.

Who is Miguel Sabido? He was born in Mexico City in a Mexican-Indian
family on November 20, 1938 (see Photo 3.1). A strong tradition of public
service over several generations permeates the Sabido family: His grandmother founded a social service order, and his mother participated in the
Mexican Revolution of 1910—"So a concern for social problems came naturally to me" (M. Sabido, personal communication, March 31, 1989).

Sabido was an unusually bright child and began reading voraciously at
age 4. Sabido's father encouraged Miguel to read a book every week, beginning with the Greek classics of Herodotus, Plato, and Aristotle. "When I
summarized the gist of the book to my father," Sabido said, "he rewarded
me by taking me for swims. I loved to swim, so I kept reading." After
finishing the Greek classics, Sabido read the classical works of Latin America,
the Middle Ages, Spain, and then Shakespeare. "My cultural education fin-

Photo 3.1. Miguel Sabido (left), the pioneer of entertainment-education *telenovelas* in Mexico, with David O. Poindexter, former president of Population Communications International, who helped diffuse Sabido's soap opera methodology to various developing countries. (*Source:* ApcoApeda, used with permission.)

ished in the classical works of the 17th century, when my father died." Sabido was 14 years old.

During Sabido's childhood, his parents regularly hosted many post-revolutionary artists and intellectuals at their Mexico City home, including such luminaries as the painter Diego Rivera and the writer Xavier Villauruttia. "My interaction with these illustrious people fueled in me a desire to rescue traditional Mexican culture from Western influences," said Sabido. He began to experiment with the social uses of theater, founding several socially conscious theater groups in Mexico City, such as *Teatro de Mexico* (Theater of Mexico) and *Teatro Campesino* (Farmer's Theater).

Sabido's stage debut was at age 13. He quickly moved to producing and directing historical-cultural plays. During the mid-1950s, Sabido studied humanities at the National Autonomous University of Mexico (in Mexico City), specializing in drama theory and in 17th century Aztec theater. During the late-1950s and 1960s, Sabido's reputation rose as a theater director. Sabido honed a technique, after much experimentation, to arouse his theater audience by having his actors channel energy through three different body zones (Nariman, 1993): One behind the eyes, one behind the base of the neck, and one in the pubic area. Sabido observed that if the actor focused energy behind the eyes, the audience was likely to be cognitively aroused; if the actor focused energy behind the base of the neck, the audience was likely to be emotionally aroused; and if the actor focused energy in the pubic area, the audience was likely to be sexually aroused[2] (Nariman, 1993).

In the mid-1960s, Miguel Aleman, the executive vice-president of Televisa (later the president), began advocating that mass media play a more active role in spawning social change in Mexico. Aleman, the son of a former president of Mexico, searched for a strategy to use commercial television to serve the public interest without sacrificing commercial objectives. Aleman commissioned Sabido to write and produce a historical-cultural program to educate the Mexican people about their rich history and foster a sense of national unity. Sabido accepted the challenge. Thus began Sabido's involvement with entertainment-education.

In 1967, Sabido wrote what he believes was an "awful" commercial soap opera called *Las Momias de Guanajuato* (The Mummies of Guanajuato). It earned satisfactory ratings, but Sabido was dissatisfied with its "vacuous" content. He became interested in creating soap operas that were beneficial for society, and which also earned high television ratings. Commissioned by Televisa to write a soap opera about the Mexican Revolution of 1910, he created a family in which the father supported President Diaz, the son supported Pancho Villa, the daughter supported Zapata, and the mother supported Madero. These characters presented contrasting viewpoints of the Mexican Revolution.

Sabido produced four historical-cultural soap operas between 1967 and 1970, each highly popular with Mexican audiences. The first was broadcast in 1967 to celebrate the 50th anniversary of the Mexican Constitution. Then from 1968 to 1970, he produced three historical-cultural *telenovelas* for Televisa (see Table 3.1). *La Tormenta* (*The Storm*), co-written by Sabido and the noted Mexican poet Eduardo Lizalde, concerned the French invasion of Mexico during the Napoleonic wars in Europe. *La Tormenta*'s success proved to Sabido that "soap operas did not have to be 'tear-jerkers' and superficial," as were most previous *telenovelas* on Mexican television (Sabido, 1989).

The late Emilio Azcarraga, then president of Televisa, asked him to prepare a plan to reorganize Mexican television along more socially responsible lines in the face of criticisms from the president of Mexico, who objected to the imported U.S. television shows that were broadcast on Mexico's commercial

---

[2]This event triggered Sabido's interest in MacLean's triune brain theory, discussed later in this chapter.

TABLE 3.1
Miguel Sabido's Entertainment-Education Soap Operas Broadcast in Mexico

Year	Title	Theme
1. 1967	*La Tormenta* (The Storm)	French invasion of Mexico
2. 1968	*Los Caudillos* (The Leaders)	Mexican struggle for independence
3. 1969	*La Constitucion* (The Constitution)	Principles underlying the drafting of Mexico's constitution
4. 1970	*El Carruaje* (The Carriage)	Story of Benito Juarez, hero of Mexico's freedom struggle
5. 1975–76	*Ven Conmigo* (Come With Me)	Adult education
6. 1977–78	*Acompáñame* (Come Along With Me)	Family planning
7. 1979–80	*Vamos Juntos* (Let's Go Together)	Responsible parenthood
8. 1980	*El Combate* (The Battle)	Adult education and literacy
9. 1980–81	*Caminemos* (Let's Walk Together)	Sexual responsibility among teenagers
10. 1981	*Nosotras las Mujeres* (We the Women)	Status of women
11. 1981–82	*Por Amor* (For Love)	Family planning
12. 1997	*Los Hijos de Nadie* (Children of No One)	Street children

Source: Compiled from Televisa's Institute for Communication Research (1981a), Singhal (1990), and other sources.

television network. Televisa canceled 35 of its most "offensive" programs in 1971, including those with the most violence and sex. Sabido proposed a reorganization of television channels in Mexico to cater to several audience groups, such as elites, the middle class, and the proletariat.

Meanwhile, Sabido continued to work on formulating a theory-based strategy to produce entertainment-education soap operas. He was especially struck by the audience effects in Mexico of the Peruvian soap opera, *Simplemente María*, broadcast in 1971. Large numbers of young women in Mexico suddenly enrolled in adult literacy classes and sewing classes. Sabido and a team of Televisa researchers analyzed the Peruvian soap opera for two years. A frame-by-frame study provided Sabido with an understanding of its strong audience effects.

In 1974, Sabido became the vice president for research at Televisa. He visited Professor Albert Bandura, the Stanford University psychologist, to learn more about social learning theory and its application in entertainment-education. Between 1975 and 1982, Sabido produced seven entertainment-education television soap operas for Televisa, each of which were popular, earned a profit, and met their educational objectives (Nariman, 1993). In 1988, Sabido and his sister Irene established Humanitas Pater, a nonprofit organization in Mexico promoting culture and education via melodrama. In 1990, Sabido resigned his position at Televisa.

In 1997, Sabido's television soap opera, *Los Hijos de Nadie* (Children of No One) was broadcast in Mexico. Supported by UNICEF, and dealing with street children, this *telenovela* will also appear in various nations. Sabido has trained individuals in India, Kenya, and China in his entertainment-education strategy. His impact is worldwide.

SABIDO'S ENTERTAINMENT-EDUCATION STRATEGY

Sabido found the television soap opera format ideal for entertainment-education. Soap operas were highly popular in Mexico, and commercial sponsors were willing to underwrite production costs. A soap opera typically was broadcast for 30 minutes daily, 5 times a week, for about 1 year, thus providing massive, ongoing exposure to an educational message. Viewers talked about the characters and plot of the soap opera at home and at work. The melodrama in a soap opera represented a confrontation of good versus bad, offering a unique opportunity to promote *good* behaviors and dissuade *bad* behaviors (Sabido, 1989).

Sabido's historical-cultural soap operas dramatized momentous epochs in Mexico's past, rejuvenating public interest in Mexican history and culture. He was pleased with the audience popularity of these programs. However, it was the unprecedented popularity of *Simplemente María* that convinced Sabido that soap operas represented a powerful means to promote educational issues.

From 1970 to 1974, Sabido worked with his sister, Irene Sabido (a teacher and television producer at Televisa), to formulate his theory-based strategy for designing commercial soap operas for educational purposes. Sabido's methodology had two components: an integrated, multi-disciplinary theoretical framework, and a well-defined production system, which preserved the qualities of a commercial soap opera while promoting an educational issue.

Sabido's ideas were revolutionary; most television officials insisted that commercial entertainment television could not be used for educational purposes. In 1975, Televisa officials gave Sabido the green light to produce *Ven Conmigo* (Come With Me), a soap opera designed to promote adult literacy.[3] *Ven Conmigo* represented the first acid test of Sabido's strategy.

Ven Conmigo

In 1975, an estimated 8 million Mexican adults, about half of Mexico's labor force, were illiterate. Their lack of formal education prevented these individuals from contributing fully to Mexico's socioeconomic development. Mexico's Ministry of Public Education created an Open Education System

---

[3] *Ven Conmigo* was written by Celia Alcántara, the Argentinean scriptwriter who penned the hit soap opera *Simplemente María* (see Chap. 2, this volume).

to enable Mexican adults to earn a primary school diploma. Sabido designed *Ven Conmigo* (Come With Me) to support the Ministry's efforts and to reinforce the value of adult education, self-teaching (to encourage illiterate adults to study), and altruism (encouraging literate adults to tutor illiterates). He wanted to take advantage of the infrastructure for adult education that the Ministry of Public Education had created.

Ven Conmigo was broadcast by Televisa from November 17, 1975 to December 10, 1976, a total of 280 half-hour episodes that were aired five times each week. The early episodes of *Ven Conmigo* tried to teach adults how to read and write. This didactic approach did not work well. The soap opera content was dull. Sabido changed *Ven Conmigo* to encourage adults to enroll in, and to continue to participate in, literacy classes. For instance, the *telenovela* centered around the lives of the dozen adults enrolled in one literacy class. One individual, a very old man, had to overcome his initial doubts about whether he could still learn to read and write. With the encouragement of other members of his class and teacher, the old man continued to study. Eventually, he became literate. He was a positive role model for the educational purpose of *Ven Conmigo*. The *telenovela* climbed in popularity, eventually achieving average audience ratings of 33%, higher than the ratings of other soap operas broadcast by Televisa (Televisa's Institute for Communication Research, 1981a). *Ven Conmigo's* average rating represented an estimated audience of 4 million people in metropolitan Mexico City.

Sabido ended each episode with a 30-second epilogue, delivered by Marga Lopez, a well-known Mexican film and television actress. She summarized the main educational point of each episode and related it to the daily lives of the *telenovela's* viewers. For instance, Lopez concluded one of the early episodes with the following: "How sweet, an old man who wants to go back to school. I have never really thought about what it must be like for older people who have not had the chance to learn how to read. Have you ever thought about it?" (Nariman, 1993, p. 66). Sabido introduced epilogues[4] to provide specific information about the infrastructure needed for a viewer to convert an intention, motivated by television, into action. For example, epilogues of *Ven Conmigo* provided the street address of the Ministry of Education building where free literacy booklets were distributed.

To assess the impacts of *Ven Conmigo*, a panel of 600 adult respondents living in Mexico City was surveyed by Televisa's Institute for Communication

---

[4]In a 1997 interview in Mexico City, Sabido told author Singhal "that epilogues are very important to the success of entertainment-education soap operas, but they are also dangerous as they can be perceived as being pedantic and boring." He believes epilogues are best delivered by a person who is perceived by the audience members as "sympathetic, charming, and a moral authority." In his latest *telenovela*, *Los Hijos de Nadie* (Children of No One), the epilogues were delivered by children.

Studies (directed by Sabido). This investigation showed that *Ven Conmigo* viewers were higher in knowledge about the Mexican National Plan for Adult Education than were non-viewers, and that exposure to the *telenovela* was related to a more positive attitude towards helping other individuals study (Televisa's Institute for Communication Research, 1981a; Berrueta, 1986). Data gathered by Mexico's Adult Education System showed that between November, 1975 and December, 1976 (the period in which *Ven Conmigo* was broadcast), 839,943 illiterates enrolled in adult literacy classes in Mexico. This number of new enrollments was 9 times the number in the previous year, and double the number of enrollments the following year, when *Ven Conmigo* was no longer broadcast (Televisa's Institute for Communication Research, 1981a). Undoubtedly, exposure to the entertainment-education soap opera was a major influence in encouraging Mexicans to enroll in literacy classes, although contemporaneous changes may have had an effect.

Televisa sold the rights to broadcast *Ven Conmigo* to 15 Spanish-speaking countries, where it also encouraged enrollment in literacy classes.

Gridlock in Mexico City

The strong effects of *Ven Conmigo* are especially demonstrated by an unintended event. In one episode of *Ven Conmigo*, the literacy students visit the Mexican government's Adult Education headquarters on Avenida Insurgentes in Mexico City to pick up their free literacy booklets and other study materials. The street address was shown in the episode. Previously, Televisa officials had queried the government's adult literacy officials regarding their capacity to handle requests for these booklets from the *telenovela*'s viewers. "No problem," said the officials, who had tens of thousands of the booklets in a warehouse at their headquarters building.

On the day following the episode's broadcast, 250,000 newly enrolled adult learners converged on the warehouse to obtain their literacy booklets. The result was complete frustration. Supplies of free booklets were soon exhausted. Then an unprecedented traffic gridlock was created in downtown Mexico City, lasting until after midnight.

The following year, when this episode of *Ven Conmigo* was broadcast in Peru, the Mexico City address for obtaining the free booklets was mistakenly left in the *telenovela*. Frustration again resulted because there is no Insurgentes Avenue in Lima.

What lesson was learned from the Mexico City gridlock? *Failure to anticipate the effects of entertainment-education can undermine its effectiveness in changing audience behavior. Providing an adequate infrastructure to support the audience's behavioral change is of critical importance in the success of entertainment-education.*

Acompáñame

Encouraged by the success of *Ven Conmigo* in 1975–1976, Miguel Sabido and his sister Irene designed a second entertainment-education *telenovela, Acompáñame* (Come Along with Me). This soap opera promoted the adoption of family planning, a sensitive topic in Catholic Mexico. *Acompáñame* was a bold step and a major innovation for Miguel Sabido, who purposely incorporated principles of Bandura's social learning theory in the series design.

Acompáñame was broadcast by Televisa from August 15, 1977 to April 21, 1978, as 180 half-hour episodes. Like *Ven Conmigo, Acompáñame* was highly popular with Mexican viewers, achieving average audience ratings of 29%, higher than the average ratings for Televisa's other soap operas (Rogers & Antola, 1985). *Acompáñame* promoted the value of family harmony, with family planning as one means for achieving this goal. Other topics, such as equal status of women and the importance of spousal communication, were also emphasized. *Acompáñame*'s specific objectives were threefold (Nariman, 1993; Televisa's Institute for Communication Research, 1981a):

1. To inform fertile couples about family planning methods, and about the infrastructure of government health clinics that provided family planning.
2. To motivate people to adopt family planning services.
3. To motivate couples who already practiced family planning to encourage other couples to do so.

The story followed the lives of three sisters from a lower class Mexico City family. Each had a distinctive marriage situation. One enjoyed a healthy, happy marriage. The second, Martha, had three children and suspected that she was pregnant again. In one scene, while her 6-month-old child is crying, a pot is boiling over on the stove, and the telephone is ringing, her son complains. Martha loses control and slaps him, just as her mother had beaten her children. Guilt-stricken, Martha moves her bed into the kitchen, vowing never to have sex again. In the following weeks, Martha and her husband talk about alternatives to abstinence. They visit a family planning clinic, where Martha learns that she is not pregnant. They are happy to begin a family planning method. The third sister represented a negative role model for family planning. She did not adopt contraception and subsequently suffered from unwanted pregnancy.

A before–after panel study of 800 adult respondents living in Mexico City showed that *Acompáñame*'s viewers were higher in knowledge about family planning methods than were non-viewers, and that exposure to *Acompáñame* was related to a positive attitude toward family planning methods

(Nariman, 1993; Televisa's Institute for Communication Research, 1981a). Data provided by Mexico's national family planning program showed that during the 1976–1977 year when *Acompáñame* was on the air, 562,464 individuals adopted family planning at government health clinics, an increase of 33% over the previous year. The number of phone calls per month to the national family planning program increased from zero to 500. Most callers said they were motivated by *Acompáñame* to seek such information (the telephone number was shown at the end of each episode). Some 2,500 Mexican women registered to work as volunteers in the Mexican national family planning program, an idea promoted by *Acompáñame* (Nariman, 1993; Televisa's Institute for Communication Research, 1981a). Exposure to the *telenovela* also influenced Mexican couples to talk about contraception.

Acompáñame was exported to 12 countries in Latin America, where it also achieved high audience ratings. The main lesson learned by Sabido from this entertainment-education *telenovela* was that his strategy could be applied to a very sensitive issue.

Sabido's Other *Telenovelas*

From 1979 to 1982, Sabido and his sister designed five more entertainment-education soap operas for Televisa:

1. *Vamos Juntos* (When We Are Together) in 1979–1980, to promote the value of responsible parenthood.
2. *El Combate* in 1980, to reinforce the value of adult literacy.
3. *Caminemos* (Let's Walk Together) in 1980–1981 to promote sexual responsibility among teenagers.
4. *Nosotras las Mujeres* (We the Women) in 1981, to promote equal status for women in Mexican society.
5. *Por Amor* (For Love) in 1981–1982, to promote family planning.

These five entertainment-education *telenovelas* earned ratings of between 11% and 16%, lower than *Ven Conmigo* and *Acompáñame*, but still high enough to be commercially viable. These five *telenovelas* were also exported to other Spanish-speaking countries in Latin America.

While Sabido's entertainment-education *telenovelas* seemed to have important educational effects on Mexican audiences, they did not find their way into the mainstream of communication research literature. Evaluation research on the effects of Sabido's entertainment-education soap operas was mainly conducted in-house by Televisa's Institute for Communication Research, leading critics to be skeptical of the results. Although Sabido is justifiably proud of formulating the entertainment-education strategy and of using it in television soap operas, he was deeply disappointed that his accomplishment was barely recognized.[5] After a dozen years, in the 1990s, Sabido's important contributions have been credited more fully as numerous countries now utilize the entertainment-education strategy.

Miguel Sabido's main contributions to the entertainment-education strategy are as follows:

1. Creating a *moral framework* of the specific educational issues to be emphasized in an entertainment-education intervention and a *values grid* for the educational messages. The moral framework is usually derived from a nation's constitution, its legal statutes, or from documents, such as the UN Declaration of Human Rights, to which the country is a signatory. For instance, a constitutional right expressed as, "All citizens will have an equal opportunity for personal and professional development," provides the moral basis to produce media messages about gender equality.[6] The values grid, in turn, is derived from the moral framework and contains various positive and negative statements, such as, "It is good to send a girl child to school," and "It is bad to not send a girl child to school." The values grid specifies the exact behavior changes that are to be encouraged or discouraged in the soap opera. It also constitutes a formal statement signed by government, religious, and media officials pledging support for the educational values promoted. For example, Sabido asked Catholic Church leaders in Mexico to help develop the values grid for his *telenovela* about family planning. Both these documents contribute to the consistency of the characters and storyline with the goals of the entertainment-education intervention.

2. Using *formative evaluation research* with the intended audience to design the entertainment-education intervention.

3. Basing the entertainment-education intervention on social science and other *theories of behavior change.*

4. Providing multiple *transitional role models,* as well as positive and negative characters for the educational issues depicted.

5. Conducting *summative evaluation research* to measure the effects of entertainment-education on behavior change.

6. Providing *epilogues* delivered by a credible individual at the end of each episode.

---

[5]In fact, Sabido has been attacked by intellectuals in Mexico for "showing Mexico's poverty in the *telenovelas,* giving a bad reputation to Mexico" (Singhal interview in Mexico City in 1997).

[6]By deriving educational values from a moral framework, which, in turn, is derived from a nation's constitution, its legal statutes, or other UN charter documents, Sabido effectively counters the ethical dilemma undergirding entertainment-education, that is, "who decides what is right for whom?"

Sabido demonstrated these six innovations in the series of *telenovelas* in Mexico that he created in the late 1970s and early 1980s, providing a model of entertainment-education for others to follow.

Why Soaps Captivate

Television soap operas in almost every country earn the highest audience ratings. For instance, in Great Britain, BBC soap operas such as *Coronation Street* and *Eastenders* for several years have been the number 1 and 2 rated shows, respectively. In India, television soap operas, beginning with *Hum Log*, enjoyed spectacular audience popularity (some achieved audience ratings of 95%).

Why are soap operas, whether on radio or television, so popular with audiences? More than 50 years ago, Hilda Herzog (1944) identified three primary reasons:

1. Audience members look forward to the emotional release they receive through the storylines and characters. They laugh, cry, and want to be surprised by a dramatic turn of events.

2. Soap operas provide the audience members with an opportunity for fantasy fulfillment (wishful thinking). Many audience members report that while their own lives are sad or tedious, they can abandon them for a short while through the lives of the fictional characters.

3. Audience members often seek information and advice from their favorite characters.

Research spanning 50 years since Herzog's (1944) classic study of daytime radio soap opera listeners indicates that emotional release, fantasy fulfillment, and information seeking still represent major reasons why people consume soap operas (Allen, 1995; Campesi, 1980; Matelski, 1988).

CONVENTIONAL VERSUS
ENTERTAINMENT-EDUCATION SOAP OPERAS

A soap opera is a dramatic serial broadcast mainly intended to entertain its audience. The term "soap opera" was coined in the United States because the sponsors of these daytime broadcasts were detergent companies like Procter & Gamble, whose advertisements were aimed at an afternoon audience of housewives (Allen, 1995; Cantor & Pingree, 1983; Chesebro & Glenn, 1982; Modleski, 1984). Fifty million Americans are regular viewers of one or more soap operas.[7]

---

[7]See Whetmore and Kielwasser (1983). This figure has remained more or less constant in the past decade.

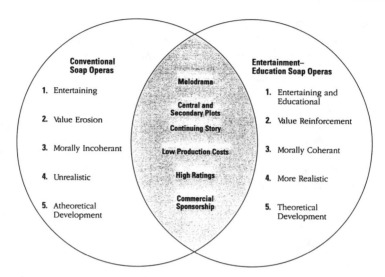

FIG. 3.2. Comparison of conventional soap operas and entertainment-education soap operas. (*Source:* Brown, Singhal, & Rogers, 1988).

In Latin America, *telenovelas* are the most popular type of television fare (Rogers & Antola, 1985). Sabido's entertainment-education *telenovelas* in Mexico differ in several important ways from U.S. soap operas. Unlike U.S. soap operas, which may continue for many years, *telenovelas* begin, build to a climax, and conclude. More importantly, Sabido's entertainment-education *telenovelas* are deliberately designed to be informative, value-specific, morally coherent, realistic, and theory-based (Fig. 3.2; Brown, Singhal, & Rogers, 1988).

Entertainment Versus Entertainment-Education

Whereas conventional soap operas are not purposely educational, the conscious aim of entertainment-education soap operas is to attract large audiences, be commercially successful, and to convey purposely an educational issue. While certain educational benefits may be realized by a conventional U.S. soap opera viewer, such learning is largely incidental.

Conventional soap operas are not intended to promote specific pro-social values. The primary purpose is to attract large audiences, hence undesirable values such as excessive sex, violence, greed, and materialism are often depicted. Entertainment-education, however, is designed to promote and reinforce particular pro-social beliefs and values.

One exception to this dreary picture of the antisocial content of conventional soap operas is provided in Brazil, which is, more than anyplace else in the world, the land of soap operas (Kottak, 1991). TV Globo, the dominant television network in Brazil, broadcasts a heavy fare of conventional soaps. They often show the good life of well-off Brazilian urban families, who enjoy nice homes and consume expensive products. Unintentionally these soap operas showed the Brazilian public *la dolce vita* (the good life), motivating them to have smaller families and to acquire money to purchase refrigerators, air conditioners, and other consumer products. Professors Joe Potter at the University of Texas and Emile McAnany at the University of Santa Clara analyzed data on the television exposure of Brazilians to determine whether it led to smaller family size over recent decades (McAnany, 1993; Potter, Assunção, Cavenaghi, & Caetano, 1998). In this case, soap operas may have been an ideal method of family planning.

Moral Confusion Versus Coherence. Conventional soap operas are often morally incoherent—as no clear moral distinctions are made between *good* and *bad* behaviors (Berrueta, 1986). Good moral characters frequently violate social norms, confusing the audience about what constitutes good versus bad behavior. Despite certain practical difficulties in clearly showing good and bad behaviors, entertainment-education programs seek to avoid sending confusing signals to their audience (audience interpretation is not always as intended, however). An attempt is made to clarify the consequences of moral choices by rewarding positive behaviors and punishing negative behaviors. Furthermore, a carefully constructed epilogue, delivered by a respected authority figure, reinforces these moral distinctions for audience individuals.

Unrealistic Versus Realistic. Conventional soap operas are usually unrealistic fantasies because they depict inaccurate portrayals of life as experienced by most viewers (Alexander, 1985; Estep & MacDonald, 1985). In contrast, entertainment-education soap operas are designed to fit the reality of the target audience conditions. Formative evaluation is conducted to assess the needs of the target audience, and details such as facial expressions, costumes, and sets are used to enhance the realistic nature of entertainment-education soap operas.

Atheoretic Versus Theoretic. The most important difference between conventional U.S. soap operas and entertainment-education television is that the former have little or no theoretical foundation, whereas Sabido's *telenovelas* are based on a multi-disciplinary framework of human communication theories.

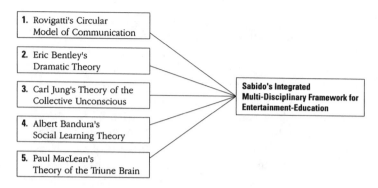

FIG. 3.3. The various theories that form the basis of Sabido's approach to designing entertainment-education soap operas. (*Source:* Singhal, 1990).

THEORETIC BASES OF SABIDO'S SOAP OPERAS[8]

Sabido's *telenovelas* were unique in that their message construction was guided by several theories of human communication: Rovigatti's circular model of communication, Bentley's dramatic theory, Jung's theory of archetypes and stereotypes, Bandura's social learning theory, and MacLean's theory of the triune brain (see Fig. 3.3).[9] Here we distill the basic tenets of Sabido's multi-disciplinary framework for entertainment-education *telenovelas*.

Rovigatti's Circular Model of Communication

Sabido modified the mathematical model of communication proposed by Claude E. Shannon in conceptualizing the effects of his *telenovelas* on their audiences (Shannon & Weaver, 1949). He was directly inspired by Rovigatti (cited in Televisa's Institute of Communication Research, 1981a), who rearranged the five basic elements in Shannon's communication model—communicator, message, medium, receiver, and response—into a circular, rather than linear, arrangement. Sabido recognized the inadequacy of a linear model and re-invented it into an interactive communication model.

Sabido proposed a layered communication model involving several communicators, messages, media, receivers, and responses. Sabido saw one communicator as the manufacturer of a product, the message as "buy my product," the medium as the soap opera, the receiver as the consumer, and

---

[8]This section draws on Bandura (1973, 1977, 1986, 1997) and Singhal (1990). The theoretical viewpoints discussed, for instance Bandura's social learning theory and MacLean's triune brain theory, are not free of limitations. Critiques of such behaviorist and sociobiological approaches exist and Sabido is well informed about them.

[9]In addition to Rovigatti, Bentley, Jung, Bandura, and Maclean, Sabido's work has been inspired foremost by Aristotle's (1961) *Poetics*. "Aristotle is the very source," he told Singhal in Mexico City in 1997. He also credited Mexican dramatists Rudolfo Usigli and Luisa Josefina Hernandez as exerting a strong influence on his work.

the response as the purchase of the advertised product. But he also added a second layer in the case of an entertainment-education television soap opera. For example, in *Ven Conmigo*, which promoted adult literacy, Sabido's second communicator was the Mexican government agency for adult education, the second message was "enroll in adult education classes" or "help others to study," the second receiver was the target audience of illiterate adults, and the second response was enrollment in adult literacy classes (Fig. 3.4). Although most television producers are probably aware of this complexity, Sabido capitalized on this conceptualization in creating his entertainment-education strategy.

Bentley's Dramatic Theory

As a theater director in Mexico, Sabido was particularly inspired by the dramatic works of Aristotle and of Eric Bentley, a playwright, performing artist, and a professor of theater and drama at Columbia University. Bentley's (1967) theory described the structure and effects of five key theater genres: tragedy, comedy, tragicomedy, farce, and melodrama. Sabido drew on Bentley's description of the structure and effects of melodrama to design the characters and plots of his *telenovelas*, which had a structure, tone, anecdote, theme, and characters organized to affect its audience.

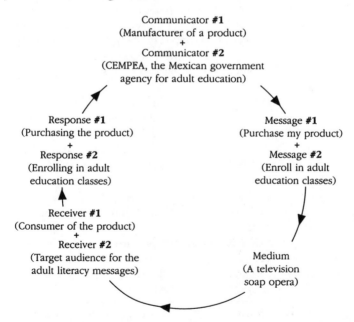

Communicator #1
(Manufacturer of a product)
+
Communicator #2
(CEMPEA, the Mexican government
agency for adult education)

Response #1
(Purchasing the product)
+
Response #2
(Enrolling in adult
education classes)

Message #1
(Purchase my product)
+
Message #2
(Enroll in adult
education classes)

Receiver #1
(Consumer of the product)
+
Receiver #2
(Target audience for the
adult literacy messages)

Medium
(A television
soap opera)

FIG. 3.4. Sabido's use of Rovigatti's model to add a second educational communication circuit to an existing commercial soap opera circuit. (*Source:* Based on Televisa's Institute of Communication Research, 1981a, 1981b; Singhal, 1990).

Sabido was convinced that melodrama was a powerful emotive genre in which *good* and *bad* moral behaviors could be contrasted. This conflict, Sabido argued, focuses audience attention on the anecdote, causing them to champion the forces of good over the forces of bad (Nariman, 1993). For instance, in *Acompáñame*, Martha, a housewife and mother, personifies the conflict between traditional expectations to produce children and the need for harmony in one's household (Nariman, 1993). Dialogues amplified Martha's emotional sentiments, eliciting high audience involvement. Suspense was created through exaggerated situations, as viewers wondered how Martha would resolve her discord. After initial difficulties, she did so by adopting a family planning method, with the agreement of her husband.

Jung's Theory of the Collective Unconscious

Sabido believed that the *telenovela's* narrative structure can provide coherence and meaning to people's lives. Humankind seeks the meaning of its existence, the origin and nature of the world, and strives for a state of well- being. Humans construct tales that model and ritualize their experiences, providing meaning to life. In contemporary society, confusion exists about the meaning of life, to which the media contribute (Berrueta, 1986). Sabido believed that drama, ritual, and stories derived from myth could counter such confusion.

The television soap opera is a potentially powerful vehicle for purveying myths—legends that express the beliefs of a people, often explaining natural phenomenon or the origins of a people (Campbell, 1988). Myths are part of the collective unconscious, which often becomes conscious (Jung, 1970). Stories and myths offer solutions to human problems as they affect conscious and unconscious minds.

Mythical stories represent a way in which collective ideas originating in the unconscious are passed from one generation to another through archetypes (Jung, 1970). An archetype is a perfect model—or an assumed exemplar—that inferior examples may resemble but can never equal. Archetypes can be observed through their recurring images, like the dream of a perfect model like Prince Charming (Jung, 1970).

Sabido based his entertainment-education soap operas on Jung's theory of the collective unconscious, archetypes, and stereotypes. Soap opera characters that imitate a myth represent archetypes; those who imitate life represent stereotypes. All of Sabido's archetypes are bi-polar, that is, they can be positive or negative role models. Sabido's soap operas typically have several male and female archetypes, each representing a different stage in the human life cycle (Berrueta, 1986).

Capitalizing on the Mythical Nature of Melodrama

Sabido's entertainment-education *telenovelas* capitalized on the mythical quality of melodramatic soap operas, which provide a fertile learning experience for audience individuals (Lozano, 1992; Lozano & Singhal, 1993):

1. They are closed at a structural level but allow audience individuals unlimited variation in their interpretation of events and actions.
2. They have a sense of historicity in that they follow the unfolding life of a community in a way that runs parallel to the lives of the audience.
3. They enact a collective imagination through the continuous discussion of their plot, characters, and situations among the audience.
4. They are re-created and re-enacted in public discussion, through oral and communal sense-making.
5. They allow audience individuals to vicariously experience the inner motivations, emotions, and inner thoughts of the characters.

The television melodramatic serial, as a mythical storyteller and as a mass entertainer, is thus endowed with a special ability to provide educational learning. The myth provides the ground, the support, the language, the characters, and the symbolic system in which instruction can make sense (Fiske, 1987; Lozano & Singhal, 1993).

Bandura's Social Learning Theory

Sabido's use of Bandura's social learning theory started with *Acompáñame*. Bandura believed that individuals learn not only in classrooms but also by observing role models in everyday life, including characters in movies and television programs (Bandura, 1977, 1986; Bandura, Grusec, & Menlove, 1966). Real-life models and television models do not differ in how people learn new behaviors (Bandura, 1962, 1965, 1973, 1977, 1986).

Imitation, Identification, and Modeling. Sabido understood modeling to be the central concept in social learning theory, which Bandura contended was broader than imitation and identification. *Imitation* is the process by which one individual matches the actions of another, usually closely in time (Bandura, 1986). *Identification* is the process through which an individual takes on a model's behavior and/or personality patterns in some form. Bandura defines *modeling* as the psychological processes in which one individual matches the actions of another, not necessarily closely in time (Bandura, 1977). Modeling influences have broader psychological effects than identification or the simple response mimicry implied by imitation.

Observational Learning From Television. Observational learning occurs when a viewer acquires new knowledge about certain rules of behavior from a model through the cognitive processing of information (Bandura, 1977). Bandura (1986) explained that observational learning is regulated by four cognitive sub-processes: *attention, retention, production,* and *motivation.*

1. *Attentional processes.* Bandura (1977) contended that people learn by attending to, and perceiving accurately, the main features of a modeled behavior. An observer's psychological attraction first to the model and then to the modeled behavior, enhances the observer's attention to the modeled activity (Bandura, 1977). Sabido used a popular entertainment format, the *telenovela*, to engage the audience's attention and designed characters to be physically and psychologically attractive and of a slightly higher status than the target audience.

2. *Retention processes.* Bandura (1977) contended (a) that people retain knowledge about modeled activities in their memories in symbolic form, as verbal or visual symbols, (b) that retention of these symbols can be facilitated by cognitive repetition or rehearsal of the modeled behavior, and (c) that if a model's actions are coded in verbal signals, they are more likely to be remembered. Sabido's *telenovela*'s provided an opportunity for viewers to retain the features of the modeled activities in both verbal and visual symbols, and to observe repeatedly a certain modeled behavior during the course of a *telenovela*'s many episodes. Sabido added an epilogue, delivered by a moral authority figure, at the end of each episode so that modeled activities could be verbally coded and easily recalled by viewers.

3. *Production processes.* A viewer converts retained symbols into behavioral action by initiation, monitoring, and refinement on the basis of feedback received on the actual performance of the modeled behavior. Sabido shows his *telenovela* models initiating, refining, and practicing new socially desirable behaviors (such as enrolling in a literacy class or visiting a family planning clinic).

4. *Motivational processes.* Bandura (1977, 1986) distinguished between acquisition and performance of a new behavior. When a television model is rewarded or punished for performing a certain behavior, the viewer cognitively (via the individual's imagination) shares the model's experience. For instance, when Martha in *Acompáñame* visited a family planning clinic, she was visibly rewarded. When a role-model in *Ven Conmigo* refused to enroll in a literacy class, he was punished.

Social Learning Theory in Sabido's Soap Operas. Table 3.2 lists how Sabido utilized Bandura's social learning theory in designing entertainment-education *telenovelas*. Viewers learned socially desirable behaviors from role models depicted in the television series. For example, when a character in an entertainment-education soap opera models a behavior that is socially desirable, the character is rewarded. If the character emulates a socially undesirable behavior, he or she is punished (Brown, Singhal, & Rogers, 1988).

Each of Sabido's entertainment-educational soap operas has three types of characters: those who support the educational value (positive role models), those who reject this value (negative role models), and those who

TABLE 3.2
Social Learning Theory Applied in an Entertainment-Education Soap Opera

Principle	Application
1. Humans have symbolic capability.	1. Viewers retain knowledge about modeled activities in verbal and visual symbols.
2. Humans have vicarious capability.	2. Viewers vicariously learn from a variety of models.
3. Psychological effects of observing a model could be: (a) Observational learning effects: acquisition of new behaviors.	3. Entertainment-education soap operas could influence viewers by: (a) Providing new information and new behavioral alternatives—family planning, for example, or adoption of vasectomy, condoms, IUDs, and so forth.
(b) Inhibitory–disinhibitory effects: weakening or strengthening inhibited responses.	(b) Overcoming resistances: Religion may forbid the use of contraceptives, but the viewer's attitude toward family planning can be strengthened by showing an improved lifestyle as a result of practicing family planning.
(c) Response facilitation effects: prompting the performance of a behavior already acquired.	(c) Prompting an observer who already knows about family planning, but has not adopted it until a TV character adopts it.
(d) Environmental enhancement effects: drawing an observer's attention to an environmental factor which may later act as a stimuli.	(d) Enhancing an environmental stimulus: An observer who usually sought a friend's advice on sexual matters is encouraged to visit a family planning clinic because he or she saw such a clinic in the soap opera.
(e) Arousal effects: emotionally arousing an observer toward a social issue.	(e) Reinforcing an emotional response: For example, a model's emotional release upon learning that she is not pregnant, may influence an observer's behavior toward contraception.
4. Observational learning effects can be enhanced by: (a) Gaining the attention of the viewer and having him or her attend to the main features of the modeled activities.	4. The effects of an entertainment-education soap opera are enhanced as: (a) Viewers' attention is gained by using a highly popular entertainment format and by presenting models who are physically and psychologically attractive for the viewers.
(b) Facilitating the cognitive repetition and rehearsal of the modeled behavior, and verbally describing the model's actions.	(b) Modeled behaviors are repeated and rehearsed several times. The epilogue helps anchor the model's actions in the viewers' minds.
(c) Helping the viewer to cognitively organize all of his or her responses that lead to the actual performance of a modeled behavior.	(c) The model is shown initiating, refining, and practicing new socially desirable behaviors in order to help viewers to cognitively order their production processes.

(Continued)

TABLE 3.2
(Continued)

Principle	Application
5. Performance of a desirable behavior can be promoted if the model's behavior is rewarded.	5. Reward the soap opera character (model) when he or she portrays a socially desirable behavior.
6. Performance of an undesirable behavior can be discouraged if the model's behavior is punished.	6. Punish the soap opera character (model) when he or she portrays a socially undesirable behavior.

Source: Adapted from Televisa's Institute for Communication Research (1981a); Brown, Singhal, and Rogers (1988); and Singhal (1990).

change from negative to positive behavior (transitional characters). Each soap opera has three or four positive role models and an equal number of negative counterparts; each also has several transitional characters (see Fig. 3.5). They are initially negative role models, or at least unsure about adopting the desired behavior. One transitional character adopts the educational value (for instance, family planning), about one third of the way through the soap opera's episodes; the second adopts about two-thirds of the way through; and the third transitional character continues doubting all the way through the soap opera and is severely punished near the end. When the first and the second transitionals gradually change their attitudes and behaviors toward the educational value, their transformation is reinforced and explained in the epilogues. Each time a positive role model or a transitional character performs the socially desirable behavior, they are rewarded immediately in the storyline. Each time a negative role model performs a socially undesirable behavior, he or she is immediately punished.

MacLean's Triune Brain Theory

To achieve their goals, entertainment-education soap operas should evoke cognitive (intellectual), affective (emotional) and animalistic (physical) responses in their audiences. Sabido drew upon the theory of the triune brain proposed by Dr. Paul D. MacLean, a leading brain researcher at the National Institutes of Health. Humans process messages in three brain centers: the neo-cortex (representing intelligence), visceral[10] (representing emotions), and reptilian (representing physical urges like sex).

MacLean (1973) wrote that human life begins with a reptilian brain, and through a process of physiological evolution, develops a visceral capability, followed by a neo-cortex capability. The reptilian brain triggers animalistic urges, such as to seek food, to experience sexual gratification, or to be aggressive. The visceral brain triggers emotional activity (the principle on

---

[10]Commonly referred to as *mammalian.*

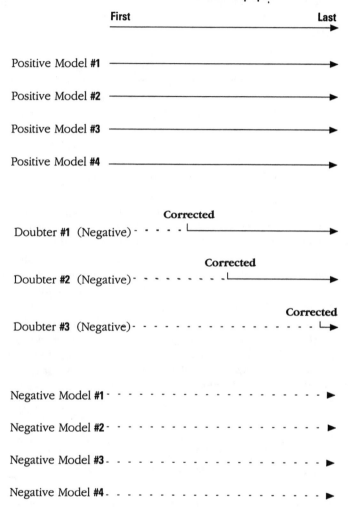

FIG. 3.5. Positive role models, negative role models, and transitional characters in Miguel Sabido's entertainment-education television soap operas. (*Source:* Singhal, 1990, and Nariman, 1993).

which a lie-detector test is based). The neo-cortex brain, which MacLean contended is only found in human beings, triggers intellectual activity. Insufficient coordination between the neo-cortex and the two older brain centers (visceral and reptilian) leads to conflict in an individual's inner drives. For instance, people sometimes behave like animals, even though they want to behave in a civilized manner.

Sabido hypothesized that sports programming, contests, slapstick comedy, and pornography elicit reptilian-type responses. Soap operas typically elicit visceral-type emotional responses. News and political analysis elicit neo-cortexial intellectual responses. In order to achieve its educational purpose, an entertainment-educational program must agitate emotions, create conflict between viewers' physical urges and prevailing social norms, and encourage viewers' intellectual activity to make judgments about moral values.

Sabido contended that most educational programs fail because they only trigger intellectual (neo-cortex) responses. An entertainment-education soap opera should evoke emotional (visceral) and physical (reptilian) responses from its viewers in order to have the desired educational effect. Sabido's strategy is to use the soap opera's plot to trigger reptilian and visceral responses from the audience and to use epilogues in each episode to stimulate the viewers' neo-cortex.

Sabido drew from social scientific and human communication theories to formulate his strategy for creating entertainment-education *telenovelas*. For Sabido, each of these theoretical perspectives served a useful function in his design of entertainment-education *telenovelas*. Rovigatti's circular model of communication detailed the process of communication through which sources, messages, receivers, and responses could be linked. Dramatic theory provided a model for orchestrating characters, their interrelationships, plot, and the various production elements. Jung's theory of archetypes and stereotypes provided a model for depicting characters that embody universal physiological and psychological energies. Social learning theory provided character models for viewers. And the triune brain theory provided a model for sending messages to the three brain centers in order to evoke desired responses.

PRODUCING ENTERTAINMENT-EDUCATION SOAP OPERAS[11]

Sabido and his sister Irene created a three-phased production system for entertainment-education *telenovelas*, which follows:

Pre-Production Activities. Conduct formative research to help design the program.

1. Identify the central educational value, such as family planning, as well as a related values grid of specific statements (worded as "It is good that

---

[11]Sabido's production techniques are described in detail in Nariman (1993) and Televisa's Institute of Communication Research (1981a, 1981b).

. . ." and "It is bad that . . .") regarding, for instance, the status of women, family harmony, or spousal communication. Sabido also organized workshops of media people, health officials, policymakers, religious leaders, commercial sponsors, and others to reach consensus on the moral framework, which these relevant leaders were asked to sign to indicate their support. Typically, a moral framework is based on legal documents, such as a national constitution, laws and policies, and United Nations declarations.

2. Evaluate the role of television in society, the television production and broadcast facilities, and the availability and appropriateness of commercial advertisers.

3. Evaluate the infrastructure that supports the educational issue to be sure it is adequate to meet expected demand.

4. Assess the appropriateness of the entertainment-education format, in light of the demographic and sociocultural characteristics of the audience.

5. Assess the physical characteristics of the intended audience to design life-like characters, sets, and costumes.

Production Activities.   These encompass the actual production of the soap opera.

1. Collaborate with social scientists and formative researchers to inform the production team about the educational issue to be promoted.
2. Foster cooperation between the creative and production personnel.
3. Design character profiles and paths based on the values grid, and write the scenes, episodes, scripts, and epilogues.
4. Shoot the episode. To reduce production costs and streamline planning, Sabido insisted that his soap operas be shot not in production studios but in a large rented house on the outskirts of Mexico City. Actors wore electronic prompting devices and concentrated on portraying the right emotions, thus minimizing the number of retakes.

Post-Production Activities.   Assess the effects of the entertainment-education soap opera.

CONCLUSIONS

Miguel Sabido, the Mexican writer and director, helped formulate the intellectual basis of the entertainment-education strategy in television soap operas. While the idea of combining entertainment with education seems straightforward, Sabido uniquely combined his skills as a communication scholar and storyteller to formulate this communication strategy. He possesses an unusual ability to translate theoretic propositions into powerful mass media messages in the form of year-long *telenovelas*.

Although none of the elements in Sabido's entertainment-education strategy were entirely new—entertainment-education is as old as Aesop's Fables—Sabido's contribution was to assemble these components into a coherent, systematic strategy, based on social scientific theories, that could be followed (or modified) by contemporary message designers to achieve desired behavioral changes.

In the following chapter, we explain how Sabido's methodology found its way to India and led to the creation of *Hum Log*.

The *Hum Log* Story in India[1]

"It was nice to finally have a TV program about the problems and welfare of ordinary Indian people."
—Ashok Bhatia (*Hum Log* letter writer)

"The audience feedback? My God, it was tremendous. We received hundreds of thousands of letters. I think some scholar should write a thesis on the audience response."
—Om Gupta (Assistant Director of *Hum Log*,
cited in Singh and Virtti, 1986)

The first effort to internationally transfer Miguel Sabido's entertainment-education methodology led to the creation of the Indian television soap opera, *Hum Log* (*We People*). When Doordarshan, the Indian government television system, began broadcasting *Hum Log* in 1984, 9 years had passed since Miguel Sabido created *Ven Conmigo*.

David Poindexter, as president of Population Communications International (PCI), played a key role in acquainting Indian government officials with Sabido's entertainment-education strategy. The *Hum Log* story began in September 1977, when Poindexter first met Sabido in Mexico City and learned about entertainment-education soap operas. The history of *Hum Log*'s creation, presented in Table 4.1, includes several fortuitous events that occurred over a 7-year time period, from 1977 to 1984, when *Hum Log* began broadcasting. The behind-the-scenes political process of launching

---

[1]This chapter draws upon Singhal (1990) and Singhal and Rogers (1989a, 1989b, 1989c).

TABLE 4.1

Hum Log Time Line

Year	Main Events
September 1977	David Poindexter, Director of Communications at the New York-based Population Institute (later Population Communications International), meets Miguel Sabido of Televisa and is intrigued by Sabido's entertainment-education methodology.
March 1980	Emilio Azcárraga, President of Televisa, tells Poindexter in Mexico City about his desire to share Sabido's methodology with Prime Minister Indira Gandhi of India.
September 1981	Poindexter meets M.S. Swaminathan, India's top agricultural scientist and a former member of India's Planning Commission, in Oslo at an international conference. Swaminathan invites Poindexter to New Delhi for a conference on the environment in December 1981.
	Poindexter meets Inder K. Gujral, former Indian Minister of Information and Broadcasting at the International Institute of Communication conference in Strasbourg, France. Gujral missed Sabido's presentation on entertainment-education soap operas at the conference but two weeks later viewed a videotape that Sabido had presented, in Poindexter's New York office. Gujral invites Poindexter to India.
December 1981	Poindexter shows Sabido's videotape to 20 Indian officials at Inder Gujral's New Delhi home. Poindexter feels that the response is unenthusiastic and returns to New York disappointed.
April 1982	S. B. Lal, Secretary in the Indian Ministry of Information and Broadcasting, invites Poindexter to return to India, where he hosts a 2-day workshop for 20 Indian scriptwriters, introducing them to Sabido's strategy.
June 1982	Manzurul Amin, a Doordarshan official, visits Mexico City and meets Sabido. Impressed, he invites Sabido to India.
June 1983	The long-awaited and often-delayed Sabido trip to India occurs. Sabido leads a 5-day workshop for scriptwriters, producers, directors, and other mass media officials in New Delhi, and meets Prime Minister Indira Gandhi, who is enthused about entertainment-education.
September 1983	Poindexter meets S. S. Gill in New Delhi, who succeeded S. B. Lal as Secretary in the Ministry of Information and Broadcasting. Indian television is expanding rapidly, and Gill is searching for attractive programming.
November 1983	Gill calls a meeting of 25 Indian writers, journalists, producers, and directors to suggest innovative television programs for Doordarshan. The participants react negatively to an entertainment-education soap opera proposal. Manohar Shyam Joshi, a novelist and newsmagazine editor, is intrigued and expresses enthusiasm.
December 1983	Gill delegates Rajendra Joshi, media officer in the Ministry of Health and Family Welfare, to attend a 10-day training workshop at Televisa in Mexico City, conducted by Sabido.

(Continued)

TABLE 4.1
(Continued)

Year	Main Events
January 1984	Gill meets with Sabido in Mexico City. Upon returning to New Delhi, he sets the ball rolling for *Hum Log*.
February 1984	Gill assembles a four-member team for *Hum Log*: Ms. Shobha Doctor, producer; Manohar Shyam Joshi, scriptwriter; Satish Garg, executive producer; and P. Kumar Vasudev, director. Work now progresses at breakneck speed on *Hum Log*.
July 7, 1984	Doordarshan begins broadcasting *Hum Log*.
Mid-July to August 1984	*Hum Log* initially obtains low ratings. The hard-sell family planning theme is modified, and related themes like gender inequality and family harmony are stressed.
September 1984 to December 1985	*Hum Log* achieves spectacular ratings and generates overwhelming audience involvement.
December 18, 1985	*Hum Log* ends.

(Source: Based on Singhal, 1990).

Hum Log involved the patronage of Prime Minister Indira Gandhi and former Minister of Information and Broadcasting, Inder Gujral, who later (in 1997) became Prime Minister (see Photo 4.1).

This chapter analyzes India's experience with *Hum Log*, which represented a turning point in the history of entertainment-education. The effects of *Hum Log* were studied by analyzing scripts and epilogues, a sample of the audience, and the 400,000 letter writers' and viewers' parasocial interaction and social modeling with the show's characters. The audience effects are presented in terms of the hierarchy-of-effects model. The various direct and indirect impacts, such as the commercialization of Indian television and the proliferation of other domestic television serials, are also discussed.

WHAT WAS *HUM LOG*?

Hum Log was an attempt to blend Doordarshan's stated objectives of providing entertainment to its audience, while promoting, within the limits of a dominant patriarchal system, such educational issues as family planning, equal status for women, and family harmony. *Hum Log* spanned 156 episodes, each lasting 22 minutes, for 17 months in 1984–1985.[2] The episodes were in Hindi, the language of North India, in which most of Doordarshan's programs are broadcast. At the end of each episode, a famous Hindi film actor, Ashok Kumar, summarized the episode in a 60-second epilogue, which

---

[2]Despite being broadcast on the national television network, one of the drawbacks of *Hum Log*, according to some of its critics, was that it upheld values that were middle class, North Indian, and Hindu. The language of broadcast, Hindi, contributed to this bias.

Photo 4.1. Miguel Sabido (second from right) briefs Indian Prime Minister Indira Gandhi (extreme left) about the potential benefits of entertainment-education soap operas in New Delhi in 1983. David O. Poindexter, a promoter of Sabido's work, is second from left. (*Source:* Population Communications International, used with permission.)

provided viewers with appropriate guides to action in their lives (Singhal & Rogers, 1988).

The first *Hum Log* episodes earned disappointing ratings. Individuals in 40 television viewing clubs, set up to provide feedback about *Hum Log*, complained of violent dramatic situations, didactic sermons about family planning, indifferent acting, and a storyline that was too slow in developing. A motion against *Hum Log* was raised in the Indian Parliament.

After the first 13 episodes, based on feedback received from the audience, scriptwriter Manohar Shyam Joshi gave *Hum Log* a mid-course correction: He diluted the family planning theme and focused on such themes as the status of women, family harmony, and national integration. A subplot addressing underworld activities and political corruption was also added, which, while popular with the audience, diminished the soap opera's major educational purpose (Singhal & Rogers, 1989c). *Hum Log* rose rapidly in popularity, earning ratings of up to 90% in Hindi-speaking North Indian towns and cities. The soap opera maintained this high attraction for the final 15 months of its broadcasts. When it ended on December 18, 1985, its departure was marked by widespread sentimental protest from *Hum Log* viewers. Videotapes of the episodes enjoyed a brisk commercial sale for the next several years, both in India and to Indians living overseas.[3]

---

[3]The videotapes were licensed by Doordarshan to a Hong Kong-based media company, Esquire Ltd., for worldwide distribution. Also, *Hum Log* has been broadcast several times on Doordarshan and on other Indian satellite cable channels during the 1990s.

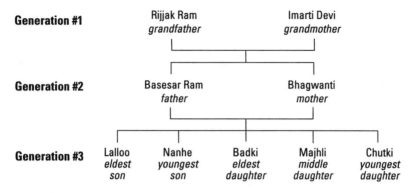

FIG. 4.1. The three-generation Ram family in *Hum Log*.

The *Hum Log* Family

Hum Log centered around the joys and sorrows of the Rams, a lower middle-class joint family of three generations, typical of many Indian households (see Fig. 4.1). Relationships between grandparents and grandchildren, mother-in-law and daughter-in-law, husband and wife, brother and sister, and parent and child were portrayed. Intergenerational differences in values about the status of women, family planning, and family harmony were addressed. The nine members of the Ram family were central to the educational issues in *Hum Log*.

DATA COLLECTION

Research began on *Hum Log* with a major handicap: By the time the research was funded by the Rockefeller Foundation (December 1986), the broadcasts had ended. While a post-hoc evaluation of a television program complicates research on its effects, a variety of methods were used to overcome these limitations. A triangulation research strategy was employed to understand the effects of *Hum Log*, by gathering five types of data:

1. Personal interviews with key officials involved in *Hum Log*
2. Content analysis of scripts
3. A survey of the Indian television audience
4. Content analysis of viewer letters written in response to *Hum Log*
5. A mailed questionnaire to a sample of the letter writers

Key Officials. We interviewed 25 key officials responsible for creating, maintaining, and sustaining *Hum Log*, among them, Miguel Sabido, David

Poindexter, and Inder Gujral; S. S. Gill, Secretary in the Indian Ministry of Information and Broadcasting and the leading promoter for *Hum Log*; Shobha Doctor, producer; Manohar Shyam Joshi, scriptwriter; Satish Garg, executive producer; Abhinav Chaturvedi and Vinod Nagpal, two *Hum Log* actors; and Harish Khanna, former Director General of Doordarshan.

Content Analysis of the Scripts. We analyzed the contents of the scripts for 149 episodes of *Hum Log*[4] (a) to identify the prosocial themes portrayed, (b) to evaluate the degree of prosocial versus antisocial behavior of the *Hum Log* characters, and (c) to identify the nature and degree of reinforcement of the prosocial messages provided in Kumar's epilogues.

Audience Survey. A survey questionnaire was developed to reflect the thematic content of the series and pretested it with 148 urban and rural respondents around Delhi. These pretest data were analyzed, and the questionnaire was further refined.

An audience survey of 1,170 adult respondents residing in three geographic regions was conducted: in and around Delhi (599 respondents), a Hindi-speaking area in North India; in and around Pune (332 respondents), a Marathi-speaking area in Western India, near Bombay; and in and around Madras (239 respondents), a Tamil-speaking area in South India. We chose Delhi, Pune, and Madras to assess how language and culture differences mediated the effects of *Hum Log*. Marathi is a close derivative of the Hindi language (the broadcast language), and there are many cognates between the two languages. Tamil is quite different from Hindi, with a completely different script and grammar.

We oversampled in urban areas, as over 80% of television sets in India were at that time located in urban households. About 83% of our total sample resided in urban areas, with 17% in rural areas. The *Hum Log* viewers, as compared with nonviewers, were characterized by urban residence, younger age, higher education, higher income, and by greater fluency in Hindi (the language of broadcast).

Content Analysis of Viewers' Letters. We content-analyzed a random sample of 500 viewers' letters written in response to *Hum Log*, out of the 20,000 viewers' letters provided to us by Manohar Shyam Joshi, the writer of the soap opera. These 20,000 letters were a nonrandom sample of an estimated 200,000 letters received by Doordarshan in response to *Hum Log*. In addition, approximately 200,000 letters were received by *Hum Log*'s actors

---

[4]Of the 156 episodes, we could not obtain the scripts for 7.

and actresses, making an overall total of 400,000 viewers' letters that were received during the 17 months in which the television series was broadcast.

Mailed Questionnaire to Letter Writers. We mailed a questionnaire about *Hum Log* to 321 of the 500 letter writers (we could not obtain adequate addresses for the other 179 letter writers) in August 1987, 20 months after the *Hum Log* broadcasts had ended. We received a response of 295 mailed questionnaires (representing a 92% response rate). As such an unusually high response rate might suggest, these letter writers were highly involved with the television soap opera.

EDUCATIONAL THEMES IN *HUM LOG*

A content analysis of 149 episodes indicated the series addressed many of the prosocial issues confronting contemporary Indian society: family harmony, status of women, character and moral development, national integration, family planning, health, problems of urban life, and public welfare services. The unit of analysis was the sub-theme. Some 10,668 sub-themes were coded in the 149 episodes in eight thematic categories, such as family harmony, status of women, character and moral development, and so on. In the category of family harmony, for instance, the most common sub-theme was "mutual respect among family members leads to family harmony" (see Fig. 4.2). In the category "status of women," the most promoted sub-theme was "women should value their self-esteem." An average episode of 22 minutes contained approximately 70 sub-themes. Looked at another way, *Hum Log* promoted an average of 3.2 prosocial sub-themes during each minute of broadcasts, representing a highly prosocial text.

Multiple Audience Readings[5]

Seventy-four percent of all *Hum Log* episodes depicted at least one sub-theme on national integration or the sustenance of indigenous traditions. Given the diversity of cultures, languages, and ethnic groups in India, scriptwriter Joshi faced a dilemma: How could the series promote a national identity while maintaining cultural pluralism, that is respect for local traditions?

An ethnographic study, conducted by Amita Malwade-Rangarajan (1991, 1992), in her doctoral dissertation at Penn State University, examined "How audiences from different ethno-linguistic groups in India accepted, opposed, ·

---

[5]This case draws upon Malwade-Rangarajan (1991, 1992). Unfortunately, the literature on broadcast television and its influence in shaping cultural identity (both national and regional) is sparse (Rota & Tremmel, 1989).

or negotiated *Hum Log*'s preferred readings of national identity." Joshi adopted a two-pronged strategy: An *Indian* identity was depicted as being in opposition to *Western* identity, and Indian identity was defined in terms of the coexistence of multiple regional identities.

Indian Identity Versus Western Identity. Episode 16 depicted a *Westernized* birthday celebration of Kamiya's[6] nephew Sonny. Guests wished Sonny "Happy Birthday" and gave him wrapped gifts. The party atmosphere was dominated by English words and phrases (like "aunty," "uncle," and "many happy returns of the day"). Handshakes and kisses were exchanged. Sonny cut a cake decorated with candles while the guests sang "Happy Birthday to You." A game of "passing the parcel" was also conducted to the tune of Western music.

Ashok Kumar's epilogue raised a question about this Western way of celebrating a birthday (Malwade-Rangarajan, 1991, 1992): "In the past, on the occasion of a child's birthday or any other celebration, we used to celebrate the occasion Indian style. . . . We touched our parents' feet and asked for blessings. Now we celebrate in a *vilayati* (foreign) way. . . . We shake hands, kiss each other on the cheeks [he laughs]. If we continue doing this, for all practical purposes we'll become Westerners and it will become difficult to locate the Indian part in us."

Malwade-Rangarajan (1991, 1992) contended that episode 16 depicted what it meant to be an Indian by explicitly describing how certain practices, rituals, and behaviors were not Indian. Touching one's parents' feet or asking for their blessings are behaviors that constitute an Indian identity. Shaking hands, kissing people on the cheek, and cutting a cake are defined as being non-Indian, as being part of an alien Western culture. Kumar's epilogue voiced concern about the possibility of Western culture wiping out Indian social identity. Content analysis showed that nearly one fourth of all *Hum Log* episodes contained at least one sub-theme that placed Indian identity in opposition to Western identity (see Fig. 4.2).

Coexistence of Multiple Regional Identities. Malwade-Rangarajan (1991, 1992) also focused her research on episode 18, in which Dadiji (the grandmother), a Hindu, sprinkled water around the house as part of her morning prayer rituals. When Mona, a Christian house guest, asked Dadiji if she could be purified by holy water, Dadiji said "No." Mona then replied: "I have more power over you. I can make you impure, but you cannot make me pure." Convinced by Mona's argument, Dadiji relented and sprinkled holy water on Mona. Dadaji (the grandfather) chastised Dadiji for her blind following of old customs: "How can any of us be impure? God made us all, and we are all children of God. Therefore, we are all equal and pure."

The purpose of episode 18, according to Joshi, was to show that various religious subgroups in India could coexist (Malwade-Rangarajan, 1991, 1992). The episode also made an indirect reference to the Indian caste system, which

---

[6]Kamya was Nanhe's girlfriend in the early episodes of *Hum Log* prior to her marriage to Prince Ajay Singh.

views lower caste people, labeled *Harijans* (Children of God) as *impure*. Dadaji not only reprimanded Dadiji for upholding the caste system, but also told viewers that being a Hindu (a regional identity) is compatible with respecting people of other religious backgrounds (a national identity). Episode 18 depicted an Indian as a member of a religious group who simultaneously respects people of other religious groups (Malwade-Rangarajan, 1991, 1992).

When Malwade-Rangarajan conducted focus-group interviews in Delhi to investigate how audiences interpreted episodes 16 and 18, she found that audience decoding was socially situated (1991, 1992). Joshi intended certain readings of the *Hum Log* text, that is, that national integration could go hand-in-hand with cultural pluralism. But audience members used their personal experiences and interactions with others to interpret the messages (Malwade-Rangarajan, 1991, 1992). For example, while *Hum Log* defined Indian identity in opposition to Western identity, many viewers saw Indian identity as a mix of East and West. A Delhi family interviewed by Malwade-Rangarajan, agreed with Dadaji on social and religious equality, not because they believed all people are born equal, but because they opposed the caste-based system of job reservations, which could deprive them of a government job (through the process of reverse discrimination).

An important lesson from Malwade-Rangarajan's research on *Hum Log* was that audience members determine how and what they "read" out of an entertainment-education text. Later in this volume, we see these different readings in the case of the Archie Bunker effect.

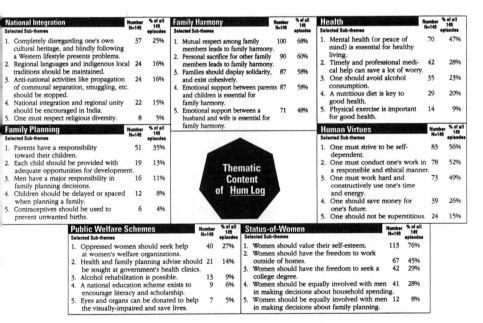

FIG. 4.2. Thematic Content of *Hum Log*. Note: This chart illustrates themes and selected sub-themes, identified by the writer Joshi and the Dube Report, as central to *Hum Log*—based on 149 episodes.

AUDIENCE POPULARITY

Hum Log was highly popular with its audience. It commanded audience ratings from 65 to 90% in North India (a predominantly Hindi-speaking area), and between 20 and 45% in the main cities of South India, where Hindi language programs cannot be understood by most television viewers. The lower ratings in South India support the notion that national television programs often have a limited appeal for India's multicultural and multilingual audience. An audience of about 60 million people watched the average *Hum Log* broadcast. At the time (1984–1985), this audience was the largest ever to watch a television program in India (Singhal & Rogers, 1988).

Results from a 1987 survey of 1,170 Indian adults showed that 96% of the respondents who had watched at least one episode of *Hum Log* liked the television soap opera. Ninety-four percent thought it was entertaining, 83% said it was educational, and 91% said that it addressed social problems. In Madras, a Tamil-speaking area, only 48% of respondents had seen at least one episode of *Hum Log*, mainly because it was broadcast in Hindi. However, the individuals who did view *Hum Log* in Madras liked the program (93%) about as much as did viewers in North India.

Why was *Hum Log* so popular with its audiences?

Timing

Hum Log was broadcast at a time (1984–1985) when Doordarshan, then a virtual monopoly in India, was experiencing an unparalleled expansion due to the launch of the Indian National Satellite (INSAT-1B) in 1983. This greatly increased public access to television (see Fig. 4.3). The increase was due to the large-scale installation of television transmitters in India: from 42 in 1983, to 175 in 1985 (Singhal, Doshi, Rogers, & Rahman, 1988). During the 18 months of *Hum Log*'s broadcast, the number of television viewers in India increased sharply from 37 to 60 million. During the same period, the number of television sets in India doubled from 3.5 million to 7 million. The rapid expansion created a need on the part of Indian government officials to broadcast attractive programming. The timing of *Hum Log*, coupled with its first-of-a-kind nature, boosted the soap opera's popularity.

Novelty

Hum Log was Indian national television's first long-running soap opera, a novel programming genre for Indian audiences. Soap operas did not appear on Doordarshan's national network until 1984, which is surprising given that similar family-centered drama dominated Indian films. Prior to *Hum Log*, short, entertainment-education television serials were only produced

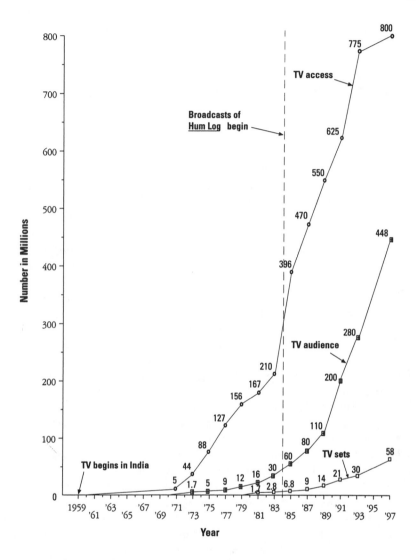

FIG. 4.3. Growth in the number of people who have access to television, the number of people who watch television, and the number of television sets in India. (*Source:* Con.piled from Singhal & Rogers, 1989a, and other sources.)

and broadcast by the Space Application Center (SAC) in Ahmedabad to raise consciousness and to initiate local development programs in Gujarat's Kheda District (Kalwachwala & Joshi, 1990; Mody, 1991). Whereas SAC's television series were relatively short (up to 40 episodes) and only broadcast locally, *Hum Log* was the first long-running soap opera broadcast to a national audience. The entertaining nature of the genre, coupled with the dull nature of existing Doordarshan programs, helped boost *Hum Log*'s audience appeal. After the *Hum Log* broadcasts were completed in 1985, a soap opera dominated Indian television for the next several years: *Buniyaad* in 1986–1987, about the 1947 separation of India and Pakistan, and *Ramayana* in 1987–1988 and *Mahabharata* in 1989–1990, were based on religious epics.

Ashok Kumar's Epilogues

While each of the ten main characters in *Hum Log* were present in only certain episodes, Kumar delivered the epilogues—written by Joshi—in all 156. Consistent with Sabido's methodology, Kumar's epilogues, each about 60 seconds, explained the moral choices that had just been presented to viewers, providing guidelines to appropriate action in their lives. Audience reaction was invited on social dilemmas, such as, "Is the role of women restricted to the household, or should it go beyond?" The epilogues provided names and addresses of infrastructural services, such as women's organizations, health clinics, alcohol rehabilitation centers, and so on, where viewers could write (or visit) to seek help. Thus, the function of the epilogues was to convert audience members' intentions into action.

Episode 98, which is typical, begins with a shot of Basesar Ram, the father, lying unconscious on a hospital bed. He became ill after drinking illicit liquor. At his side is his wife Bhagwanti, who prays for his recovery, pleading with God to help her husband overcome his drinking problem. When Basesar regains consciousness, he complains of physical weakness, and cajoles Bhagwanti to fetch him a drink of whiskey so he can regain his strength. Unable to bear her husband's suffering, Bhagwanti asks Badki, their eldest daughter, if Basesar could be given a little whiskey. Badki is angry at Bhagwanti for indulging Basesar. The self-negating Bhagwanti blames herself for her husband's drinking problem.

Basesar is sedated by the doctor and dreams about his youth, when he aspired to be a famous singer. He sees himself embodied in his favorite singer, K. L. Sehgal, who in real life was an alcoholic who died of cirrhosis of the liver. Nauseated by his dream, Basesar wakes abruptly and vomits. Bhagwanti wipes his face. Fearful of losing his life, Basesar asks Bhagwanti if he vomited blood. He pleads with Bhagwanti to save him, at least until Badki's wedding (only two episodes away). Kumar concludes episode 98 as follows:

> Well, if nothing, Basesar Ram is thinking about staying away from the bottle due to fear of death. Let us pray that he has the strength and the willpower to stay away from alcohol. For such alcohol addicts like Basesar, it is very difficult and problematic to leave drinking. But it is possible.
>
> You may call it a coincidence, or an irony, but throughout I have received letters from women who say that their fathers or husbands are alcoholics. They write that whichever days Basesar Ram features on *Hum Log*, that day the alcoholic in their family sits in front of the TV set.

On behalf of Basesar Ram can I say "cheers" and request these alcoholics to attempt to give up drinking? Lalloo has invited Badki and Ashwini to his village home for a picnic in this beautiful month of May. In the next episode, *Hum Log* will attend this picnic armed with umbrellas and ice cubes.

Contents of Kumar's Epilogues. A content analysis of 114 epilogues (42 were unavailable) showed that 40% provided a commentary on human virtues and vices, 14% clarified status-of-women issues, 12% addressed family harmony issues, 8% highlighted the need to preserve local cultural traditions, and 2% promoted family planning.

Twenty-eight percent of the epilogues encouraged viewers to write letters to Doordarshan (or to Kumar) in response to a social or moral dilemma raised in the episode, and 25% encouraged viewers to either write to or visit a public agency or service organization, for example, a women's organization. The epilogues encouraged viewers to become efficacious in controlling their future. Ninety-nine percent of Kumar's epilogues provided a hook for the next episode, encouraging viewers to tune in, often to resolve a suspenseful situation: For example, "Let us find out whether Badki will resolve her indecision to marry Ashwini in the next episode of *Hum Log.*"

Ashok Kumar: The Grand Old Man of *Hum Log*

A favorite in Indian cinema, Ashok Kumar also became the grand old man of Indian television during 1984–1985, when he delivered the *Hum Log* epilogues. "Eighteen months of *Hum Log* did more to my nationwide popularity, than 50 years of film acting," said Kumar (cited in Prasad, 1986, p. 75). During *Hum Log*'s period of broadcasting, 60 to 70 viewer letters arrived at Kumar's Bombay residence each day, in addition to the several hundred addressed to him at Doordarshan headquarters in Delhi. "I threatened Doordarshan with dire consequences if they dared send these letters to my home. I had a hard enough time dealing with the ones I got at home," said Kumar (cited in Prasad, 1986, p. 75).

Kumar's influence was profound. Young boys and girls wrote pleading with him to convince their parents that they be allowed to marry the man or woman of their choice. Several parents, in turn, sent horoscopes of their daughters to Kumar, requesting that he find a suitable match. Many viewer letters pleaded with Kumar to be their family counselor, while others indicated how important *Hum Log* had become in their daily lives. Even though the series ended in 1985, 13 years later Kumar was still receiving occasional letters.

Hum Log was a high point in his life: "The serial was a most enlightening time for me, and I was amazed by how television mobilized the Indian viewers" (cited in Prasad, 1986, p. 75). But the work took a heavy toll on Kumar's free time. "Had I known the serial was going to be so long, I would have thought twice before accepting this responsibility. . . . I accepted because H. K. L. Bhagat, the then Minister of Information and Broadcasting, requested me to inaugurate the serial, and summarize the first ten episodes or so. Then somebody else was to take over, but this never happened" (cited in Prasad, 1986, p. 75). Not wanting to desert the series midway, Kumar continued—without payment.

"My most discerning and critical fans in *Hum Log* were children," says Kumar. "I seem to have become a universal *'dada'* [grandfather]" (cited in Prasad, 1986, p. 77). Several letters addressed Kumar as *Dada Moni, Dadu Moni, Munni Dada*, Ashok *Dada* (all implying lovable or respectable grandfather). Although Kumar encouraged viewers to write, "It was physically impossible to cope with all this mail" (cited in Prasad, 1986, p. 75). Tens of thousands of letters were never opened.[7]

Learning from elders is a cherished Indian value, and father figure Kumar doled out words of wisdom in his epilogues in a form of a *meta-communication*, that is, communication about communication (Singhal & Rogers, 1989a). Ashok Kumar's popularity, credibility, and friendliness, coupled with his words of wisdom, added to *Hum Log*'s audience popularity and to its educational effects.

Use of Rustic Hindi Language

Joshi creatively combined *Khadi Boli*, a much used, rustic, yet popular derivative of the Hindi language in North India, with conventional Hindi. There are more than 125 dialects in North India alone, where the Hindi language is dominant. The combination of *Khadi Boli* and conventional Hindi served as the lowest common denominator for North Indian viewers.

The script is the most important single factor in the success or failure of an entertainment-education television series.[8] The invisible power behind any popular television show is its scriptwriter, in this case, Manohar Shyam Joshi.

Joshi, a bespectacled, articulate, and well-read man, in his mid-sixties, had never written a television soap opera script before *Hum Log*. He had been editor of a popular Hindi magazine and then of an English magazine.

In 1983, S. S. Gill, Secretary in the Ministry of Information and Broadcasting, invited Joshi to a writers workshop to discuss plans for *Hum Log*. Gill envisioned a family-based entertainment-education drama like Sabido's. The dozen other writers in the India workshop were skeptical of combining entertainment and education. They said the public had tired of family planning and doubted that a soap opera format was appropriate for Indian television.

---

[7]Most of the 20,000 viewer letters given to us by Joshi were unopened.

[8]See Esta de Fossard's (1996) manual on writing entertainment-education scripts.

Joshi was intrigued with the idea, even though he had not met Sabido during his May 1983 visit to India. Gill found Joshi an office in the Doordarshan headquarters building in New Delhi and told him to design the television serial, complete with character portfolios and storylines. Joshi was provided with a report on Indian family values by Dr. S. C. Dube and Sabido's 1981 paper presented at the Institute for International Communication conference in Strasbourg, France. Joshi also viewed the videotape that accompanied the paper.

Joshi wasted no time. He wrote the synopses for 39 episodes in one month. *Hum Log* went on the air on July 7, 1984. Usually Doordarshan had only three or four episodes in the can. Joshi was under tremendous pressure to deliver two scripts every week. He single-handedly wrote the entire script for *Hum Log*, a task that in the United States would require a team of perhaps 10 writers and a support staff of another 15 to 20 secretaries, editors, receptionists, and clerks. Joshi worked in a 10-by-12-foot study in his modest apartment in a Delhi suburb, dictating each script to his steno-typist, who then typed it on a manual typewriter. Joshi believes in dictating dialogue so he can hear the lines.

Joshi created lifelike characters with a realistic quality missing in most Hindi entertainment films. His use of the commoner's language (*Khadi Boli*), and his ability to portray the life of a lower middle-class family helped endear the *Hum Log* family to millions of Indian viewers.

A Skilled Scriptwriter

Hum Log was only the first step in Joshi's experience as a successful television scriptwriter. After *Hum Log*, he wrote a 104-episode saga about India's Partition, *Buniyaad* (*Foundation*), which achieved even higher audience ratings than *Hum Log*. In *Buniyaad*, Joshi took Indian television viewers through the life and times of a four-generation Punjabi family, focusing on the tumultuous years following India's Partition with Pakistan in 1947. Several of the *Buniyaad* characters had appeared previously in *Hum Log* (like Nanhe), so there was a certain commonality in the two hit television series. After *Buniyaad*, Joshi created two more popular serials: *Mungeri Lal Ke Haseen Sapne* (Mungeri Lal's Romantic Dreams) in 1988, an indigenous version of *The Secret Life of Walter Mitty*, and *Kakkaji Kahin* (Says Kakkaji) in 1989, drawing upon the BBC series *Yes Minister*. *Kakkaji Kahin* became such a powerful critique of Indian politics, that the Indian government discontinued it. In 1992–93, Joshi wrote *Hum Raahi* (*Co-Travelers*), which was also patterned on Sabido's entertainment-education strategy.

While Joshi has earned fame and a lucrative income from his success in television serials, his lifestyle has not changed. His living room floor now has wall-to-wall carpeting. But Joshi still wears traditional clothing and lives a modest, unassuming lifestyle.

Audience Identification and Involvement

Many viewers empathized with the *Hum Log* family, becoming vicariously involved in their daily affairs. Badki, the eldest daughter, and a positive role model for female equality, was mobbed on several occasions by young college girls, who said, "They had also rebelled and she should advise them what to do next" (M. S. Joshi, personal communication, July 16, 1986). Sudhir Dar, India's foremost cartoonist, who made a guest appearance on *Hum Log*, said: "I was surprised to see how the various characters were coming to life and the way they held sway over every type of person" (cited in Singh & Virtti, 1986, p. 6).

Hum Log was also unusual in that audience feedback via viewer letters helped Joshi to write and rewrite the storyline, suggesting new twists to the plot and new characterizations. Three avid viewers wrote in October, 1985: "Please have mercy on Samdar [the police inspector who lost his eyesight]. Poor fellow has got all the bad things in life. Allow some good things to happen in his life, for instance, give back his eyesight, please." Joshi promptly restored Samdar's eyesight, "How could I not?"

On some occasions, Joshi could not fill viewer requests. Many letters pleaded that Grandmother be cured of terminal cancer (she died in the final episode). Viewers also asked Joshi to have Nanhe marry Kamia, when Kamia's marriage was not working out with Prince Ajay Singh. Doordarshan received hundreds of thousands of letters, so many that Joshi could not read them all (Doordarshan did not have a unit to tabulate the letters' suggestions). But he frequently altered his storyline to allow for certain viewer reactions.

VIEWER LETTERS

The viewer outpouring of 400,000 letters was unprecedented in Indian television. An estimated 150,000 were addressed to Ashok Kumar. They voiced concerns about such social ills as dowry and alcoholism. Viewer V. C. Raju, in a 3-page, single-spaced, 1989 letter to Kumar, commented on Basesar Ram's drunken behavior at the time of his daughter's marriage ceremony:

> All over the country many eagerly awaited the coming of 28th May [1985], the date of Badki's and Ashwini's marriage. . . . While the ceremony got off to a good start, the auspicious occasion was marred by the appearance of Badki's drunken father [Basesar].
> . . . For a girl, the most solemn occasion is her marriage, but cruel fate took to robes in the form of her [Badki's] father. . . . The blank stare on Badki's face would have left many viewers fathoming her thoughts and feelings. . . . This hangover would last a very long time.

I feel the portrayal of Basesar Ram as the drunken entity, and the immeasurable harm he brings about, has been given too long a play. It is high time that his proclivities come to an end. Otherwise, society would believe that such a scourge [alcoholism] could never be removed.

Many letters pleaded for more women's organizations, encouraged eye donations, and demanded improved treatment for cancer patients (both an eye transplant and a cancer death were part of the *Hum Log* story). Sarla Mudgal, president of Kalyani, a women's organization, said in her letter to Kumar: "In *Hum Log* you call for names of social organizations. Ours is such an organization working for the welfare of women and other downtroddens. We are enclosing a brief resume of our activities, and hope that we will be of some benefit to the needy women through *Hum Log*."

Characteristics of Letter Writers

A content analysis of 500 letters written to Doordarshan (0.5% of all letters) shows that most were written in Hindi, came from cities and towns, were fairly detailed in content, came mainly from North Indian viewers, and were written by young, well-educated people. These characteristics reinforce the finding that *Hum Log* was more popular in Hindi-speaking North India.

More than 99% of viewers did not write to *Hum Log*. The letter writers are therefore atypical of the viewing audience. Nevertheless, they represent one important measure in assessing the hierarchy of *Hum Log*'s effects. Entertainment-education programs, especially those with epilogues, have a tremendous potential for viewer involvement.

A questionnaire mailed to 321 of the 500 letter writers yielded 295 replies, a response rate of 92%: 34% were less than 20 years old, 41% were between 21 and 30 years old, and 25% were more than 31 years old. Some 77% had earned a university degree, while 21% had a high school diploma. Forty-two percent of the letter writers were students, 15% were government employees, 13% unemployed, 10% housewives, and 9% in business. Most were middle class.

Approximately 20% of respondents said they had written two or more letters to *Hum Log* (some as many as four); 95% of these watched most or all episodes, reinforcing the notion that they constituted a highly involved group of viewers.

Parasocial Interaction

Many *Hum Log* viewers felt that they knew the television characters, even though they had never met them (see Table 4.2). A perceived parasocial relationship can lead audience members to actually establish contact with a television performer (Horton & Wohl, 1956). Prior to his marriage to Badki,

TABLE 4.2
Feedback Provided by *Hum Log* Letter Writers

Feedback	Percent Who Provided Each Type (N = 500)
1. Likes *Hum Log*.	94
2. Expresses opinion about the behavior of characters.	76
3. Identifies with characters.	66
4. Expresses opinion about a social issue raised.	39
5. Responds to a social conundrum raised by Ashok Kumar's epilogue.	36
6. Suggests new twists in the plot.	34

Source: Singhal (1990).

TABLE 4.3
Degree of Parasocial Interaction Indicated
in Letters From *Hum Log* Viewers

Indicators of Parasocial Interaction	Percent of Letters That Indicate Parasocial Interaction (N = 500)
1. Strong involvement with characters.	93
2. Likes and respects Ashok Kumar's epilogues.	83
3. Compares personal ideas with those of characters.	65
4. Perceives a character as a down-to-earth, good person.	43
5. Talks to favorite character while watching.	39
6. Feels that Ashok Kumar helps them make various decisions and looks to him for guidance.	39
7. Adjusts time schedule to watch, to have a regular relationship with a television character.	30

Source: Singhal (1990).

for instance, Ashwini received the following letter from a 21-year-old college girl: "Why haven't you replied to my several letters? Do not be so intoxicated in your love for Badki that you do not have time for friends like me. I know Badki will not let you write to me after your marriage. So please, why don't you write before?" *Hum Log* obviously blurred the line between fantasy and reality for such viewers.

Past research (Horton & Wohl, 1956; Levy, 1979; Nordlund, 1978; Perse & Rubin, 1987; Rubin & Perse, 1987; Turner, 1992, 1993) suggests that television viewers can exhibit parasocial interaction in at least seven ways. Table 4.3 shows these seven indicators as exhibited by the 500 letter writers—39% reported talking to their favorite character via their television sets, a high degree of parasocial interaction.[9]

---

[9]The *Hum Log* study was the first on the effects of entertainment-education by means of parasocial interaction (see Chap. 8, this volume).

From Rejection to Stardom for Nanhe

When the *Hum Log* cast was selected in early 1984, few of the actors or actresses were established stars. *Hum Log* introduced them to millions of Indian television households. One was Abhinav Chaturvedi, who played Nanhe, the fun-loving younger son. While a student at the University of Delhi, Chaturvedi achieved recognition in cricket. But he also had acting experience. Joshi had created one character, Nanhe, as the younger son of the *Hum Log* family and a cricketer. He heard about Chaturvedi's acting and cricketing from his two sons, who also attended Modern School, an elite private school in New Delhi where Chaturvedi performed. Chaturvedi successfully auditioned for the role. More than 20,000 letters were sent to his home address in New Delhi, most of which began "Dear Nanhe" (suggesting a high degree of parasocial interaction). Chaturvedi also endorsed such consumer products as dress shirts and motorcycles and earned various acting awards.

When Chaturvedi married in New Delhi in 1993, his wedding reception was attended by 1,500 people, including many colleagues from the *Hum Log* cast. Chaturvedi (personal communication, August 17, 1993) said, "I became so involved with the *Hum Log* family that even to this day I find it difficult to distinguish between my 'real' and 'reel' family."

MODELING IN *HUM LOG*

Social learning theory explains how humans learn behaviors by modeling others with whom they interact or observe in the mass media (Bandura, 1977, 1986). Joshi intuited that television viewers learn educational behaviors from positive and negative role models. He read Sabido's paper from the 1981 Strasbourg Conference and grasped the general idea. "I did not rigorously utilize social learning theory in designing *Hum Log*," Joshi explained in a 1987 interview. "The idea of having positive and negative role models is common sense." Perhaps so, but our impression is that Joshi followed each of the main elements in Sabido's approach to entertainment-education (see Chap. 3, this volume).

Did viewers model their behavior after the television soap opera characters? Content analysis of 149 scripts reveals the extent of prosocial and antisocial behaviors performed by the various characters (see Table 4.4). Grandfather, Bhagwanti, Badki, Chutki, and Ashwini performed mainly prosocial behaviors. *Prosocial behaviors* are those that are desirable and beneficial to other individuals and/or to society at large (Rushton, 1982). Essentially, they are positive role models. Basesar Ram, grandmother, and Majhli displayed anti-social behaviors, and were intended to be negative role models. *Anti-social behaviors* are those that are undesirable or detrimental to other individuals and/or to society at large. Measurement of prosocial and antisocial behavior obviously involves a value judgment based on

TABLE 4.4
Degree of Prosocial/Antisocial Behavior Exhibited
by the 10 Main *Hum Log* Characters

Character	Role-Modeling Effect	Percent of 149 Hum Log Episodes in Which the Characters' Behavior Was Judged by Content Analysts as:			
		Prosocial	Neutral	Antisocial	Totals
1. Grandfather, Rijjak Ram	Positive	97%	3%	0%	100%
2. Grandmother, Imarti Devi	Transitional	55%	21%	24%	100%
3. Father, Basesar Ram	Negative	27%	20%	53%	100%
4. Mother, Bhagwanti	Transitional	75%	22%	3%	100%
5. Eldest son, Lalloo	Positive	39%	54%	7%	100%
6. Youngest son, Nanhe	Positive	66%	27%	7%	100%
7. Eldest daughter, Badki	Positive	67%	25%	8%	100%
8. Middle daughter, Majhli	Transitional	36%	50%	14%	100%
9. Youngest daughter, Chutki	Positive	70%	30%	0%	100%
10. Badki's husband, Ashwini	Positive	77%	15%	8%	100%

Underlined percentages indicate whether each character was predominantly prosocial, transitional, or antisocial. (*Source:* Singhal, 1990).

the wider social context, as is acknowledged by communication scholars (Comstock et al., 1978; Rushton, 1982).

Hum Log viewers reported learning more prosocial behavior from positive role models, often expressing a desire to emulate them in real life (see Table 4.5).

Multiple Readings of Bhagwanti's Character

Joshi conceived Bhagwanti as a negative role model for female equality.[10] She submissively allowed her husband and mother-in-law to berate her for her unknown family lineage, her lack of cooking skills, and so forth. However, some viewers sympathized with Bhagwanti's character (see Photo 4.2), viewing her as a positive role model for tolerance, compromise, and patience. One 75-year-old woman wrote: "Bhagwanti is the epitome of tolerance. She suffers, but quietly. Young Indian women should learn a lesson in patience from Bhagwanti. How I wish I could have a Bhagwanti as my daughter-in-law."

The audience survey showed that 80% of viewers who chose Bhagwanti as a positive role model were women. Seventy-six percent of homemakers, compared to 7% of employed women, chose to emulate Bhagwanti. These viewer perceptions suggest that modeling effects were mediated by prior attitudes and age, lifestyle, and occupational experiences.

---

[10]Our content analysis of *Hum Log's* episodes showed that Bhagwanti's behavior in three fourths of the 149 episodes was assessed as prosocial (see Table 4.4). Bhagwanti was depicted as polite, accommodating, caring, and always putting the interests of others before her own.

The case of Bhagwanti reinforces the notion that viewers actively negotiate multiple meanings from a soap opera text (Fiske & Hartley, 1978; Livingstone, 1990). The entertainment-education strategy recognizes that audience readings are varied. The intention of the text may not always correspond with the interpretation by audience individuals. Formative research and pretesting episodes with audience members can limit, but not eliminate, oppositional readings of an entertainment-education text.

Photo 4.2. Joyshree Arora in the role of Bhagwanti in *Hum Log*. Bhagwanti was intended to represent a negative role model for the educational value of gender equality; however, certain *Hum Log* viewers believed that she was an ideal homemaker. (*Source:* Personal files of the authors).

Implications of Role-Modeling

Survey respondents were able to recall the perceived prosocial–antisocial qualities of the 10 *Hum Log* characters, 18 months after the final broadcast (Singhal, 1988). We conclude the following:

1. Viewer perceptions of the prosocialness of television models in *Hum Log* were positively related to viewers learning prosocial behaviors from the

TABLE 4.5

Hum Log Characterizations and the Degree of Audience Learning and Modeling

Family Member (Role-Modeling Effect)	Characterization*	Percentage of Respondents Who Report Learning Prosocial Behaviors (N = 1,170)	Percentage of Respondents Who Said This Character Was the Best Role Model to Copy in Real Life (N = 1,170)
1. Grandfather, Rijak Ram (Positive)	A World War II veteran, strict disciplinarian, highly moral, and hardworking.	63%	37%
2. Grandmother, Imarti Devi (Transitional)	A beautiful, indulgent person believing in tradition and rituals. Somewhat selfish and sarcastic.	42%	6%
3. Father, Basesar Ram (Negative)	A boorish drunkard who mistreats his wife and children, is superstitious, and tries to make a fast buck.	39%	4%
4. Mother, Bhagwanti (Transitional)	A self-effacing woman. She suffers quietly at the hands of her husband and mother-in-law. Portrays the stereotype of the traditional Indian wife/mother. A negative role model for gender equality, but a positive model for family harmony.		
5. Eldest son, Lalloo (Positive)	Lethargic, timid, and stupid to the extent of being hilarious. Moves from the city to a village to confront corrupt politicians.	53%	18%
		36%	6%

94

6. Youngest son, Nanhe (Positive)	A fun-loving sportsman, and a know-it-all in wheeling and dealing. A smart lovable rascal.	46%	10%
7. Eldest daughter, Badki (Positive)	Hard-working, brilliant, and proficient in sewing. She is rejected by prospective grooms because her parents cannot afford a large dowry, and because she is plain. She works hard, establishes her own identity by becoming an official in a women's organization, and later marries a handsome medical doctor.	52%	11%
8. Middle daughter, Majhli (Transitional)	Beautiful and glamor-struck. A failure in school, displays a warped sense of modernity. Initially, a negative role model, she mends her ways and marries a police inspector.	33%	1%
9. Youngest daughter, Chutki (Positive)	A studious, no-nonsense, practical person who studies medicine. Although adopted by a Muslim couple, she lives with her original family.	44%	5%
10. Badki's husband, Ashwini (Positive)	A handsome medical doctor, who respects his wife's feminist views, and cares for her family.	42%	5%
		Total	2% 100%

*Based on character profiles prepared by scriptwriter Manohar Shyam Joshi while designing *Hum Log*. Our content analysis of the scripts of 149 episodes confirms that Joshi designed the characters based on his initial profiles. (*Source:* Singhal, 1990).

televised models in *Hum Log*. Viewers reported learning prosocial behaviors from those characters perceived as prosocial and not from those perceived as antisocial.

2. The viewers' degree of exposure to *Hum Log* was positively related to viewers learning prosocial behaviors from the televised models. Frequent viewers of *Hum Log* reported learning more prosocial behaviors from the characters than did occasional viewers.

3. Viewer proficiency in the Hindi language was positively related to learning prosocial behaviors from the televised models. Those living in Hindi-speaking North India reported learning more prosocial behaviors from television characters than did those living in the non-Hindi-speaking regions of South India.

In summary, the degree of exposure to the program, the level of Hindi-language fluency, and place of residence were found to be important mediators of *Hum Log*'s modeling effects. A multiple regression analysis of learning from each of the ten main *Hum Log* characters indicated that viewers reported learning prosocial behaviors from characters of the same sex, age, and socioeconomic status (Singhal, 1988). For higher socioeconomic class viewers, the modeling effects were not as pronounced, which makes sense given that the *Hum Log* television family was a lower income family (Singhal, 1988).

Our *Hum Log* study was one of the first on how entertainment-education soap operas have their effects through role modeling. What implications does our research on social modeling in *Hum Log* hold for designers of entertainment-education? Viewer learning of certain prosocial behaviors from media models can be enhanced: if the models are perceived as prosocial by the audience, if audience individuals are exposed to the television model over a long duration of time, if the audience shares relevant sociodemographic characteristics with the media models, and if viewers comprehend the language and actions (Singhal, 1988).

Social learning theory has been criticized for being primarily used to demonstrate observational learning by children, in laboratory settings, and with aggressive behavior measures as the dependent variable (Comstock et al., 1978). Our research on social modeling in *Hum Log* clarifies the potential of utilizing social learning theory for observational learning effects with a total population, in a natural field setting, and with prosocial learning measures as dependent variables.

IMPACTS OF *HUM LOG* ON VIEWERS

Here we analyze, within the limits of the existing patriarchal, patrilineal, and patrilocal social structure of India, how viewers' exposure to *Hum Log* affected their knowledge, attitudes, and behaviors toward an equal status for women, and the issue of family planning. Our analysis is based on William McGuire's (1981) classification of the hierarchy of effects.

The Hierarchy of Effects

One of the most important fronts in communication research deals with the effects of the mass media. Several thousand communication effects studies are published each year. Out of this huge body of research has come a conceptualization of possible media impacts in terms of a hierarchy of effects (McGuire, 1981). Figure 4.4 shows the main components of the hierarchy-of-effects model and the corresponding stages an individual typically experiences in learning a new behavior. These elements are cumulative; an individual must progress from the first to the later stages. For instance, an individual would not usually change overt behavior without first being exposed to a communication message about this change.

Typically, we expect an entertainment-education message like a soap opera to have its strongest effects near the top of the hierarchical model. We expect entertainment-education to create widespread exposure (Stage 1), awareness (Stage 2), and comprehension about the message content (Stage 3). Fewer individuals are typically persuaded to change attitudes toward the message content (Stage 4), or intend to change their behavior (Stage 5). Few individuals (perhaps a small percentage) will change their overt behavior, such as by adopting a family planning method (Stage 6), or maintain the behavior change (Stage 7). These latter effects are the bottom line for most national policymakers. An individual changes behavior, and maintains this change, not only due to exposure to entertainment-education messages, but also if the appropriate infrastructure is available, and if the individual feels efficacious in being able to implement the behavior change.

As indicated in Fig. 4.4, different research methods are more appropriate for gathering data at each level in the hierarchy of effects. An audience survey can measure the degree to which individuals are informed about an educational issue, but point-of-referral monitoring data (as might be gathered from new clients in a family planning clinic) are better for measuring behavior change.

Hierarchy of *Hum Log*'s Effects

About 50 million people watched each *Hum Log* broadcast, with audience ratings of up to 90% in Hindi-speaking areas. Eighty-three percent of our 1,170 respondents watched at least one episode. A high proportion of respondents (between 64 and 75%) reported becoming aware, and being informed, about such educational contents of *Hum Log* as family harmony, limiting family size, gender equality, and cultural diversity. Regression analy-

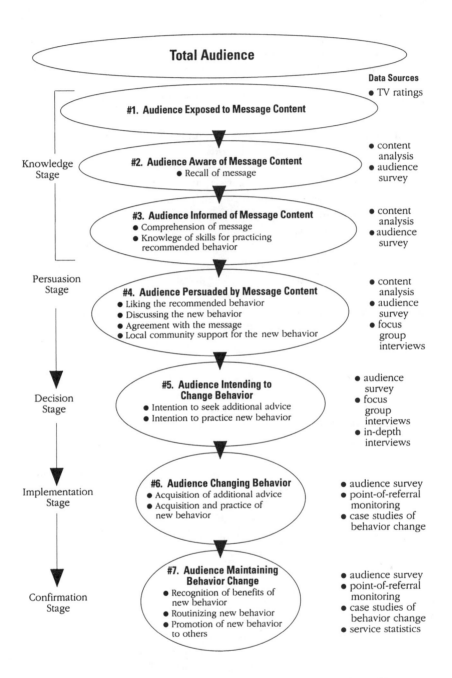

Total Audience

Data Sources
● TV ratings

#1. Audience Exposed to Message Content

Knowledge
Stage

#2. Audience Aware of Message Content
● Recall of message

● content
analysis
● audience
survey

#3. Audience Informed of Message Content
● Comprehension of message
● Knowlege of skills for practicing
recommended behavior

● content
analysis
● audience
survey

Persuasion
Stage

#4. Audience Persuaded by Message Content
● Liking the recommended behavior
● Discussing the new behavior
● Agreement with the message
● Local community support for the new behavior

● content
analysis
● audience
survey
● focus
group
interviews

Decision
Stage

**#5. Audience Intending to
Change Behavior**
● Intention to seek additional advice
● Intention to practice new behavior

● audience
survey
● focus
group
interviews
● in-depth
interviews

Implementation
Stage

#6. Audience Changing Behavior
● Acquisition of additional advice
● Acquisition and practice of
new behavior

● audience survey
● point-of-referral
monitoring
● case studies of
behavior change

Confirmation
Stage

**#7. Audience Maintaining
Behavior Change**
● Recognition of benefits of
new behavior
● Routinizing new behavior
● Promotion of new behavior
to others

● audience survey
● point-of-referral
monitoring
● case studies of
behavior change
● service statistics

FIG. 4.4. The hierarchy of media effects, its various stages, and possible
sources of data about these effects at each stage. (*Source:* This figure draws
upon McGuire, 1981; Piotrow et al., 1997; Rogers, 1995; and Shefner, Valente,
and Bardini, 1993).

sis was conducted to determine the degree to which exposure to *Hum Log* predicted attitudes and behaviors related to the status of women and to family planning. Exposure to *Hum Log* was found to be positively related to attitudes toward freedom of choice for women (for instance, women having a say in choosing a career or a life partner), toward equal opportunities for women (for instance, educating both the female and the male child past high school), and toward smaller family size norms, while controlling for several sociodemographic characteristics of our respondents: rural–urban background, age, sex, formal education, family income, and Hindi-language fluency (Brown & Cody, 1991; Singhal, 1990; Singhal, Rogers, & Cozzens, 1989). The magnitude of these effects, although statistically significant, was found to be very small.

Exposure to *Hum Log* was positively related to behaviors indicating freedom of choice for women, but not to behaviors indicating equal opportunities for women or smaller family size norms (Brown, 1988, 1991; Brown & Cody, 1991; Singhal, 1990; Singhal, Rogers, & Cozzens, 1989). Again, the magnitude of the behavioral effects on freedom of choice for women was small (Singhal, Rogers, & Cozzens, 1989).

Content analysis of the 500 *Hum Log* viewer letters provided additional support for the hierarchy-of-effects model. The effects were stronger for letter writers than for other viewers, not surprising given that the letter writers represent a unique audience segment. Most letter writers, for instance, were heavy viewers of *Hum Log*. Our content analysis showed that *Hum Log* influenced 92% of the letter writers in a prosocial direction. Some 47% of the 500 letters indicated that *Hum Log* affected the writers' cognitions regarding the educational issues, 33% showed that *Hum Log* influenced attitudes regarding these issues, and 7% showed that *Hum Log* resulted in overt behavioral change on the part of the letter writer.

These findings fit our conceptualization of the hierarchy-of-media effects (McGuire, 1981). We expected it to create widespread audience exposure and a high level of message awareness and comprehension. Exposure to the entertainment-education broadcasts were less likely to change attitudes about the issues promoted, and even fewer individuals were expected to change their overt behavior.

Certain effects of *Hum Log* could not be measured by our evaluation methods. Point-of-referral data (such as, from women's organizations) could not be systematically gathered, a limitation of our ex post facto research design. However, there were documented reports that the series stimulated eye and organ donation campaigns, increased attendance at women's organizations, and led to neighborhood clean-up drives. Support for such overt behavioral changes was found in the viewer letters. The president of the Legal Aid Centre for Women, in New Delhi, in a letter to Kumar said: "Your encouragement on *Hum Log* boosts our organization's morale. During June and July, 1985 [when *Hum Log* was being broadcast], a record number of women's cases (152) were handled by our office, out of which 56 were new." The president of a youth club in Chandigarh in his letter said: "After getting an inspiration from the *Hum Log* television series about eye donation, we the members of Chandigarh's Youth Club, have launched a campaign to sign up eye donors. We plan to enroll 5,000 prospective eye donors in the next one month. . . . To date we have enrolled 982 members." While organ donation is extremely rare in India, *Hum Log* spurred several eye and organ donation campaigns.

The research on *Hum Log* was limited by reliance on an ex post facto design. We could not determine that the hierarchy-of-effects variables measured indicated only the changes due to exposure, because we were unable to collect benchmark data before the soap opera was broadcast. Our research was also limited by our inability to measure whether the viewers actually performed the behaviors they reported learning. When the India research was concluded in the late 1980s, we began to look for an opportunity to conduct a more rigorous evaluation of an entertainment-education soap opera. Future research on an entertainment-education soap opera in Tanzania in the mid-1990s overcame such limitations by gathering point-of-referral data from health clinics (see Chap. 7, this volume).

IMPACTS OF *HUM LOG* ON THE INDIAN
TELEVISION SYSTEM

Hum Log indirectly impacted the Indian television system in two major ways: the commercialization of Doordarshan, and the proliferation of serials on Doordarshan.

Commercialization

Hum Log launched the era of commercially sponsored programs on Doordarshan. A sponsored television program is one for which an advertiser pays the production costs of a program, in return for several minutes of spot advertisements, before, during, or immediately following the broadcast. Here lies a unique sustenance quality of entertainment-education programs: Their production costs can be underwritten, making the educational message pay for itself. Commercial interests can be served without sacrificing social interests. The sponsor of *Hum Log* was Food Specialties Limited. The product advertised was Maggi 2-Minute Noodles, a radical consumer innovation in India.

Maggi 2-Minute Noodles. The story of Maggi 2-Minute Noodles in India demonstrates how the rapid diffusion of television, the popularity of

Hum Log, and organizational innovations in marketing and advertising can launch an alien product in a developing country. Food Specialties Limited (FSL), who marketed Maggi Noodles in India, is a subsidiary of Nestle, the Swiss multinational corporation. In 1984, Food Specialties introduced Maggi 2-Minute Noodles, a new food product in India. For many years, Nestle had sold Maggi Noodles in Malaysia, Singapore, Hong Kong, China, and Japan. So FSL executives said: "Why not in India?"

Noodles were perceived in India as a very Chinese product. So FSL's task was to portray noodles as an *Indian* product. FSL developed *tastemakers,* a small packet of flavoring, including masala, chicken, capsicum, and garlic, making the taste of Maggi Noodles Indian. An effective marketing and advertising strategy was needed next. The noodles were marketed in India as a snack food. Most Indian hot snacks, for example, *samosas* and *jalebis,* are difficult to prepare. The appeal of Maggi Noodles was convenience. The slogan was: "Fast to cook, and good to eat."

Initially, FSL executives doubted whether an Indian homemaker would accept the idea of a quick-preparation hot snack. Hence, television advertising was aimed at persuading children to ask their mothers for Maggi Noodles. Thus the homemaker prepared noodles because her children wanted them. Television spots showed children engaged in some physical activity, like playing sports, who then rushed home to ask their mother for a quick hot snack. Mother served them Maggi 2-Minute Noodles.

Food Specialties began to advertise Maggi 2-Minute Noodles during the *Hum Log* broadcasts, which in 1984–1985 reached an audience of 60 million people.[11] *Hum Log's* high viewership, coupled with the rapid diffusion of television sets in India, helped Maggi Noodles get off to a fast start in the Indian market. The volume of Maggi Noodles increased from none in 1982 to 1,600 tons in 1983, 4,200 tons in 1985, 10,000 tons in 1990, and 15,000 tons in 1998. The marketing of Maggi Noodles became a case study of how to effectively market a new product.[12] The positive experience of Food Specialties Limited convinced other Indian advertisers that program sponsorship could be attractive. Advertisers lined up at Doordarshan, eager to buy time. Advertising rates for television spots rose accordingly, and advertising revenues poured into Doordarshan.

Hum Log represented a turning point in the commercialization of Doordarshan (see Fig. 4.5). It also demonstrated that entertainment-education programs could be self-supporting.

---

[11]FSL wanted to be associated with a long-running television program that was broadcast frequently, rather than buy isolated advertising spots that would appear in a continuous series of 35 to 40 spots each evening, leading to clutter.

[12]It is ironic that *Hum Log* promoted Indian culture and national identity, while its advertising introduced a Chinese food marketed by a Western corporation.

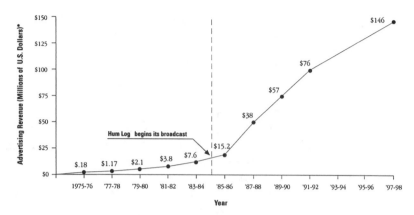

FIG. 4.5. The growth of advertising revenue on Doordarshan. (*Source:* Compiled from Singhal & Rogers, 1989a and Doordarshan press releases.)
*One U.S. dollar equals 42 Indian rupees.

The Revolution of Television Serials. *Hum Log*'s commercial success led to a proliferation of domestically produced television serials on Doordarshan by demonstrating that indigenous soap operas could attract large audiences. *Hum Log* was the original long-running indigenous serial broadcast on Indian television in 1984. When it ended 18 months later, several dozen serials were being broadcast on Doordarshan (Jain, 1985).

Hum Log was a watershed. By 1998, Doordarshan had broadcast several hundred television serials dealing with a wide variety of social issues. While these serials varied in length, popularity, production quality, and impact, they generally did not glamorize violence, sex, or crime.

WHY DID *HUM LOG* END?

Unlike U.S. soap operas, which continue almost endlessly, *Hum Log* was based on the Mexican *telenovela* format, which usually has a pre-defined beginning, middle, and end. *Hum Log* was originally slated for 300 episodes spanning a 3-year period, but it ended in 17 months, after 156 episodes.

Why did *Hum Log* end earlier than planned? The actors and actresses had become stars. Some had offers to perform in other serials at salaries 5 to 10 times what they earned from *Hum Log*. *Hum Log* also faced increasing competition from other popular serials on Doordarshan during 1985 (most of them produced in Bombay). Doordarshan was under considerable pressure from private television producers who wanted their new serials to replace existing programs like *Hum Log*. S. S. Gill's patronage of *Hum Log* waned as he became heavily involved in implementing the (one-television-transmitter-a-day) expansion program of Doordarshan in 1984–1985. Shortly thereafter, he retired from public office. Finally, the *Hum Log* story reached a natural ending point when Grandmother died of cancer, Basesar Ram mended his errant ways, Nanhe got a decent job, Chutki entered medical college, and Majhli had found Samdar.

Beyond *Hum Log*

Although *Hum Log* has been off the air since late 1985, its indirect effects continue to this day. *Hum Log* demonstrated that India could produce a commercially viable entertainment television program, which, despite its many limitations, could address educational issues (Singhal & Rogers, 1989a). Once that fundamental point was demonstrated, other developing countries began to follow India's lead: In 1987, Kenya broadcast its first entertainment-education television soap opera centered around family planning, *Tushauriane* (*Let's Discuss*), followed by a family planning radio soap opera, *Ushikwapo Shikimana* (see Chap. 5, this volume). During 1992–1993, an entertainment-education soap opera, *Hum Raahi*, patterned on the Sabido methodology and written by Joshi, was broadcast in India. Beginning in 1993, a family planning–HIV prevention radio soap opera, *Twende na Wakati* (Let's Go with the Times) was broadcast in Tanzania, and a similar radio soap opera, *Tinka Tinka Sukh* (Happiness Lies in Small Things) was broadcast in India in 1996–1997.

Hum Log is of historic importance as it occurred 9 years after Miguel Sabido's first entertainment-education soap opera (*Ven Conmigo* in 1975–1976), and was the first non-Mexican use of the entertainment-education strategy in television. Its greatest impact may have been to break the temporary logjam in the early 1980s in the international diffusion of entertainment-education soap operas.

CONCLUSIONS

Hum Log was of historic importance in the evolution of Miguel Sabido's methodology for creating entertainment-education soap operas. Despite the best of intentions, certain elements of Sabido's methodology were compromised in *Hum Log*. The main educational purpose of *Hum Log*, to promote family planning, was greatly diminished after 13 episodes. Subsequently, *Hum Log* became a compromise between Doordarshan's goals, Joshi's scriptwriting, the producer's profits, sponsors' ratings, and the audience's expectations. *Hum Log* had a skilled scriptwriter in Manohar Shyam Joshi, who, with a somewhat limited knowledge of Sabido's methodology, maintained, for the most part, the educational themes in the soap opera's broadcasts. Thanks to Joshi's scriptwriting, the lower middle-class Ram family of *Hum Log* became the nation's first television family.

Hum Log was also historically important in terms of independent, theory-based evaluation research on entertainment-education programs. Multiple research methods represented a triangulation strategy in assessing the effects of *Hum Log*, although we were limited by our ex post facto design in assessing effects. Our content analysis indicated the series de-emphasized family planning compared to the degree initially planned.

Hum Log promoted an average of 3.2 prosocial sub-themes during each minute of its broadcasts. However, this prosocial content was subjected to varied interpretations by the audience based on personal experiences and beliefs.

Ashok Kumar's epilogues helped clarify moral choices for *Hum Log* viewers, and provided guidelines for action. By providing the address of a public welfare agency or a women's organization, epilogues helped viewers convert intentions into action, which aided the educational purpose of *Hum Log*. Kumar's credibility also facilitated the educational effects.

Hum Log's popularity provided broad exposure to educational issues. A high degree of parasocial interaction also occurred between viewers and the characters. The outpouring of letters was unprecedented, and modeling effects of viewers with role models were observed. Survey respondents connected with positive role models and expressed a desire to emulate them in their daily lives.

Our findings verify our conceptualization of the hierarchy of effects: widespread exposure assured high awareness of the message, with less success in influencing the audience attitudes, and even less in influencing overt behavior change.

Hum Log indirectly impacted the Indian television system by launching an era of commercialization on Doordarshan, and causing a proliferation of domestically produced television serials in India.

The Entertainment-Education
Strategy in Music[1]

Music, not television, is the most important medium for adolescents.
—Kathleen Roe (1987, p. 216)

The entertainment-education strategy dates back thousands of years in various music traditions, including protest and reform music, folk music,[2] and devotional music[3] (see Fig. 5.1). These ancient customs have been utilized in recent years for educational issues. Rock music, music videos, and celebrity concerts[4] are used for advocacy, educational issues, and fund-raising. Most noteworthy, in recent years, is Johns Hopkins University's use of rock music to promote sexual responsibility for youth in Latin America and the Philippines, and for adults in Nigeria. In creating the rock-music based campaigns,

---

[1]This chapter draws upon Singhal (1990), Singhal and Rogers (1989a, 1989b), and Rogers et al. (1989). We thank Johns Hopkins University's Patrick L. Coleman for his comments.

[2]There are several advantages to using folk music to educate rural audiences: It is popular, can provide immediate feedback, is inexpensive, and comes from perceived credible sources (Dissanayake, 1977; Parmar, 1979; Sujan, 1993). Examples of this approach include the Bauls, who live on the border of India and Bangladesh, and the Brazilian *cantadores* (singing poets), who travel from village to village to entertain and educate their audiences.

[3]Religious music serves multiple purposes of devotion, motivation, and recreation. For instance, in India, *Bhajan-Mandlis*, *Hari-Kathas*, *Kabigans*, and *Pandvani* provide a forum for social interaction, reflection, and informal education (Parmar, 1979; Sujan, 1993). Gospel songs serve a similar purpose in other countries.

[4]Celebrities have raised funds for humane causes. Examples are the Bangladesh-Aid Concert in 1971 to support refugees, the "We Are the World" concert in 1985 for Ethiopian famine relief, and "Farm-Aid" to raise money for the Midwest's ailing farm economy (Rogers et al., 1989).

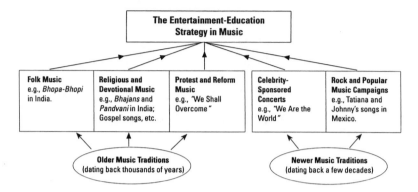

FIG. 5.1. The older and newer music traditions that illustrate the entertainment-education strategy in music.

Patrick L. Coleman and his colleagues at Johns Hopkins University's Population Communication Services (PCS) were influenced by Miguel Sabido's entertainment-education strategy, along with lessons drawn from MTV and commercial advertising.

Johns Hopkins University's PCS

Johns Hopkins University, located in Baltimore, Maryland, is the first research university in America. Its School of Hygiene and Public Health was the first in the United States. Population Communication Services (PCS) is a large unit in the public health school, established 15 years ago by Dr. Phyllis Tilson Piotrow with funding from the U.S. Agency for International Development. PCS employs approximately 75 professionals, most with graduate degrees in communication or public health, who manage some 50 projects at any one time in Latin America, Africa, and Asia. The research and evaluation division of PCS studies the effects of these projects, with about 10% of a project budget typically allocated for evaluation research.

PCS is involved in a larger number of entertainment-education projects than any other world organization. Almost from its beginning, PCS embraced entertainment-education, with Patrick Coleman inviting Miguel Sabido to train the PCS staff and their collaborators in this strategy (Piotrow, 1994; Piotrow & Rimon, 1994). The Johns Hopkins people then modified Sabido's approach as they applied entertainment-education to a variety of popular music, radio and television soap operas, and folk theater projects. What is distinctive about the PCS use of entertainment-education?

1. PCS often inserts the entertainment-education intervention, perhaps a soap opera, into an ongoing radio or television program. For example, a 43-episode drama about family planning was incorporated in an established television variety show called *In a Lighter Mood*, broadcast in Enugu, Nigeria (Piotrow et al., 1990). Similarly, PCS produced a radio soap opera, *Fakube*

Jarra (Wise Man), whose episodes about family planning were inserted into an existing radio show in The Gambia (Valente et al., 1994). The object is to get the entertainment-education intervention off to a fast start by inheriting a large audience of listeners or viewers.

2. PCS frequently incorporates an entertainment-education program as the main component of a communication campaign, to achieve a synergy of effects. An example is the Green Star campaign in the mid-1990s organized by Johns Hopkins consultants in collaboration with the Tanzanian Ministry of Health's Family Planning Unit. At the heart of this family planning campaign was a radio soap opera, *Zinduka!* (Awake!) broadcast intermittently by Radio Tanzania from 1993 to 1996. The Green Star elements included: training the clinic staff to treat patients with more consideration to win a green star for high quality service, posters, radio advertisements for *Zinduka!* and for the campaign, pamphlets, audio cassettes of *Zinduka!*, and other communication activities. This comprehensive approach achieves a greater number of family planning adopters than the radio soap opera alone, although at a greater cost. One disadvantage of this approach is that summative research faces the complex difficulty of separating audience effects due to the radio soap opera from the effects of other campaign elements.

3. PCS has a high degree of control over the entertainment-education project being implemented and evaluated because, to a large extent, PCS controls the funding from U.S. AID. Thus, in the Green Star campaign in Tanzania, Johns Hopkins could withhold funds from the Tanzania Ministry of Health whenever Ministry officials reneged on their agreement. Such control could be of considerable value in such research activities as gathering clinic data from new family planning adopters, or ensuring that project interventions were timely.

4. PCS has long-term funding from U.S. AID, so communication interventions can be planned for a number of years. On the other hand, a political upheaval in a nation (as in the change of government in Indonesia in 1998) can lead to disruption of a PCS project.

In comparison to the PCS modus operandi, the field projects of Population Communications International—which also applies Sabido's methodology in developing countries—usually consist of entertainment-education broadcasts that mostly stand alone[5] (rather than being inserted into existing radio or television programs), are not accompanied by other major campaign activities, and are characterized by less control by PCI or the evaluation researchers

---

[5]PCI in recent decades has helped insert entertainment-education messages on Brazilian and Mexican television shows. David Poindexter, former president of PCI and a Hollywood lobbyist in the 1970s, influenced Norman Lear to incorporate prosocial messages in his ongoing TV shows, for example, in *Maude* (see Chap. 1, this volume). Furthermore, every few years, PCI organizes a Soap Summit in Hollywood, an event designed to educate and challenge executive producers, scriptwriters, and senior network television executives to employ television's potential to effect positive social changes. The PCI-sponsored Soap Summits are an innovative way to extend the concept of Hollywood lobbying.

over their in-country counterparts. One advantage of the PCI approach is that the effects of the intervention are more easily distinguished from simultaneous communication activities. Nevertheless, the PCS and the PCI approaches share a common origin in Sabido's formula for entertainment-education.

MUSIC, A PERVASIVE MEDIUM

Audiences participate in music in ways that are physical, by singing along, tapping, clapping, dancing, or through sexual arousal; emotional, feeling the music, reminiscing, or romanticizing; and cognitive, processing information, learning, stimulating thought, or framing perceptions (Lull, 1992). Because music is so widely popular, it is an attractive medium for delivering messages.

Music and musicians have played key roles for various health issues. In 1984, singer and musician Philly Bongoley Lutaaya left Uganda as a political refugee. Proud of his African heritage, Lutaaya wrote a song "Born in Africa," which became an anthem for his countrymen when he returned from exile in 1988. He was hailed as a national hero, and concerts of "Born in Africa" were sold out throughout the African continent. A year later, Lutaaya shocked his fans when he announced he was dying of AIDS. Lutaaya was the first prominent African to disclose publicly that he had AIDS. His admission placed a spotlight on a taboo topic that few would discuss publicly. Lutaaya launched a national AIDS education campaign in Uganda through his popular songs, prior to his death in 1989.

In November 1991, basketball superstar Magic Johnson disclosed that he had contracted HIV. Like Lutaaya, Johnson's disclosure increased AIDS awareness in the United States (Dearing & Rogers, 1996). The number of telephone inquiries to the National AIDS Hotline jumped 30-fold, swamping the capacity of the information service (see Fig. 5.2). In 1992, Johnson teamed with his television entertainer friend, Arsenio Hall, to release a 42-minute videotape "Time Out: The Truth about HIV, AIDS, and You." Employing rock, rap, and comedy, and featuring numerous celebrities, "Time Out" was Johnson's way of personally communicating with his millions of fans about how to avoid HIV/AIDS infections. Popular musicians and other celebrities whose lives are personally intertwined with an issue represent a very special educational resource for that topic.

Music's influence on public opinion was recognized more than 4,000 years ago when the emperors of China's Hsia dynasty commanded court officials to listen carefully to workers' songs to gauge their level of unrest (Ashraf, 1975; Dunaway, 1987; Wang, 1935). A contemporary example of

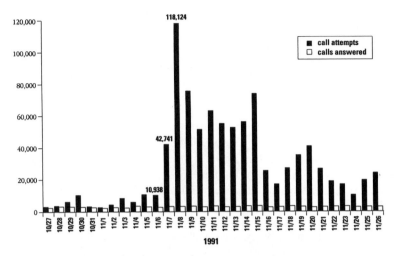

FIG. 5.2. The effects of Magic Johnson's news conference of November 7, 1991, on the number of call-attempts made to the National AIDS Hotline (only English-language calls are shown here). Only a small percentage could be answered. (*Source:* CDC National AIDS Hotline.)

music's role in an important political movement, the civil rights protest in the United States in the 1960s, is represented by the traditional hymn "I'll Overcome." The lyrics and tempo of the hymn were suitably revised for mass singing, leading to "We Shall Overcome," which became the theme song for the civil rights movement (Carawan & Carawan, 1965).

Ringing the Democracy Bell in Mongolia

A democratic movement toppled the ruling Communist Party in Mongolia in 1990. Street demonstrations and hunger strikes played an important role in the protest, but popular support for the pro-democracy movement was mainly garnered via rock-and-roll music (Kristof, 1990). A popular Mongolian rock band, *Hongk* (which in Mongolian means *Bell*), led the dissidents' struggle for democracy through their song, "The Ring of the Bell." The lyrics, which became the dissidents' anthem, argued for a national awakening: "The ring of the bell rouses us, let it toll across the broad steppes, reverberating mile after mile, let the bell carry our yearning, and revive all our hopes" (Kristof, 1990). As "The Ring of the Bell" gained in popularity, protests against the Communist Party mounted, eventually leading to the ouster of party officials, and the establishment of a democratic government in Mongolia.

ENTERTAINMENT-EDUCATION MUSIC[6]

Since the mid-1980s, JHU/PCS has used music videos[7] to promote sexual responsibility among young adults in developing countries.[8]

Tatiana and Johnny

Teenage pregnancy is a major social problem in developing countries, especially the 20 Latin American republics. Teenagers are difficult to reach through most mass communication channels (Avery, 1979). This audience segment has a low degree of media exposure—except to music.

In 1986, a unique communication project was launched in Spanish-speaking Latin America: Two rock music videos promoting teenage sexual responsibility, "*Cuando Estemos Juntos*" (When We Are Together) and *Détente* (Wait) were produced by PCS (see Photo 5.1). "*Cuando Estemos Juntos*" was number one on popular music charts within six weeks of its release in Mexico, and soon was a top-rated song in 11 other Spanish-speaking Latin American countries (Kincaid, Jara, Coleman, & Segura, 1988).

The story of these music videos goes back to 1977, when Coleman, a former music industry official in Los Angeles, was serving as a communication advisor to the National Family Planning Program in El Salvador. Coleman observed the audience effects of Sabido's soap operas (see Chap. 2, this volume): "Everyone in El Salvador was abuzz over *Ven Conmigo*. . . . It was a tremendous inspiration to me," recalled Coleman. "There's something great here. I bet we can do even more [with entertainment-education]" (cited in Coleman & Meyer, 1990, p. 19).

In 1983, Coleman joined JHU/PCS. He organized a three-day international conference in Quito, Ecuador, inviting Sabido and 77 other experts from 17 countries to gauge the status of communication strategies for family planning. Also present at the Quito conference was Xavier de la Cueva, an expert on global advertising from McCaan Erickson. The strategy of producing a message for all of Latin America, instead of a different message in each nation, impressed Coleman (personal communication, August 14, 1998). The 1983

---

[6]This section is based on interviews with Patrick Coleman (1988), Tatiana Palacios (1989), Lea Salonga (1989), King Sunny Ade (1989), and Onyeka Onwenu (1989).

[7]Refer to Abt (1987) for a detailed discussion on music videos.

[8]The idea of utilizing popular music for education pre-dates the JHU/PCS music campaigns. In the early 1980s, the Jamaican Family Planning Board ran a communication campaign, which included songs about sexual responsibility ("Before You Be a Mother, You Got to Be a Woman"), radio and television commercials, and newspaper, billboard, and cinema advertisements (*Population Reports*, 1986). However, the JHU/PCS efforts were unique in their use of formative and summative research to inform campaign design and measure its effects, their involvement of creative professionals in program production and marketing, and their orchestration of multimedia channels.

Photo 5.1. Tatiana (second from left) and Johnny (third from left), the two rock music singers who promoted sexual responsibility among teenagers in Latin America in 1986, with Patrick L. Coleman (extreme left) and Dr. Phyllis T. Piotrow (extreme right) of Johns Hopkins University's Population Communication Services. (*Source:* JHU/PCS Media/Materials Center, used with permission.)

Quito conference also convinced Coleman of the potential of the entertainment-education strategy.

In the mid-1980s, with funding provided by the U.S. Agency for International Development, JHU/PCS launched a campaign to promote sexual responsibility among teenagers in Mexico and other Spanish-speaking Latin American countries. Coleman knew from formative evaluation research (and from his own professional experience) that the common denominator for young people throughout Latin America was rock music (Church & Geller, 1989). He hired Fuentes y Fomento Intercontinentales (FFI), a Mexican marketing and music record company, to produce two music videos with an educational message about teenagers saying "no" to sex. The needs of the target audience were assessed, and a marketing plan was developed. Record companies in Mexico recommended 32 composers and writers, each of whom was asked to write two songs as part of a nationwide contest. Out of 30 entries, 6 were pretested with adolescents for their acceptability and content (Kincaid et al., 1988). The lyrics and the various attributes of the musical presentation were tested in focus-group interviews with Mexican teenagers, and this feedback led to fine-grained changes in the song (Church & Geller, 1989).

The artists were selected carefully, because their image is a key factor in the effects of entertainment-education music. Several prominent Mexican singers refused to be involved in the adolescent pregnancy prevention project, due to the sensitive nature of the topic, which they feared might damage their careers. Tatiana, a beautiful 16-year-old singer from Mexico who was just launching her career, and Johnny, a 17-year-old Puerto Rican singer (already popular in Latin America as a Menudo[9] graduate), agreed to perform "*Cuando Estemos Juntos*" and "*Détente.*" The two songs were produced with special care: The music was recorded in a sound studio in Spain, the voices were recorded in Los Angeles, and the music video was filmed in Mexico. Every effort was made to obtain high production quality.

In "*Cuando Estemos Juntos,*" the teenage singers told their audience not to have sex, a much more effective strategy than having a preachy message emanate from parents or priests. The lyrics were: "You will see that I am right when I say 'no,' even though my heart is burning." The tune was catchy, and the sensitive nature of the teenage-sex topic was suitably handled by having Tatiana and Johnny dance with life-sized male and female dolls, respectively, in the music video. Near the end of the video, they discard the dolls and dance with each other in a pelvis-thrusting motion that is daringly sexy. Their nonverbal communication certainly attracts the attention of their intended audience, reinforcing the message that one can be "sexy" but still say "no."

The songs were released in two phases. A commercial release came first, in 1986, with the premier of the music video of "*Cuando Estemos Juntos*" on a popular Latin American television variety show, *Siempre en Domingo* (Only on Sunday), watched by an estimated 150 million Spanish-speaking viewers throughout Latin America (Kincaid et al., 1988). Raul Velasco, the influential host of the show, interviewed Tatiana and Johnny about the topic of teenage sexual abstinence. Then the song was released for sale throughout Latin America in the form of records, tapes, and videos.

As the commercial release of "*Cuando Estemos Juntos*" gained huge sales for the song, the second phase, an institutional effort, began. Press conferences were held, news clippings of the artists were provided free to radio and television stations, and Tatiana and Johnny made numerous personal appearances, both live and on television talk shows (Coleman, 1988). The two teenagers were frequently asked whether or not they were virgins (both Tatiana and Johnny said they were), suggesting their importance as positive role models.

---

[9]Menudo is a youth rock music group from Puerto Rico popular in Latin America and the Philippines in the mid-1980s. Group members graduate from Menudo at age 17, ensuring that members are always young teenagers.

Public service announcements on radio and television accompanied the two songs. Radio and television stations could play the songs without paying a broadcast fee if they agreed to accompany the music with an announcement of the address and telephone number of a local family planning clinic that offered contraceptive services to teenagers. This information helped channel the teenage audiences' knowledge and attitudes into action. An estimated 1 million hours of free radio and television time were provided by broadcasting stations in Latin America for playing and discussing the song (Coleman, 1988). The typical Mexican radio station played "*Cuando Estemos Juntos*" about 14 times daily for the four months of the song's greatest popularity. (A typical hit song was played five times per day). Thus listeners were repeatedly exposed to the educational content of these entertainment-education songs. Six months after the peak popularity of "*Cuando Estemos Juntos*," Mexican adolescents could still recite the words (Kincaid et al., 1988).

A summative evaluation of the rock music campaign in Mexico—which included a sample survey of teenagers, focus-group interviews, content analysis of listener letters, and personal interviews with media professionals—showed that the two songs disseminated information about contraception to teenagers, encouraged teenagers to talk more freely about sex, reinforced teenagers who already had decided on sexual restraint, sensitized younger viewers to the importance of the topic, and led to a modest increase in demand for services at family planning clinics (Kincaid et al., 1988). Perhaps the greatest compliment to Tatiana and Johnny's entertainment-education music came not just from its observed effects, but from its competition. While the number one hit song "*Cuando Estemos Juntos*" was promoting sexual abstinence to teenagers in Mexico, the second most popular song in Mexico was "No Control," which promoted exactly the opposite message. Here we see an illustration of how contemporaneous activities might affect the impacts of an entertainment-education intervention. Fortunately, the effects of "No Control" were minimal.

"*Cuando Estemos Juntos*" demonstrated that it is possible to use an entertainment format for educational purposes without sacrificing commercial objectives, and without degrading the message content.[10] What lessons were learned about creating effective entertainment-education messages from the Tatiana and Johnny music campaign in Latin America?

---

[10]The Indonesian national family planning agency, inspired by JHU/PCS's Tatiana and Johnny music campaign, in 1987 created "*Jangan Dulu*" ("Wait a While, My Love"), Indonesia's first popular song that promoted sexual responsibility (Pekerti & Musa, 1989). A compressed version of "*Jangan Dulu*" became a highly popular radio spot for family planning. The creation of "*Jangan Dulu*" and the accompanying advertising spots cost only $3,000 (U.S.), while the record album including "*Jangan Dulu*," sold more than 100,000 copies, yielding large profits (Pekerti & Musa, 1989).

1. Launching an effective entertainment-education campaign requires money, time, and expertise. An estimated $300,000 and 2½ years of planning were invested in the Mexican music project, plus $100,000 for evaluation research (Church & Geller, 1989). However, record sales, donated airtime, and corporate sponsorship offset these production costs many times over.

2. Choosing the most appropriate mass medium to reach the target audience is important.

3. Enlisting the services of skilled professionals to develop the message products is crucial.

4. Producing a high-quality campaign to ensure a high level of commercial support from program sponsors is important.

5. Selecting celebrities who can serve as personal role models for the educational issue that is being promoted is crucial and often difficult.

6. Formative and summative evaluation research can help in creating highly effective entertainment-education messages and in measuring the audience effects of such messages.

Six months after the two songs were popular, Johnny called a press conference to announce he had impregnated a young woman, but would not marry her. Suddenly, he became a negative role model for sexual responsibility. The fallout from this negative action was probably minimal, given the time of his announcement. But it shows the importance of the personal behavior of role models in entertainment-education. Since Johnny's fall from grace, much greater care has been given to checking out the lifestyle of musicians, actors, and other individuals who are involved in entertainment-education.

Tatiana Palacios

Born in Philadelphia in 1969, Tatiana Palacios spent her early childhood years in the United States, while her father earned a PhD degree in economics from the Wharton School of Business at the University of Pennsylvania. Tatiana's musical training started at age 4, when she began violin lessons, followed by piano, guitar, and dance. She was also a child gymnast of unusual ability. Coached by her mother, a gymnastics coach, Tatiana in 1980 won first place in the Mexican National Championships. She was a youthful celebrity at age 11.

At age 15, Tatiana played Jane in *Kuman*, a popular musical opera based on Tarzan's adventures, produced by Irene Sabido, Miguel's sister. *Kuman*'s popularity launched Tatiana's singing career. At about the same time, Coleman was searching for a popular teenage singer to represent responsible sexual behavior. In JHU/PCS-sponsored field research, Mexican teenagers overwhelmingly chose Tatiana.

Tatiana's record album *Chicas de Hoy* (Today's Girls), which contained the two JHU/PCS sexual responsibility songs, sold more than 600,000 copies (a spectacular achievement by Mexican standards), earning her five gold records and one platinum record. Tatiana donated the royalties from her two songs about sexual responsibility (more than $50,000 U.S.) for community outreach efforts to promote responsible parenthood. She strongly believes in the entertainment-education strategy and advocates greater social responsibility by creative artists.

Rock Music for Sexual Responsibility in the Philippines

Building on Tatiana and Johnny's experience in Latin America, JHU/PCS, jointly with the Philippine's Population Center Foundation (PCF), launched a music campaign to promote sexual responsibility among youth in 1987. The first song, "That Situation," was sung by a 16-year-old Filipino artist, Lea Salonga, and the rock group Menudo. The song was launched via a live Menudo concert in December 1987. Within a month, "That Situation" was number one on the popular music charts of the Manila and Cebu City radio stations (Rimon, 1990). "That Situation" promoted sexually responsible behavior among teenagers: "It's up to us not to jump into that situation, I'm too young, not ready yet."

In May 1988, a second song, "I Still Believe," was sung by Salonga and ex-Menudo singer Charlie Masso. It instantly became the number one song on the popular music stations of Manila and Cebu City (Rimon, 1989). A survey of youths in Manila revealed that "I Still Believe" was the only Filipino music video among the top 10 most recalled in 1988. Its lyrics included such lines as "I still believe in love at first sight, I don't think it's right to need me just for a lonely night." The message to young adults was: "Be sexually responsible. Sex can wait!"

PCS's multimedia campaign attempted to establish each song as a commercial hit with an educational message and to link the song and its message to a telephone hotline providing information, counseling, and referrals for sexual or pregnancy problems. The hotline, Dial-a-Friend, was an improvement over the Mexican "*Cuando Estemos Juntos*" project in that it yielded data on the song's effects, measured by the number of phone calls received, and provided a route to behavior change for individual callers.

PCS's efforts in the Philippines received support from multinational corporations like Pepsi Cola, Nestle, and Close-Up, and from several Filipino companies including the Philippines Long Distance and Telegraph Company (PLDT), which donated broadcast time and underwrote certain project costs (Rimon, 1989). Companies like Nike, AGFA, Close-Up, and Johnson & Johnson donated products given away during the song's promotion. An estimated $1.2 million were provided in free broadcasting time and donated materials like posters, cards, calendars, T-shirts, and discounted telephone charges (Kincaid et al., 1991; Kincaid et al., 1992; Rimon, 1989). The Filipino media provided free broadcast time for these songs on radio and for the two music videos on Filipino television. Lea Salonga visited high schools in Manila to promote the songs and to discuss their messages with teenagers (Rimon, 1990). These high schools held an essay-writing contest in which students discussed the social message in "That Situation," and how this message affected their lives. The winning essays received awards from prominent personalities.

Television advertisements used segments from the music video and radio advertisements used audio clips from the songs to introduce the telephone hotline in Manila. The telephone hotlines were also promoted by Dial-a-Friend advertisements featuring Salonga. These television spots showed teenage crisis situations associated with premarital sex and unwanted pregnancy, encouraging the teenagers to Dial-a-Friend for counseling. Trained professional counselors maintained four hotlines, which averaged 1,000 calls per week. The hotlines were so popular that PLDT agreed to continue funding when PCS's Philippines project ended in May 1989, and to donate prime-time television spots for continuing the Dial-a-Friend campaign on Filipino television (Rimon, 1989).

Research showed that "That Situation" and "I Still Believe" positively influenced knowledge, attitude, and behaviors related to sexual responsibility among Filipino teenagers (Kincaid et al., 1991; Silayan-Go, 1990). The Filipino music campaign resulted in an expected hierarchy of effects: Some 92% of youths (aged 13 to 24) in Manila recalled the songs, 90% liked the songs, 70% interpreted the sexual responsibility messages correctly, 51% were influenced in some way, 44% talked to friends or parents about the songs, and about 25% sought information about contraceptives as a result of hearing the songs (Kincaid et al., 1991). Eleven percent of the respondents, an estimated 150,000 in Manila, used the Dial-a-Friend hotlines. This widespread response was unexpected: Fewer than 1% of callers (13,000 youths) succeeded in getting through. The importance of adequate infrastructure was again emphasized.

Salonga appeared live on television 22 times, and the music video of "I Still Believe" was broadcast 126 times on television (Rimon, 1989). Salonga and members of the Menudo group received thousands of letters from Filipino teenagers about the educational message in the two songs.

Lea Salonga

Born in Manila in 1971, Lea Salonga began singing professionally at age 6. A year later, she was invited to join the Filipino Repertoire Group (the only professional Western theater group in the Philippines). By age 12, Lea had recorded three music albums for children and hosted her own television show "Love Lea."

In 1986, Coleman selected Salonga from among several dozen Filipinos to perform "That Situation" and "I Still Believe." Coleman said the videotape submitted by Salonga was of inferior quality, recorded in a tiny studio with her brother providing accompaniment on a guitar. But Coleman heard a wonderful voice, he invited Salonga for a personal try-out, and offered her the opportunity to record the two songs.

Like Tatiana in Mexico, Salonga became a celebrity role model for the educational issue of teenage sexual responsibility. She was especially happy to be associated with the teenage sexual responsibility project, which also "boosted my career tremendously" (L. Salonga, personal communication, March 31, 1989).

In 1988, the President of the Organization of Filipino Singers called Salonga's mother to invite Lea to audition for *Miss Saigon*, a musical theatrical production. In a worldwide search, Lea won the lead role of a Vietnamese girl (Kim), who in the show is unwillingly forced into prostitution. *Miss Saigon* opened to packed audiences in a major London theater in Fall 1989, and was immediately a resounding success. In 1990, Lea and *Miss Saigon* moved to the New York stage and even greater success. Lea won the prestigious Tony Award and the Sir Lawrence Olivier Award for her acting and singing. *Miss Saigon*'s composer, Claude-Michel Boublil, said: "Lea is the most amazing and intuitive professional I have ever met" (cited in Joffee, 1990).

In 1993, Lea was selected to record songs for *Aladdin*, the Walt Disney animated movie. The popularity of *Miss Saigon* and *Aladdin* made Lea Salonga a world celebrity. And it all began with an entertainment-education music video in the Philippines.

Karina and Charlie: Failure

In 1989, two rock songs and music videos, *"Creo en Ti"* ("I Think of You"), a Spanish translation of "I Still Believe" and *"Frena"* ("Stop"), were produced and distributed in Latin America by FFI in collaboration with PCS. The two singers were Karina, formerly a Venezuelan soap opera actress, and Charlie Masso, a Puerto Rican singer, formerly with Menudo.

An estimated 1,000,000 Mexican teenagers heard the two songs, so a considerable audience was reached. Despite this promising beginning, everything went wrong. Evaluation research on the effects of the two songs conducted in Mexico and Peru showed the music videos were unsuccessful from both a commercial or educational perspective.

The songs were poorly translated and inadequate in musical quality. Karina was not perceived by the audiences as a credible source for espousing sexual responsibility. Charlie Masso's other songs were then popular in Latin America, which crowded out his entertainment-education songs with Karina. Young adolescents had trouble comprehending the educational messages of *"Creo en Ti"* and *"Frena,"* and confused the lyrics of the two songs with other popular songs (Church & Geller, 1989).

What lessons can be learned from the relatively unsuccessful experience of the Karina and Charlie music campaign? Entertainment-education messages developed for a specific context in one country may have limited appeal in another context. Audience-based formative research and pretesting are crucial in designing effective entertainment-education. Furthermore, high-quality production, and performers who are perceived by the target audiences as credible role models for the issue being promoted, are crucial. Finally, the Karina and Charlie music campaign showed that *entertainment-education can fail, just like any other communication approach, if it is not implemented effectively.* This conclusion was a sobering, and useful, lesson for everyone involved in entertainment-education.

Promoting Sexual Responsibility in Nigeria

Building on the successes in Mexico and the Philippines, and learning from the mistakes of the Karina and Charlie campaign, JHU/PCS officials next focused their attention on Nigeria, a West African country with a high population growth rate and a high degree of male sexual irresponsibility. Under the direction of Coleman, King Sunny Ade and Onyeka Onwenu, two of Nigeria's best-known singers, recorded "Choices," a song aimed at adult men, and "Wait for Me," targeted at adolescents, in 1989 in London (see Photo 5.2). About half of Sunny Ade's 100-plus albums deliver an educational

Photo 5.2. Sunny Ade, the "King" of Juju music, with Onyeka Onwenu promoting sexual responsibility in Nigeria through popular music. (*Source:* JHU/PCS Media/Materials Center, used with permission.)

message, such as integration of the different cultures and religions of Nigeria (Graham, 1988): "Popular music is the best means to reach the public with such educational messages" (Ade in Singhal, 1990). The two songs were released in Nigeria five months later and became big hits.[11] Music videos of the two songs were shot in Nigeria and broadcast on national network television. Listeners learned the importance of making decisions about contraception and responsible sexual behavior.

The audience effects of PCS's Nigerian music campaign supported the hierarchy-of-effects model: 64% of men and women in the 15- to 35-year age group (the intended audience) in the cities of Lagos, Enugu, and Kano recalled the songs; 61% comprehended the family planning message; 49% liked the song; 34% talked to someone about the song; 16% talked to their spouse about family planning; and 12% talked to family planning clinic staff (campaign messages accompanying the songs promoted these clinics) (Kincaid et al., 1992). Contraceptive usage increased to 26% after the campaign from 16% before the music campaign (Kincaid et al., 1992).

CONCLUSIONS

Music is one of the oldest entertainment traditions, and attracts large audiences. However, its educational potential remains largely untapped and underutilized. The PCS-sponsored music campaigns in Mexico and Latin America, the Philippines, and Nigeria show that music can promote educational issues without sacrificing commercial objectives. However creating an effective entertainment-education music campaign is complex: an integrated multimedia effort involving government leaders, communication researchers, health officials, international donor agencies, entertainment industry executives, rock musicians, broadcast media, commercial sponsors, religious groups, and infrastructure.

---

[11]The music videos played an important role in this popularity (Coleman, personal correspondence, August 14, 1998).

The Entertainment-Education
Strategy in Radio

Radio soap operas allow you to eavesdrop on the lives of people you care about.

—Elaine Perkins, Jamaican scriptwriter
(personal communication, March 30, 1989)

The entertainment-education strategy in radio preceded its use on television, which is not surprising given that radio broadcasts began more than two decades before television broadcasts in most nations. The potential of the entertainment-education strategy in radio remains largely untapped in most countries, although radio projects in Tanzania and in India in the mid-1990s have proven to be promising. A historical basis for the entertainment-education strategy in radio is provided by the BBC's long-running radio soap opera, *The Archers*. Some other notable illustrations[1] of entertainment-edu-

---

[1] Johns Hopkins University's Population Communication Services' (JHU/PCS) has also promoted family planning and public health messages through entertainment-education radio soap operas. Notable examples in Africa include *Fakube Jarra* (Wise Man) in The Gambia, *Family Affair* in Ghana, *Ezi na Uno* (Our Family) in Nigeria, and *Akarumwa Nechekuchera* in Zimbabwe. Research evaluations of these radio soaps, which included a pre-broadcast baseline survey, a post-broadcast survey, a survey of new adopters of family planning, clinic statistics, listener interviews, and marketing surveys, showed that listenership was high for each of these four radio soap operas. For instance, *Akarumwa Nechekuchera* was regularly heard by 62% of all radio-owning households in Zimbabwe (Lettenmaier et al., 1993). The four soap operas spurred a great deal of interpersonal discussion about family planning between the listeners and their spouses and friends. For instance, in Nigeria, 60% of the men and women who had listened to *Ezi na Uno* the previous night said they had spoken about it with another person (Lettenmaier et al., 1993). Listeners to these four radio soap operas demonstrated sharp

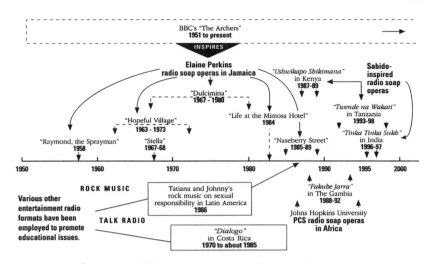

FIG. 6.1.   Some well-known entertainment-education radio soap operas.

cation in radio are Elaine Perkins' soap operas in Jamaica, and the Sabido-inspired *Ushikwapo Shikimana* in Kenya, *Twende na Wakati* in Tanzania, and *Tinka Tinka Sukh* in India (see Fig. 6.1).

THE PROMISE OF RADIO

Radio is the most widely available mass medium worldwide. In 1993, there were 2 billion radio receivers in the world, roughly one for every three people (Lettenmaier et al., 1993),[2] one third in the developing countries of Asia, Africa, and Latin America. In developing countries, where only 20% of households own a radio receiver, the rate of radio adoption is much higher in some than in others: 85% in Egypt, in India the figure is 35%, and in several African countries, it is lower.[3] Worldwide, radio reaches larger audiences than does television, print, or any other mass media (Epskamp, 1985; George, 1990; Lettenmaier et al., 1993; Singhal, 1990).

---

increases in knowledge and more favorable attitudes toward family planning. After listening to *Fakube Jarra*, 91% of the respondents knew that contraception does not cause sterility, up from 41% prior to the soap operas broadcast. Important behavioral changes were also observed in the audiences of these four radio soap operas. For instance, after regularly listening to *Akaraumwa Nechekuchera*, 7% of male listeners adopted a family planning method.

[2]Data on the worldwide diffusion of radio sets come from *Population Reports* (1986) and the BBC's *World Radio and Television Receivers* (1989).

[3]Radio listenership is high in most Latin American countries. In the more developed countries of Africa, for instance in South Africa, radio listenership is more than 90% of the population.

The "little" medium of radio offers several advantages over the "big" media of television and film, especially in developing countries (Schramm, 1977). Radio programming can be produced cheaply, quickly, and messages can be tailored to specific local needs (*Population Reports*, 1986). Radio uniquely reaches low-income and less educated people, who have the highest fertility, the greatest risk of AIDS, and, more generally, whose lives are plagued by social problems that entertainment-education can alleviate. Radio is not as glamorous as television, and it appeals only to one's sense of hearing. But it is more portable than television (for instance, it can be carried to agricultural fields) and one can listen to radio while doing something else. Unlike television, which depends on the availability of central-station electricity, radio can be battery operated. In certain developing countries like India, the recent rapid rise of television in the 1980s has undermined the importance of radio as the dominant mass medium in delivering news and entertainment.

One of the most notable illustrations of entertainment-education in radio is *The Archers*, a soap opera that began broadcasting in England[4] in 1951.

THE ARCHERS[5]

The British Broadcasting Corporation (BBC) radio serial *The Archers: An Everyday Story of Country Folk*, was designed to promote the diffusion of agricultural innovations to British farmers, and to help urban listeners understand rural problems. Created at a critical time for British agriculture in 1951, *The Archers* is still broadcast, and it has grown in popularity.

During World War II, food imports were restricted, and the British government made food production a top priority. Radio programs about agriculture were highly technical, uninteresting, and seldom heard (Food and Agriculture Organization, 1987). When Godfrey Baseley, who organized rural programs for the BBC from 1942 to 1965,[6] conceived of a radio drama

---

[4]In recent decades, several other entertainment-education projects have been implemented in Europe, most notably in the Netherlands. During 1987 to 1991, a highly popular television comedy series, *Family Oudenrijn*, incorporated messages about traffic safety, drinking and driving, and others (Wittink & Hagenzieker, 1991). In 1991, a 13-episode television drama series, *Villa Borghese* promoted a healthy lifestyle (Bouman & Wieberdink, 1993). Lessons learned from the *Villa Borghese* experience encouraged the Netherlands Heart Foundation in 1992–1993 to insert messages on cardiovascular health in *Medisch Centrum West*, an existing and highly popular television drama series (Bouman, Mass, & Kok, 1998). Various other variety and game shows in European nations have also utilized the entertainment-education strategy, for instance, the 1988 *Way of Life Show* on Netherlands television (Bouman, 1989; Bouman, 1998), the 1992 *Health Show* on BBC-TV (Wallace, 1993), and others.

[5]This section draws on Food and Agriculture Organization (1987).

[6]Before implementing *The Archers*, Baseley hosted a talking head radio program on agriculture. He soon realized that it was boring his target audience and ineffective.

centering around agricultural innovations, his supervisors were skeptical. But after 2 years of negotiation, Baseley received the go-ahead to produce *The Archers.*

The first episode was broadcast on January 1, 1951. The program airs every weekday evening, and on Saturday morning, an omnibus program summarizing the week's episodes is broadcast. In 1998, 47 years and 12,350 episodes later, *The Archers* holds the record as the longest running radio serial in the world (Thank You, 1998).

The plot initially centered around Dan Archer, a progressive farmer; his wife, Doris, a kind, gentle homemaker; and their three children. Baseley insisted the characters be authentic, so he detailed their personal characteristics, providing a history for Dan and Doris Archer back several generations. A fictional village, Ambridge, was invented with farms, a school, church, chapel, shops, and pubs. Ambridge was geographically located in the Midlands of England, and its nearest market town was Borchester. The Archers' farm, Brookfield, represented a typical mid-sized dairy farm that employed crop production and raised pigs, sheep, and poultry.

Baseley instructed the soap opera's scriptwriters to avoid didactic lectures at all costs, and instead to feature short, crisp dialogue. A prime consideration was to attract and hold the audience, so a formula of 60% entertainment and 40% education was followed. Each 15-minute episode contains three scenes, each no longer than 6 minutes. Each episode ends with a cliff-hanger.

Music introduces the program, enhances emotional effects, creates transitions in time and location, and ends each episode. Thirty to 90 seconds of material peripheral to the storyline is usually included in each episode. Current news topics inserted at the last minute, like a farm price change or the score of a major sporting event are included in each episode, providing authenticity. The topicality of *The Archers* requires that final decisions are made after the 6 p.m. evening news, just 45 minutes before airtime.

The Archers quickly built a regular audience of 2 million listeners. When the program was moved to prime time, its audience swelled to 4 million (Food and Agriculture Organization, 1987). In 1955, when *The Archers* was at its peak popularity (before television diffused widely in Britain), two out of three adults in Britain, about 20 million people, were regular listeners. In the mid-1990s, *The Archers* commanded a regular audience of about 8 million. The educational content kept up with the times. During the 1990s, issues such as organic farming and HIV/AIDS were addressed (James, 1992).

"But Did the Cow Have Warbles?"

Godfrey Baseley left no stone unturned to maintain the authenticity of *The Archers.* For example, Baseley knew that different tractors make different sounds. So, once established, a tractor recording on *The Archers* was not changed unless it had been specifically mentioned that a new tractor had been bought.

So punctilious was Baseley about sound effects that once he sent a BBC sound technician many miles into the countryside to record the sound of brushing a cow's back, for an episode about the control of the Ox Warble Fly (whose larva live in swellings on a cow's back). When the technician returned, Baseley quizzed him as to whether the recording was properly done. When the technician assured him that it was, Baseley asked: "But did the cow have Warbles?" The technician, shaking his head, left to search for a cow with Ox Warbles.

Well into his 80s, Baseley presently lives in retirement in a comfortable home in Gloucester, England. Every evening, he tunes his radio dial to hear *The Archers*, the program that he created 47 years ago.

Effects of *The Archers*

The Archers met several of its educational goals. Millions of urban dwellers learned of happenings in the countryside and about the problems of farmers and farming, which gained prestige for agriculture and understanding of its problems. *The Archers* provided useful information to farm families about animal diseases, how to increase farm productivity, and new crop practices. Research conducted by the BBC indicates that *The Archers* played an important role in helping a relatively inefficient agriculture in the post-war years become one of the most efficient in the world (Food and Agriculture Organization, 1987).

On one occasion, Britain's Fire Fighting Services, disappointed with their own efforts, requested that Baseley promote the idea of farm ponds for both fire fighting and irrigation. The result was a barn fire on Brookfield Farm in which Dan Archer's daughter-in-law Grace died while trying to save her horse. The BBC's telephone switchboard was jammed by sympathetic callers, and mourners' letters arrived in large sacks at BBC headquarters. English newspapers ran banner headlines, "GRACE ARCHER DIES IN STABLE FIRE." Several hundred suggestions were received by the BBC on how to resurrect Grace Archer.

Efforts to transfer the idea of *The Archers* to other countries, though, has yielded mixed results. Attempts to copy *The Archers* in the Netherlands failed, as Dutch Ministry of Agriculture officials had an inadequate understanding of the entertainment-education principles coined by Baseley (Van den Ban, personal communication, August 3, 1988). Nigeria had better success with a television soap opera, *Cock Crow at Dawn*, and a radio soap opera, *Don Manuma* (For Farmers), both patterned after *The Archers* (De-Goshie, 1986; Ume-Nwagbo, 1986). The plot of *Don Manuma* revolved around a farming village (like Ambridge), and it too promoted agricultural innovations among Nigerian farmers (Ugboajah, 1980).

Photo 6.1.   Elaine Perkins (second from right) recording an episode of *Nase-berry Street*, a family planning radio soap opera, at the Kingston studios of the Jamaican Broadcasting Corporation in 1989. (*Source:* Elaine Perkins, used with permission.)

But the most important progeny of *The Archers* were the several radio soap operas created by Elaine Perkins in Jamaica.

THE JAMAICAN RADIO SOAP OPERAS
OF ELAINE PERKINS[7]

Elaine Perkins was born in Kingston, Jamaica in a family of professional journalists (see Photo 6.1). Her grandfather and father were on the editorial staff of *The Gleaner*, an elite English newspaper widely read throughout the Caribbean area. In 1958, *The Gleaner* hired Perkins to write short stories and features. That same year, one of Perkins' friends, an official of the Jamaican Information Service, invited her to write a script for a radio drama. Her approach involved extensive formative research and a clear definition of the target audience (Cambridge, 1992). She wandered into the neighbor-hoods with an audio cassette recorder to tape sound effects, snatches of

---

[7]This section draws on Cambridge (1992), Hazzard and Cambridge (1988), *Population Reports* (1986), and Singhal's interviews with Elaine Perkins and Maisha Hazzard, in Los Angeles on March 30, 1989.

conversation, and local lingo. She sought to create credible locales and use common colloquial language (Cambridge, 1992).

Raymond, the Sprayman

Perkins' first well-known radio program, *Raymond, the Sprayman* (1958–1959), was designed to promote the Jamaican Government's mosquito eradication campaign. The Aedes Egypti mosquito was causing widespread dengue fever and malaria in Jamaica. Many people thought spraying would poison their children and destroy crops and gardens. Perkins' series was designed to help Jamaicans overcome their fears.

Raymond the Sprayman went from home to home allaying fears about mosquito spraying. He was a likable character—he often mixed the wrong sprays keeping the audience in high humor through his bumbling efforts—important in softening audience attitudes toward malaria health inspectors. *Raymond, the Sprayman* was immensely popular among radio listeners in Jamaica and appears to have contributed to the success of the mosquito eradication campaign, although no summative evaluation research was conducted.

In 1960, Perkins trained at the BBC in London. She was especially intrigued by the popularity of *The Archers*. Then in 1963, she was appointed Chief Broadcasting Officer in the Jamaican Information Service (JIS), the government communication agency. She had a dynamic staff but lacked money to produce quality programs. Perkins searched for creative ways to disseminate information about government health services, literacy efforts, agricultural innovations, and other development activities. Overwhelmed by the task of creating separate programs for each development issue, Perkins decided to create one radio serial, *Hopeful Village*.

Hopeful Village (1963–1973) was the story of a typical Jamaican village. Through this fictional venue Perkins sought to boost the self-efficacy of listeners and promote self-determination, self-respect, and self-sufficiency. *Hopeful Village* was popular with its intended listeners and earned Jamaica's prestigious Musgrave Medal.

Perkins became a consummate creator of believable radio characters, as corroborated by the audience reaction to her two radio series: *Life at the Mimosa Hotel* (1984) and *Naseberry Street* (1985–1989).

Perkins created *Life at the Mimosa Hotel* at the request of the Jamaican Tourist Board. This soap opera centered around a small hotel located on Jamaica's Northern Coast and was designed to modify attitudes and behaviors of the street vendors who frequently harassed foreign tourists. The series portrayed the conflict between the higglers (nonlicensed street vendors) and foreign tourists, hotel officials, and local shop owners. It earned very high audience ratings before it was canceled by Jamaican government officials within a year.

Naseberry Street

From 1985 to 1989, Perkins wrote and produced a family planning soap opera, Naseberry Street. Funded by the Jamaica Family Planning Association and by a private commercial sponsor, Naseberry Street followed characters who lived in a low-income neighborhood on Kingston's fictitious Naseberry Street. A question-and-answer talk show followed each episode and dealt with listeners' questions about family planning.

Perkins' characters were spokespersons for contrasting worldviews of family planning. Typical of her style she wrote crisp dialogues and made creative use of music and sound effects to be commercially appealing (Cambridge, 1992; Hazzard & Cambridge, 1988). Nana, a superstitious older midwife, represented traditional beliefs and superstitions about family planning. Nana's neighbor was Nurse Hugget, a health educator, employed by a family planning clinic located on Naseberry Street. Hugget was Nana's antithesis, and provided advice on family planning methods.

Perkins deliberately allowed her listeners to be privy to intimate details of each character's life. Listeners heard the infamous Scattershot luring naïve young women into sexual relationships. Scattershot laughed about his sexual conquests and bragged to his male friends about his many children, whose names he could not even remember. Perkins knew that Scattershot would be perceived by a minority of male listeners as a cult hero, but she was convinced that mothers would shield their daughters from such a rogue (George, 1990). The power of the program lay in the parasocial interaction created between the characters and the audience.

Naseberry Street reached about one million people, 40% of Jamaica's total population. More than 75% of 2,000 respondents in a 1986 survey reported listening to Naseberry Street, many on a regular basis (Stone, 1986). More women listened to the radio show than men, and people of lower socioeconomic status listened more regularly than those of higher status (ideal for a program about family planning). The 1986 audience survey suggested that Naseberry Street was effective in promoting the adoption of family planning (Hazzard & Cambridge, 1988). Contraceptive use was higher among listeners than among non-listeners. Listeners reported learning that unwanted pregnancies could be prevented by adopting family planning methods, that men should be sexually responsible, and that teenagers should delay sexual activity until marriage (Population Reports, 1986).

A second national survey of 2,000 respondents in 1988 showed the effects of Naseberry Street continued and grew (Stone, 1988). Scattershot, a negative role model for family planning, was more disliked by women than by men.

A few male listeners perceived Scattershot as a positive role model, naming pet dogs and race horses after the famous skirt-chaser.[8] Furthermore, *Scattershot* became a common term in Jamaican discourse, as in "Oh, you Scattershot you." *Naseberry Street* was discontinued by the Jamaican government in 1989, perhaps because Elaine Perkins' husband Wilmot engaged in provocative journalism, which led him to fall into disfavor with politicians.

While Perkins' approach to entertainment-education is totally consistent with the strategy pioneered by Godfrey Baseley and Miguel Sabido, each of these three individuals created their entertainment-education formula independently, learning of each others' approach only in recent years (partly through the efforts of the present authors). In creating her radio soap operas, Perkins did not think of them as entertainment-education: "It was just the most convenient way of telling people about development issues."

What Miguel Sabido did for entertainment-education in television, Elaine Perkins did for this strategy in radio.

COSTA RICA'S *DIALOGO*

In addition to radio soap operas, certain other entertainment radio formats— like talk radio—are well-suited to address educational issues (Aufderheide, 1990). The essence of talk radio is controversy, which can help spur audience participation in important social issues. Several radio talk show hosts in the United States focus on social issues like abortion rights, substance abuse, and teenage pregnancy.

A clear example of talk radio that addresses sensitive educational topics was *Dialogo* in Costa Rica. This 10-minute radio program was broadcast each weekday morning at 7 a.m. to promote sex education in Costa Rica. *Dialogo* was broadcast by five national and regional radio stations in Costa Rica; most were commercial. About 4,000 *Dialogo* broadcasts occurred from 1970 to the mid-1980s.

Dialogo was produced by the Centro de Orientación Familiar (COF), a private Costa Rican family planning organization. David Poindexter played an important role in *Dialogo*. COF underwrote the production costs by selling family planning booklets and audio cassettes of the programs, with funds provided by local and international donor agencies, such as the Population Institute.

Dialogo was hosted by Padre Carlos,[9] an Episcopalian Minister who became interested in population issues. It featured frank dialogues about sex

---

[8]These Jamaican men provide an example of the *Archie Bunker* effect (Vidmar & Rokeach, 1974), a phenomena also observed in other entertainment-education projects.

[9]Padre Carlos was much loved and respected by *Dialogo*'s listeners, much like the epiloguist Ashok Kumar in the Indian soap opera *Hum Log*.

education, such as between a parent and a child, a doctor and a patient, a professor and a student, or between friends. Dramatized life stories of women, couples, and families were presented to educate viewers about family planning. Thousands participated in the program via letters and phone calls. Questions were answered on *Dialogo*; in a daily newspaper column, *Dialogo Abierto* (Open Dialogue); and by direct mail. *Dialogo* helped remove the taboo from family planning in Costa Rica (Risopatron & Spain, 1980).

An amazing 40% of Costa Rica's adults regularly listened to *Dialogo*. The program's reach was higher in rural, low-income, and poorly educated Costa Rican households, the target audience (*Population Reports*, 1986; Risopatron & Spain, 1980). Half of *Dialogo's* audience were males, even though it focused on human sexuality and family life education, subjects usually of greater interest to women. Research on the effects of *Dialogo* in the late 1970s, showed that listeners had greater knowledge about family planning methods than did non-listeners, displayed more positive attitudes toward family planning, and were more likely to adopt family planning (Risopatron & Spain, 1980).

In the mid-1980s, JHU/PCS helped restructure the content and production quality of *Dialogo*, further enhancing the radio program's educational value. Themes like the role of women in development were emphasized. Women's groups and health organizations were actively involved in providing follow-up counseling services to listeners.

One of the most important and indirect impacts of *Dialogo* was to deepen David Poindexter's involvement in promoting the entertainment-education strategy, a path that eventually led him to Miguel Sabido in Mexico (see Chap. 3, this volume).

KENYA'S *USHIKWAPO SHIKIMANA*[10]

Kenyans have heard about family planning since 1962, when the Kenyan Family Planning Association was established. But relatively few Kenyans had adopted family planning methods by 1987 (Rogers et al., 1989). The average Kenyan women bore eight children. Polygamy is common, so a Kenyan man with four wives could easily father 30 or more children.

To address this population growth problem, Tom Kazungu, a radio producer at the government radio network, Voice of Kenya, was asked to create a family planning radio soap opera, *Ushikwapo Shikimana* (Hold on to He Who Holds You). *Ushikwapo Shikimana* is a popular Swahili saying meaning, "when given advice, take it." Kazungu's plans grew out of a 1983 Sabido

---

[10]This section is based on Singhal's interview with Tom Kazungu, producer of *Ushikwapo Shikimana*, in Los Angeles on March 31, 1989.

workshop on entertainment-education soap opera design arranged in Mexico by Poindexter. Plans for *Tushauriane* (Let's Discuss),[11] an entertainment-education television soap opera in Kenya were also conceived then.

Upon their return, the *Ushikwapo Shikimana* team, led by Kazungu, and the *Tushauriane* team, led by Greg Adambo, each worked to create a soap opera. Their challenge was to adapt Sabido's methodology to the Kenyan situation. Voice of Kenya producers, writers, and researchers traveled through rural Kenya to conduct formative evaluation. Anecdotes, folk sayings, and information about obstacles to family planning were obtained, and the plot, storyline, and characters developed. *Ushikwapo Shikimana* was targeted to audiences in six Kenyan states with very high fertility and infant mortality rates, although the soap opera was designed to appeal to the nation's general radio audience.

From 1987 to 1989, 219 episodes of *Ushikwapo Shikimana* were broadcast. Television appeals to urban audience in Kenya, so the radio soap opera was aimed at rural people. The family of Mzee Gogo, a traditional Kenyan man who had four wives, several children, and many grandchildren, formed the main characters. Old man Gogo derived esteem and security from his large family, who lived on a small farm in Pambazuko village. The smaller family of Jaka and Lulu and their two children represented a monogamous marriage. The two families, representing negative and positive role models, were contrasted in terms of family harmony and opportunities for their children.

Funded by the Kenyan National Council for Population and Development (NCPD), each episode of *Ushikwapo Shikimana* cost 10,000 Kenyan shillings, about $500 (U.S.), to produce. *Ushikwapo Shikimana* did not convey specific details about family planning methods, but instead was designed to motivate listeners to adopt family planning (Rogers et al., 1989). The soap opera also promoted such educational issues as reducing poverty, increasing personal self-efficacy, raising agricultural productivity, and eliminating child abuse, a growing problem in Kenya.

The three scriptwriters—Dr. Jay Kitsao wrote the early episodes, Dr. Kimani Njogu wrote the middle episodes, and Kadenge Kazungu wrote the last several episodes—were linguistics professors at the University of Nairobi. No epilogue was provided. Instead a summary of the educational messages in each episode was delivered by Kazungu.

A 1988 evaluation of *Ushikwapo Shikimana* estimated a regular audience of 7 million people, 40% of Kenya's population (Mazrui & Kitsao, 1988). Seventy-five percent accurately comprehended the family planning mes-

---

[11] *Tushauriane*, the first long-running indigenous television soap opera in Kenya achieved very high viewer ratings and its audience popularity was discussed extensively in the Kenyan press (Andere, 1987; Muchiri, 1989; Muroki, 1989; Odindo, 1987). Unfortunately, no summative evaluation was conducted of its audience effects.

sages. A post-hoc research evaluation[12] in 1990 indicated that by the time *Ushikwapo Shikimana* ended in 1989, its audience had increased to an estimated 60% of the Kenyan population. Listeners reported learning the following from the soap opera: the need for family planning, the disadvantages of polygamy, the advantages of fewer children, the importance of family harmony, how to raise healthy children, and the importance of mutual respect between husband and wife. Several thousand audience letters were received at Voice of Kenya headquarters in Nairobi, mostly from women who told how *Ushikwapo Shikimana* had affected their lives.

Ushwikapo Shikimana's impact might have been greater with adequate family planning infrastructure in Kenya's rural areas. "We could not wait for the infrastructure," said Kazungu. "We put out the message, hoping at least some listeners will benefit" (Singhal interview, 1989). The program's popularity led to *Ushikwapo Shikimana II*, broadcast by the Voice of Kenya after 1997. Perhaps the Kenya soap opera helped influence neighboring Tanzania's decision to broadcast a radio soap, *Twende na Wakati*, in 1993.

TANZANIA'S *TWENDE NA WAKATI*

The entertainment-education strategy did not spread widely in the 1980s, as a rigorous evaluation of its effects that could convince policymakers of its potential was lacking. Although Sabido's Mexican soap operas (1975 to 1982) seemed highly effective, national officials in Mexico and elsewhere were not persuaded to expand the concept. The evaluation of *Hum Log* in India lacked pre–post measures of effects. Evaluations of entertainment-education projects by JHU/PCS represented an important step forward in using before–after (and midterm) surveys of audience effects (Piotrow et al., 1997). But these studies did not include a control group, which allows researchers to eliminate the effects of contemporaneous influences on audience members. *Twende na Wakati* helped advance the evaluation process.

Twende na Wakati (Let's Go with the Times), was a family planning and HIV prevention radio soap opera broadcast twice weekly in the evening hours. The series began broadcasting in Tanzania on July 9, 1993, and continued through December 1998. Its purpose was to slow population growth and the spread of disease.

Population Growth and the AIDS Epidemic in Tanzania

The population of Tanzania was approximately 27 million in 1992 and expected to double in 20 years. In addition, per capita income in Tanzania in 1992 was only $100 and had been declining over the previous decade.

---

[12]The report that documents the post-hoc evaluation of *Ushikwapo Shikimana* does not indicate an author or source; it was made available by PCI.

Realizing the harmful consequences of rapid population growth on the nation's social and economic development, the government adopted a National Population Policy in 1992. This led to a major expansion of the national family planning program. Contraceptive services were provided free of charge at 3,000 Ministry of Health clinics, so most couples had access to family planning methods. But the 1991–1992 Demographic and Health Survey (DHS) in 1995 found a contraceptive prevalence rate for married women of only 10%.

The AIDS epidemic probably spread to Tanzania from neighboring countries in East Africa via long distance truck drivers. They infected commercial sex workers at truck stops along Tanzania's Trans-African Highway. The first three AIDS cases in Tanzania were reported in 1983. A 1991 study at seven main truck stops found that 28% of the truckers and 56% of the commercial sex workers were HIV positive (AMREF, 1992). The National AIDS Control Programme estimated the number of AIDS cases at about 400,000 (2.6% of the approximately 15 million adults on the Tanzanian mainland). However, on the basis of blood donor data, the National AIDS Control Programme estimated that 1.2 million Tanzanians were infected with HIV in 1995, 8% of the adult population and 2% above 1994.

Implementing the Entertainment-Education Strategy

In 1993, when broadcasts of *Twende na Wakati* began, most adult Tanzanians were aware of AIDS, had knowledge of the means of HIV transmission, and had favorable attitudes toward HIV prevention. However, a nationwide survey conducted a year earlier had shown a low level of HIV prevention behavior, despite widespread fear concerning the epidemic. A *KAP-gap*—high knowledge and favorable attitudes but not accompanied by widespread use or practice—existed for both family planning and HIV prevention in Tanzania in 1993.

Poindexter, then president of PCI, convinced officials in Radio Tanzania to produce an entertainment-education radio soap opera (there was no television broadcasting in mainland Tanzania). The writers and producer were trained by Kenyans Kazungu and Njogu. Extensive pre-production research was completed: 4,800 interviews and 160 focus-group interviews with the target audience.

Twende na Wakati is the most thoroughly researched program in the history of the entertainment-education genre. The formative research provided scriptwriters and producers with a detailed understanding of the educational issues to be addressed, and with the nature of message content that would be appropriate for the audience. Based on the pre-production research, a Values Grid was formulated in February 1993 to guide the content of *Twende na Wakati* at a workshop of religious, governmental, educational, and other organizations. The Values Grid comprised 57 statements, such as:

"It is not right that boy children be favored over girl children." Statements from the Values Grid formed a basis for the storyline, and roles played by the main characters. The workshop also produced the name for the radio soap opera, *Twende na Wakati* (Let's Go with the Times). AIDS prevention was selected as an educational theme along with family planning.[13]

Negative, Positive, and Transitional Role Models

Patterned after Sabido's methodology, three character types are featured in *Twende na Wakati*: Positive and negative role models who share or reject the educational values and transitional characters, whose attitudes and behaviors change and who eventually adopt the positive educational value. Positive role models are rewarded in the storyline; negative role models are punished. For example, Mkwaju is a long-distance truck driver, who is promiscuous, contracts HIV, and eventually suffers from AIDS. Mkwaju also prefers male children, but is punished by having daughters—at one point his wife and two girlfriends deliver five daughters, to his great disappointment. Thus opposition to son preference, one of 57 themes listed in the Values Grid, is conveyed through positive, negative, and transitional role models who act out the educational values.

Tunu, Mkwaju's wife, is a compliant, submissive spouse during the early months of the broadcasts. After tolerating her husband's infidelity and alcoholism, Tunu becomes a positive role model for female equality, economic self-sufficiency, and HIV prevention. She separates from Mkwaju and establishes a small business to support herself and her children. Tunu is positively rewarded by being spared from HIV infection and by prospering economically.

The messages conveyed are subtle. No preaching about family planning or HIV prevention occurs. The role models provide the vehicle for the educational message as Bandura's (1977, 1997) social learning theory dictates.

Effects of *Twende na Wakati*

The effects of *Twende na Wakati* were measured in a field experiment[14] in which most of Tanzania was exposed to the program (the treatment), while the broadcasts were blocked from a large central region of the country,

---

[13]The radio soap opera in Tanzania may be one of the first entertainment-education projects focusing on both family planning and HIV prevention. In most nations, family planning and HIV prevention projects are conducted separately, although both promote the use of condoms and are usually organized as programs in the national ministry of health.

[14]The research design for *Twende na Wakati* may not be the first entertainment-education project to include a control group: The JHU/PCS radio soap opera in The Gambia, *Fakube Jarra*, included a control group. However, the eight types of data gathered for *Twende na Wakati* (including data from a control group), make it an unusually rigorous research evaluation of the effects of entertainment-education.

Dodoma, for 2 years from 1993 to 1995 (the control). Eight types of evaluation data were gathered, including before–during–after interviews with 3,000 respondents in the control and treatment area each year for 5 years; point-of-referral data on family planning adoption at 79 clinics; focus-group and in-depth interviews with new family planning adopters; and a content analysis of audience letters in response to *Twende na Wakati* (Rogers et al., 1997). The evaluation study was carried out by Everett M. Rogers and Dr. Peter Vaughan at the University of New Mexico, and by Population Family Life Education Programme (POFLEP), a research center headquartered in Arusha, Tanzania, led by Ramadhan Swalehe and Verhan Bakari.

Twende na Wakati was popular. Fifty-five percent of Tanzanians listened to the radio soap opera and half of those listened to at least one or both of the episodes broadcast each week. The serial had strong effects, with 23% of listeners reporting the adoption of family planning methods because of exposure to *Twende na Wakati*; 82% reported adopting a method of HIV prevention. Most changed to monogamous sexual relationships, while others adopted condoms or stopped sharing razors or needles.

The cost-benefits of *Twende na Wakati* were impressive: less than $1 (U.S.) per adopter of family planning and less than 10 cents (U.S.) per adopter of HIV prevention. These figures are very important in a desperately poor nation like Tanzania, where the per capita income in 1998 was only $150 per year.

The evaluation research on effects were convincing to many national policymakers in the population field. After the first 2 years of broadcasting *Twende na Wakati* in Tanzania, radio soap operas were also broadcast in the Caribbean island nation St. Lucia, Madagascar,[15] and India. So one effect of *Twende na Wakati* was to revive interest in entertainment-education radio.

TINKA TINKA SUKH IN INDIA[16]

Tinka Tinka Sukh (Happiness Lies in Small Things) was a 104-episode entertainment-education radio soap opera broadcast in India from February 1996 to February 1997. Its purpose was to promote gender equality, women's empowerment, small family size, family harmony, environmental conservation, and HIV prevention.

---

[15]The soap opera *Sarivolana* (Reflections of the Moon) began broadcasting in spring 1997, with funding from the Dodwell Trust and with technical assistance from PCI.

[16]This section draws upon Papa et al. (1998); Sood, Law, and Singhal (1998); and Sood, Singhal, and Law (1997).

An evaluation of *Tinka Tinka Sukh* was conducted by Singhal and Rogers and others at Ohio University and the University of New Mexico. Multiple types of data were collected in a methodological triangulation to evaluate the effects of *Tinka Tinka Sukh*: content analyses of scripts; interviews with key officials involved in the production; a before–after survey in a treatment area (Gonda District) and a control area (Allahabad District) in Uttar Pradesh State in India (see Fig. 6.2); content analyses of a random sample of 237 of the 150,000 letters written by listeners; a questionnaire of letter writers; and an in-depth case study of Village Lutsaan in the state of Uttar Pradesh, India where the radio program seemed to have especially strong community effects.

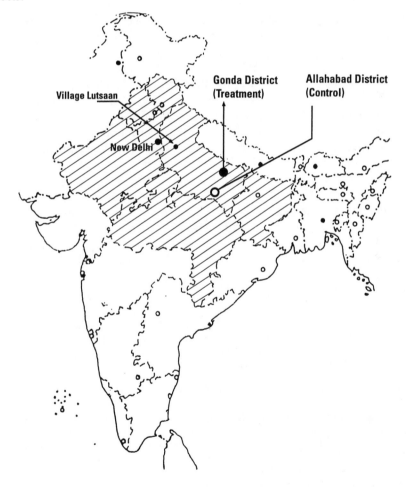

FIG. 6.2.   The radio soap opera *Tinka Tinka Sukh* was broadcast by 27 stations of All India Radio in the Hindi belt of North India (shaded).

The Creation

The idea for *Tinka Tinka Sukh* was mooted in a 1994 meeting between David Poindexter and Shashi Kapoor, director-general of All India Radio (AIR) in New Delhi. Poindexter's organization had previously helped launch two popular entertainment-education television serials in India—*Hum Log* in 1984–1985 and *Hum Raahi* in 1992–1993—on Doordarshan, the national network (see Chap. 4, this volume). Both serials attracted large audiences in the Hindi-speaking area of North India, with ratings approaching 90%. Both dealt with gender equality, family harmony, and family size (Rogers et al., 1994; Singhal, Rogers, & Brown, 1993). Kapoor entrusted the task of producing *Tinka Tinka Sukh* to Mrs. Usha Bhasin, then director of pro-grammes at AIR. Bhasin had previously produced three popular, provocative radio serials on adolescence, *Jeevan Saurabh* in 1988; marriage incompati-bility, *Jeevan Saurabh II* in 1989; and teenage sexuality, *Dehleez* in 1994–1995[17] (Bhasin & Singhal, 1998). Bhasin, like Elaine Perkins, was trained at the BBC and was familiar with *The Archers* and entertainment-education.[18]

PCI helped conduct a workshop at AIR in June 1995 to share with Bhasin and her team Sabido's methodology. The AIR workshop produced the gen-eral outline for *Tinka Tinka Sukh*, including delineation of educational val-ues, positive and negative characters, and the locale. Bhasin identified 11 scriptwriters and 6 producers, several of whom had participated in previous AIR series. The writing of *Tinka Tinka Sukh* began soon after the workshop and production began in September 1995. Based on feedback from the listeners of previous AIR serials, the producers decided to make the serial "music heavy," with music carefully selected to appeal to audiences in the entire Hindi-speaking belt. India's renowned poet Gulzaar, known for his Hindi film lyrics, wrote the theme song for *Tinka Tinka Sukh*. The famous Bombay music director Vishal Bharadwaj, composed the catchy tune, and well-known playback singer Kavita Krishnamoorthy lent her voice.[19]

---

[17]In 1998, Bhasin produced another popular entertainment-education radio serial on the environment, *Yeh Kahan Aa Gaye Hum* (Where Have We Arrived?), which was broadcast by AIR on 31 radio stations in the seven Hindi-speaking states of North India. The epilogues in this serial were delivered by Shabana Azmi, a popular Indian film actress, a social activist, and a member of parliament.

[18]Bhasin, like Elaine Perkins in Jamaica, realized (on her own) the effectiveness of the entertainment-education strategy and kept honing it through experimentation in recent decades. At AIR, she pioneered the idea of registering thousands of active listeners for each entertainment-education radio serial, whose feedback was used to fine tune ongoing programs. This approach of registering listeners also helped carry the audience of one radio serial to the next radio serial, reducing the *audience lag*, the time taken to build a sizable and dedicated audience for a media program. This audience lag is also limited in the Soul City health promotion initiatives in South Africa (see Chap. 9, this volume).

[19]A playback singer actually sings the songs in Indian films that are mouthed by the actors seen on screen.

Bhasin and her team also decided to use different music for the epilogues concluding each episode, written in the form of *dohas* (couplets). *Dohas* are universally popular in Hindi-speaking India. Religious and educational sermons are commonly associated with this genre of song and poetry. The *dohas* for *Tinka Tinka Sukh* were written by Acchar Singh Parmar, a producer and artist for *Tinka Tinka Sukh*.

Several well-known artists from radio and theater were chosen to play the major characters. Each writer brought unique strengths to the storyline, for instance, a writer with a legal background was hired for episodes dealing with women's rights and divorce law. Production began in September 1995 at a radio studio outside of AIR. The sponsor, Primetime, in turn sold episodes to other commercial sponsors. Each episode cost approximately Rs. 20,000 ($500 U.S.).

A 6-month publicity blitz preceded the first broadcast. Promotional spots, featuring the catchy theme song, character voices, jingles, and narration, were broadcast on all 27 stations where the series would air. These spots were also broadcast on AIR's commercial channels, the youth channel, and the national network radio channel. Similar spots were broadcast on Doordarshan, emphasizing the family orientation of the forthcoming serial and its long duration (by Indian standards) of 12 months.

AIR broadcast *Tinka Tinka Sukh* for one year, beginning February 19, 1996, to seven Indian states in population-rich, Hindi-speaking northern India: Uttar Pradesh, Bihar, Madhya Pradesh, Rajasthan, Haryana, Himachal Pradesh, and Delhi (see Fig. 6.2). Six hundred million people comprising 100 million households live in these seven states. Based on a 1997 survey, regular listenership was estimated at 6%,[20] an audience of 36 to 40 million people—the largest audience for any AIR soap opera, and perhaps worldwide.

The Storyline

As the title suggests, *Tinka Tinka Sukh* explores how everyday, ordinary acts of human interaction hold happiness. Navgaon is a farming community struggling to understand the value of modern traditions and moving in progressive directions. Suraj, his father Chaudhri, and mother Chaudhrain, represent an ideal family. Whereas Chaudhri and his wife understand the role of tradition, progressive ways are growing in importance. The couple represents women's causes—anti-dowry, marriage and divorce, women's empowerment—and the importance of an integrated harmonious community

---

[20]Estimates of *Tinka Tinka Sukh*'s listenership are derived from the random sample survey conducted in Gonda District, which according to AIR's Audience Research Unit lags behind other districts in the Hindi-speaking region in radio listenership. So the estimate of 36 to 40 million regular listeners represents a modest one.

based on cooperation and self-sufficiency. They raised their son, Suraj, to appreciate the importance of agriculture and individuals' relationships with their environment, particularly the community. This family's virtuous ways earn the loyal support of their poor workers, Jumman and his wife Rukhsana. Jumman is a farmhand in the Chaudhri's fields, while Rukhsana does housework.

Chacha, his wife Chachi, and their children Ramlal, Champa, Sundar, Suman, and Pappu, are the antithesis of the Chaudhris. As breadwinner, Chacha believes he is absolved of all parental responsibilities. Chachi is domineering, blindly traditional, and very vocal—the village gossip. She indulges her eldest son Ramlal, a delinquent, and is critical of her daughters. Her eldest daughter Champa quietly grows out of the family's shadows to become a famous singer.

The lives of Gareebo, a widow, and her daughters Nandini, Kusum, and Lali show the trials of being a woman in a patriarchal society. Gareebo feels societal pressure to get her daughters married since they have come of age. Nandini, the eldest, will not marry until she becomes self-dependent as a teacher. Kusum gets married early and dies during childbirth. Lali becomes a medical doctor, the first in Navgaon.

Tragedy occurs when Poonam is abused by her husband and his parents because her family lacks an adequate dowry. Poonam commits suicide. Sushma, sister-in-law of Kusum, finds herself abandoned by her husband, also for dowry. Encouraged by Nandini, Champa, and Suraj and supported by her parents, Sushma overcomes her trials and establishes a sewing school, which provides her with economic independence.

Ramlal is transformed by the quiet determination of Nandini and realizes his delinquent acts upset the peace of the community. He becomes a Block Development Officer in Navgaon so that he can contribute to his village. Champa starts an adult nightschool, and Sushma's school expands and creates economic opportunities for women. Jumman, momentarily swayed by urban glamour, contracts AIDS and disrupts his family's harmony. But he finally accepts his wife's view that life's happiness lies in small things.

Educational Themes

Tinka Tinka Sukh promoted women's issues. Women's empowerment was addressed in 80% of all episodes, 86% discussed ways for suppressed women to restore self-confidence. Women's education was featured in 51% of all episodes, 32% addressed women becoming self-reliant. Women's right to equal nutrition with men was dealt with in 18% the episodes and equal access to health care in 15%.

Although it is illegal to give or receive dowry in India, the custom is widely practiced. The negative consequences of the dowry system were examined in 21% of the radio soap opera's episodes. Torture of a bride (Poonam) for an insufficient dowry was emphasized in 25%; 8% dealt with not victimizing a woman if she does not become pregnant and deliver a son; 41% showed harmonious relationships between a woman and her husband's parents and family.

In 62% of the episodes, parents were encouraged to talk to their children about education, future plans, and so on. The soap opera also dealt with the preferential treatment of male children in half of its episodes. And in 29% of the programs, *Tinka Tinka Sukh* proposed that sons should participate in domestic chores. This attitude is demonstrated by the model youth, Suraj, and reinforced by his parents and by his friends.

Letter Writing

Approximately 150,000 letters were received by AIR in response to *Tinka Tinka Sukh*. Although only 0.4% of the listeners wrote to AIR, the notion of writing letters is an important part of Indian culture—reinforced by the involving nature of entertainment-education interventions.[21]

We randomly selected 260 letters from the 5,000 obtained from AIR. They were content-analyzed (23 were illegible) for perceptions of the letter writers regarding the radio soap opera. Audience members who wrote were atypical, both of all listeners and of the Indian population. Nevertheless, the letters were valuable in understanding the effects of the entertainment-education strategy employed by *Tinka Tinka Sukh*. The high percentage (67%) of male correspondents is particularly noteworthy, given that men might be expected to be less interested in women's issues. Ninety percent of the letters were written by individuals, and the remaining 10% were written jointly by family members, groups, and organizations. A male writer from Uttar Pradesh wrote on behalf of a conference where the participants took the following oath: "We swear that to our very last breath we will work for the upliftment of women (self-reliance, courage). We will keep in mind the problems raised by *Tinka Tinka Sukh* and will work to eradicate these problems from our country. This is our decision, our right, and our duty."

The main educational themes in *Tinka Tinka Sukh* (see Table 6.1) explicated by the letter writers dealt with gender equality, including empowerment and status of women before and after marriage. One letter, responding to Poonam's suicide, indicated that "Poonam had a number of options. She could have learned from the examples of Sushma who is running a successful sewing school, or Nandini, who despite being born into a poor

---

[21]The animated entertainment-education television series, *Superbook*, based on Bible stories, engendered a high degree of letter writing from viewers in several of the 50 countries where it has been broadcast to date (Fraser & Brown, 1997).

TABLE 6.1

Educational Themes Explicated in Letters to *Tinka Tinka Sukh*

Themes	% Mentioning Theme (N = 237)
1. Status of women in developing skills and capability	42
2. Dowry-related issues	29
3. Youth issues	27
4. Substance abuse (alcohol)	25
5. Status of women before marriage	25
6. Marriage and fertility	23
7. Community living	21
8. Status of women after marriage	19
9. Family life communication	16
10. Divorce, separation, and legal issues	15
11. Preferential treatment of boys	10
12. Family planning	8
13. Breast feeding and pregnancy	6
14. HIV/AIDS-related information	6

Source: Sood, Law, and Singhal (1998).

family is strong, brave and very firm in her decisions, or Champa who is doing so well in life."

One writer suggested that *Tinka Tinka Sukh* should "Show Champa gathering strength to stand up for her rights, thus also portraying the importance of education for girls." Many letters mentioned dowry issues after Poonam committed suicide. Kusum's death in teenage childbirth also triggered responses.

Substance abuse, specifically alcohol, was a main educational theme. As one of the letter writers indicated that "Sundar abused his own parents after he had consumed alcohol. It is difficult to imagine a sweet boy like Sundar behaving in this negative fashion. This is what alcohol does to a man." Some letter writers connected alcohol with HIV/AIDS by stating that alcohol consumption made Jumman more prone to promiscuous behavior, which in turn led to his HIV infection.

Letter writers also exhibited a high degree of parasocial interaction with the radio soap opera and its characters (discussed in greater detail in Chap. 7, this volume): rearranged schedules to listen to *Tinka Tinka Sukh*, claimed that they heard each episode twice, and listened to it daily as broadcast by the various radio stations across Uttar Pradesh. One writer was amazed that *Tinka Tinka Sukh* was always on target with what was on the listener's mind. Others compared their ideas with those presented on the program: "A few episodes ago, I disagreed with the Chaudhri and thought he was in the wrong, however, subsequent episodes have helped me understand and empathize with him. He is a great man and I apologize to him for mistrusting him and questioning his motives."

Listeners reacted to characters as natural and down-to-earth people, and they made up their minds based on the opinion presented by the radio characters. As one letter-writer stated: "Poonam's suicide, Kusum's death at childbirth, Sushma's struggle to stand on her own feet and Rukhsana's life and problems have filled my heart with sentiments, Nandini has taught me to stick to my ideals and fight against injustice, Champa has inspired me to realize my inner potential, Suraj has taught me to be proud of heritage and culture."

Comparing Listeners Versus Non-Listeners

As mentioned previously, the research design of effects included a before–after survey in a treatment and a control area. The broadcasts were blocked in Allahabad District, which served as the control area. Gonda District in Uttar Pradesh was selected as the treatment site, since it was comparable to Allahabad on key demographic variables. *Tinka Tinka Sukh's* broadcasts ended in mid-February 1997 and the post-broadcast survey for *Tinka Tinka Sukh* was conducted in March–April 1997.

The sample for the post-broadcast survey was 1,950—1,472 respondents in Gonda District and 478 in Allahabad District, 63% men and 37% women. Only 6% of respondents in the treatment area ($n = 88$) listened to *Tinka Tinka Sukh* (no listeners were found in Allahabad District which suggests the control area was preserved). The listeners represented a priority audience for the soap opera's educational messages: 90% based in rural areas, 75% had monthly household incomes of less than 1,500 Rupees ($38 U.S.), and 49% illiterate. Among those who listened, there was a high level of involvement with *Tinka Tinka Sukh* and its characters. At least 66% of the listeners had heard *Tinka Tinka Sukh* at least once a week. Respondents indicated that fairly high levels of interpersonal communication about *Tinka Tinka Sukh* occurred after the episodes; 36% discussed it with others, 25% their spouses.

Fifty percent of listeners made changes in their daily schedules to listen to the episodes; 60% found *Tinka Tinka Sukh* both entertaining and educational; 70% indicated that *Tinka Tinka Sukh* was realistic and reflected the daily life in their villages. The listeners exhibited a high degree of involvement with the individual characters in *Tinka Tinka Sukh*: 43% wanted to give advice to some character, 36% chose Suraj as the character they wanted to advise, 56% indicated they were most familiar with Suraj, a positive role model, and 39% stated Suraj was closest to them in character.

The low numbers of listeners ($n = 88$) in Gonda District makes it problematic to assess causal changes as a result of listening to *Tinka Tinka Sukh*. However, an analysis showed that listeners ($n = 88$) differed from non-listeners ($n = 1,384$) in Gonda District with respect to:

1. "Starting to send a daughter to school," with more listeners (57%) than nonlisteners (46%) responding in the affirmative.

2. "Participation in community activities" with more listeners (11%) than nonlisteners (5%) responding in the affirmative.

3. "Visiting [health] sub-centers or clinics more often" with more listeners (47%) than nonlisteners (35%) responding in the affirmative.

4. "Seeking family planning information" with more listeners (42%) than nonlisteners (20%) responding in the affirmative.

5. "Adopting family planning methods" with more listeners (43%) than nonlisteners (25%) responding in the affirmative.

As mentioned previously, these differences in Gonda District were probably not due solely to listening to *Tinka Tinka Sukh*.

CONCLUSIONS

Radio's portability, low cost, and ability to tailor a message to specific local needs provide this medium with a unique advantage in diffusing entertainment-education messages. Radio can effectively reach individuals with less formal education and lower socioeconomic status who are usually the priority audience segment for family planning and other development programs. But the potential of entertainment-education radio programming has hardly been tapped in most countries. Notable exceptions include the BBC's *The Archers*, Elaine Perkins' radio soap operas in Jamaica, *Dialogo* in Costa Rica, *Ushikwapo Shikimana* in Kenya, *Twende na Wakati* in Tanzania, and *Tinka Tinka Sukh* in India.[22] These later two projects, implemented in the mid-1990s, represent increased interest by policymakers in applying the entertainment-education strategy to radio, and more rigorous evaluations of the effects of entertainment-education through experimental research designs.

---

[22]And the JHU/PCS radio soap operas in Africa, reviewed previously in footnote 1.

The Effects of
Entertainment-Education[1]

> *Used deliberately, entertainment can be as effective in realizing political, social, and economic aims as conventional tools of persuasion.*
> —H. Fischer and S. R. Melnik (1979, p. xiv)

During the early decades of research on the entertainment-education strategy, the main question pursued by scholars was to determine the effects on audience individuals. Policymakers were unconvinced that investment in entertainment-education was sound. During the 1990s, little doubt remained about whether entertainment-education had an effect. Instead, scholarly attention turned to how entertainment-education has its effects in creating knowledge, changing attitudes, and in influencing individuals to adopt family planning, HIV prevention, and other behavior changes. In recent years, scholars have found that an entertainment-education message often serves as a catalyst for interpersonal peer communication, which in turn leads to behavior change in other audience members.

This chapter traces the evolution of the entertainment-education strategy during the past two decades, with special attention to the important role of social modeling, self-efficacy, parasocial interaction, and media-stimulated peer communication in stimulating behavior change. We particularly utilize findings from research on the effects of *Twende na Wakati* in Tanzania and on *Tinka Tinka Sukh* in India.[2]

---

[1]This chapter draws on Rogers et al. (1997, 1998) and Singhal et al. (1999). Also, we especially thank our University of New Mexico colleague, Dr. Peter Vaughan, for his extensive comments.

[2]The main body of communication research on the effects of entertainment-education has also been conducted in developing countries.

143

WHAT EFFECTS HAVE BEEN FOUND?

Research on the effects of entertainment-education in developing countries confirms that the strategy changes behavior. The effects investigated are mainly individual-level, short-term behavior changes, such as the adoption of family planning methods and HIV prevention (see Table 7.1).

The entertainment-education strategy usually involves more than just message transmission for purposes of increasing knowledge and changing attitudes. The bottom line for entertainment-education is to cause changes in overt behavior. This means the entertainment-education strategy is mainly motivational, rather than informational. Table 7.2 shows the stages individuals are expected to experience as their behavior changes. The hierarchy-of-effects model (see Chap. 4, this volume) shows that most individuals pass from knowledge of a new idea, through forming a positive attitude toward the idea, to adoption and use of the idea (McGuire, 1981; Prochaska et al., 1992; Rogers, 1995). The implication is that an individual must be informed about a new idea (say HIV prevention) and develop a favorable attitude toward the idea, before changing behavior.[3]

Research and theorizing in recent years suggest that entertainment-education has certain of its effects as a catalyst for triggering interpersonal peer communication leading to changes in the social discourse of the audience[4] (Storey, 1995), to motivate audience individuals to talk to each other about what they learned from the entertainment-education message (Rogers, 1995; Valente et al., 1994, 1997), and to engage audience individuals in socially supporting behavior change (Sood & Rogers, 1996; Vaughan & Rogers, 1996). The effects of the entertainment-education strategy occur particularly as a result of parasocial interaction and role modeling by audience individuals with positive and negative media characters. Audience individuals incorporate the language of their role models in talking to others about the entertainment-education message, and in carrying out new behaviors in their real-life contexts.

Critics of using the entertainment-education strategy to communicate preventive health messages point out that exposure to a radio drama designed to disseminate AIDS information in Zambia did not have important measurable effects in changing high-risk sexual behavior (Yoder, Hornik, & Chirwa, 1996). This evaluation might have found stronger effects if it had used triangulation

---

[3]Other behavior change models also exist depending on the relative ordering of knowledge, attitudes, and practices in behavior change research (Valente et al., 1998). For instance, one may argue that soap operas work more through emotional appeals than rational ones and hence can be expected to change attitudes before knowledge. We hope that future research on entertainment-education will more closely evaluate the relative merits and demerits of these alternative behavior change models.

[4]For example, the broadcasts of *Simplemente María* in Peru in 1969–1970 led the public to begin calling all housemaids María (Singhal et al., 1994). Similarly, in Tanzania in the mid-1990s the public began to refer to sexually promiscuous males as Mkwajus, the name of the main negative role model in the radio soap opera *Twende na Wakati*.

TABLE 7.1

Effects of Entertainment–Education Interventions in Various Developing Countries

Country	Study	Medium	Program (Date)	Data-Gathering	Educational Purpose	Degree of Effect
1. Mexico	Nariman (1993)	TV	*Ven Conmigo, Acompáñame, Vamos Juntos,* and others (1975–1982)	Surveys, other methods	Adult literacy, family planning, others	Strong
2. India	Singhal & Rogers (1989a; 1989c)	TV	*Hum Log* (1984–1985)	Survey, content analysis of episodes and letters	Gender equality, family planning	Fairly strong
3. Mexico	Kincaid et al. (1988)	Music	*Cuando Estemos Juntos* (1986)	Survey, content analysis of letters	Sexual responsibility of youth	Strong
4. Nigeria	Piotrow et al. (1990)	TV	*In a Lighter Mood* (1986–1987)	Survey, clinic data	Family planning	Strong
5. The Gambia, Ghana, Nigeria, and Zimbabwe	Lettenmaier et al. (1993)	Radio	*Fakube Jarra, Family Affair, Ezi na Uno,* and *Akarumuva Necbekucbera* (1988–1992)	Surveys, clinic data, other methods	Family planning	Strong
6. Turkey	Kincaid et al. (1993)	TV and other media	*Sparrows Don't Migrate* (1988, 1990)	Surveys, focus groups	Family planning	Strong
7. The Gambia	Valente et al. (1994)	Radio	*Fakube Jarra* (1988–1991)	Surveys, focus groups, clinic data	Family planning	Strong
8. India	Rogers et al. (1994)	TV	*Hum Raabi* (1992–1993)	Focus groups	Gender equality	Fairly strong

(Continued)

TABLE 7.1
(Continued)

Country	Study	Medium	Program (Date)	Data-Gathering	Educational Purpose	Degree of Effect
9. Zambia	Yoder et al. (1996); Valente (1997)	Radio	*Nshilakamona* (1991–1992)	Surveys	HIV prevention	Weak
10. Tanzania	Rogers et al. (1998)	Radio	*Twende na Wakati* (1993–1998)	Surveys, clinic data, content analysis of episodes and letters, focus group	Family planning, HIV prevention	Strong
11. India	Singhal et al. (1999)	Radio	*Tinka Tinka Sukh* (1996–1997)	Surveys, clinic data, content analysis of episodes and letters, focus group, case study	Gender equality, family planning, community harmony, HIV prevention	Fairly* strong
12. St. Lucia	Vaughan (1998)	Radio	*Apwe Plezi* (1996–1997)	Surveys, focus groups, telephone calls	Family planning, environment, HIV prevention	Fairly strong
13. India	Valente & Bharath (in press)	Street theater	Nalamdana's Plays (1996)	Surveys	HIV prevention	Strong

*Survey data indicated modest effects, but the content analysis of the letters written and the community case study in Village Lutsaan indicated strong effects.

(*Source:* Based on Shefner and Rogers, 1997.)

TABLE 7.2
The Hierarchy-of-Effects in the Behavior Change Process

Stage	McGuire's Hierarchy-of-Effects Levels	Prochaska's Stages Of Change
I. Knowledge	1. Recall of information	I. Precontemplation
	2. Comprehension of messages	
	3. Knowledge or skill for effective adoption of the innovation.	
II. Persuasion	4. Liking the innovation.	II. Contemplation
	5. Discussion of the new behavior with others.	
	6. Acceptance of the message about the innovation.	
	7. Formation of a positive image of the message and the innovation	
	8. Support for the innovative behavior from the system.	
III. Decision	9. Intention to seek additional information about the innovation.	III. Preparation
	10. Intention to try the innovation.	
IV. Implementation	11. Acquisition of additional information about the innovation.	IV. Action
	12. Use of the innovation on a regular basis.	
	13. Continued use of the innovation.	
V. Confirmation	14. Recognition of the benefits of using the innovation.	V. Maintenance
	15. Integration of the innovation into one's ongoing routine.	
	16. Promotion of the innovation to others.	

Source: Based on McGuire's (1981) hierarchy of effects, as modified by JHU/PCS and with the addition of Prochaska's stages of change (Prochaska et al., 1992; Rogers, 1995).

research methods for evaluating the knowledge, attitudes, and behavior changes and had investigated the role of peer communication and parasocial interaction in changing behavior, thus focusing on the persuasion and confirmation stages in the hierarchy of effects. A re-analysis of the data from the Zambia study, using respondents' exposure to the radio program, rather than access (measured as owning a working radio and listening to it at least once per week), showed that the entertainment-education evaluation had somewhat stronger effects when measured as change scores in the KAP dependent variables from the benchmark to the follow-up survey (Valente, 1997).[5]

---

[5]One of the puzzles of the Zambia investigation remained, however: Respondents reported that they changed their HIV prevention behavior (such as their number of sexual partners), but the number using condoms did not increase. Valente (1997) suggested that a possible reason is that a shipment of condoms destined for Zambia was mistakenly rerouted to neighboring Tanzania, so that condoms were not readily available in Zambia during the period when the entertainment-education radio drama was broadcast. Here we see the importance of infrastructural factors in the effects of entertainment-education.

A HISTORY OF ENTERTAINMENT-EDUCATION
EFFECTS RESEARCH

Important changes in effects research on the entertainment-education strategy occurred since Sabido formulated the basic elements of this strategy in the mid-1970s, based in part on his analysis of the Peruvian *telenovela Simplemente María* (Nariman, 1993). Early evaluations were conducted in-house by the Mexican television network, Televisa, and did not utilize the rigorous research designs of the 1990s.

The 1980s and 1990s have seen important advances in improved understanding of the effects of entertainment-education interventions. Only since the mid-1980s have university-based communication scholars become involved in research on entertainment-education, beginning with *Hum Log* in India (Singhal & Rogers, 1988). Academic scholars have brought in key concepts of study like (a) the social modeling by audience individuals with the behavior of positive and negative role models presented in media messages, (b) individuals' self-efficacy, and (c) parasocial interaction. Furthermore, these university-based scholars have often been independent of the producing organization for the program being evaluated. Findings are thus more likely to be perceived as highly credible and the impact of results on policymakers stronger.[6]

Social Modeling Theory

Bandura (1977, 1997) proposed that an individual learns behavior changes by observing and imitating the overt behavior of other individuals who serve as models.[7] He identified three types of social modeling[8]:

1. *Prestige modeling:* Characters who exhibit culturally admired behaviors.
2. *Similarity modeling:* Various media characters who appeal to different audience segments and who portray the benefits of adopting prosocial behaviors.[9]

---

[6]The evaluation researcher who is an insider to the organization implementing the entertainment-education program has certain advantages in carrying out the evaluation, such as intimate knowledge of how the program is implemented. There are often offsetting advantages and disadvantages of the insider and the outsider roles.

[7]Miguel Sabido was the first to recognize the importance of transitional characters and to incorporate them in his television soap operas in the mid-1970s.

[8]These types of modeling are directly related to positive, negative, and transitional role models.

[9]Similarity modeling compares to *homophily*, the degree to which two or more individuals who communicate are similar (Rogers, 1995). Sabido suggested that an entertainment-education soap opera might include about a dozen main characters, including those of both genders and a variety of ages (youth, young adults, middle-aged, and elderly), so that each audience individual can identify with a media character that is homophilous.

3. *Transitional modeling*: Characters that exhibit positive behaviors, negative behaviors, or transitional behavior, in which a negative role model adopts a prosocial behavior.

Bandura (1997) specified two motivational influences of social modeling in entertainment-education programs: *vicarious motivation*, presenting behavior change as a cost-beneficial decision for the individual, and *attentional involvement*, using emotional appeals to sustain parasocial interaction between the audience and the role model. The desired behavior change depends upon four factors: self-efficacy, outcome expectations, aspirations, and perceived impediments.[10]

A final component in Bandura's social modeling process is coding aids, which include: *symbolic coding*, such as epilogues at the end of broadcasts[11] to summarize the message, and *environmental support*, in which influences in the environment of the audience individual are used to sustain a behavior promoted in the program. For example, the Green Star campaign in Tanzania, conducted by JHU/PCS in collaboration with the Tanzanian Ministry of Health, embedded an entertainment-education radio soap opera as the main component of a family planning campaign that also included training clinic staff, radio spots, and other communication activities (Ministry of Health Report, 1995; Rogers et al., 1997). The JHU/PCS approach usually involves embedding the program as one component in a multimedia, multi-pronged communication campaign, which may also involve training clinic providers, advertisement, and other communication activities.[12]

Miguel Sabido based his formula for creating entertainment-education soap operas, in part, on Bandura's (1997) social learning theory. In recent years, Bandura has become increasingly interested in the entertainment-education applications of his theory and has made important intellectual advances toward sharpening the strategy. Bandura (1997) is also the main

---

[10]Real-world impediments, such as a lack of access to health services, can also play a role in determining behavior changes resulting from an entertainment-education soap opera about adult literacymly planning or HIV prevention, as the misrouted shipment of condoms to Zambia suggests (Valente, 1997).

[11]Sabido was the first to use epilogues as part of the entertainment-education strategy in his adult literacy *telenovela*, *Ven Conmigo*, broadcast in Mexico in 1975–1976 (Nariman, 1993).

[12]Piotrow et al. (1997, p. 180) concluded that one reason for the relatively modest effects of the entertainment-education radio soap opera on HIV prevention in Zambia may have occurred because the radio drama was not incorporated within a larger communication campaign: "The lesson was clear: A single, freestanding show not supported by grassroots community mobilization activities or other forms of social mobilization has a relatively small impact. . . . Reinforcing radio soap operas and other mass media entertainment with additional promotion and community activities is now standard procedure for [Johns Hopkins University's] Population Communication Services."

theorizer about the concept of self-efficacy, a key to understanding how entertainment-education has its effects.

Self–Efficacy

Self-efficacy is an individual's perception of his or her capability to deal effectively with a situation, and a sense of perceived control over a situation (Bandura, 1977, 1997; Rogers, 1995).[13] An individual who perceives herself as efficacious is more likely to adopt a family planning method because she believes that she can control how many children she has during her lifetime. Efficacy has level, strength, and generality (Bandura, 1995). Individuals with a relatively low degree of self-efficacy will avoid difficult tasks, have low aspirations, attribute their failures to others or to extraneous circumstances, decrease their efforts when they are disappointed, and are more vulnerable to stress and depression. Individuals with a strong sense of efficacy perceive threats as challenges and are more resilient to disappointments. Low self-efficacy individuals can raise their resilience through social modeling by emulating individuals who exhibit effective coping strategies, and by learning from models how to gain support from their peers.

Social change, according to Bandura (1997), often requires a strong sense of collective efficacy on the part of individuals and collectivities. *Collective efficacy* is the degree to which individuals in a system believe they can organize and execute courses of action required to achieve collective goals (Bandura, 1997). Particularly in *collectivistic cultures*, defined as those in which the collectivity's goals are more important than the individual's goals (Rogers & Steinfatt, 1999), collective efficacy is important. Even in *individualistic cultures*, defined as those in which the individual's goals are more important than the collectivity's (Rogers & Steinfatt, 1999), many types of social change can only occur in response to collective efforts. For example, a development program in India seeks to empower Indian female dairy farmers by encouraging them to receive and manage the income from their dairy enterprise (Shefner-Rogers et al., 1998). Husbands typically collect the milk payments and often squander the money on alcohol, gambling, and cigarettes. If a woman seeks to gain control over the milk payments, the response is likely to be failure, and perhaps, in some cases, even a beating from her husband. But if all of the women dairy farmers in an Indian village gain collective efficacy, form a women's group, and together demand control of their earnings, they are much more likely to be successful.

Many types of desired behavior change, however, can result from individual-level self-efficacy. Often entertainment-education projects, especially those implemented in recent years, seek to increase individuals' self-efficacy

---

[13]A more specific definition of *self-efficacy* is an individual's belief that she or he can complete a specific task (Maibach & Murphy, 1995), such as use a condom.

to bring about such behavior changes as the adoption of family planning methods or HIV prevention. The radio soap opera broadcast in Tanzania, *Let's Go with the Times*, was designed to increase self-efficacy regarding family planning, as the name implies. Individuals with higher self-efficacy regarding their fertility outcomes were more likely to adopt family planning as a result of exposure to the soap opera (as we show later in this chapter).

Parasocial Interaction

Parasocial interaction was pioneered by Merton with others (1971) in research on the Kate Smith War Bond Drive, broadcast by the CBS Radio Network in 1943. An incredible $39 million of purchases and pledges for U.S. War Bonds resulted from the popular singer's 18-hour marathon. Merton used the term *pseudo-gemeinschaft* to describe the concept of feigning personal concern for another individual in order to manipulate the individual more effectively. The designers and producers of the Kate Smith marathon were called "technicians of deceit" by Merton, because they created the impression of the singer's sincerity and sacrifice, in order to motivate individuals to buy Bonds. At this point, parasocial interaction was considered a negative quality.

Merton's work influenced Horton and Wohl (1956) to propose their concept of parasocial interaction. Rubin et al. (1985) and other scholars (for example, Rubin & McHugh, 1987), then measured parasocial interaction of television viewers with a scale composed of several items (such as "Do you talk to your favorite television character during the broadcast?").[14] A high degree of parasocial interaction between audience members and television role models was found.[15] Research illuminated how parasocial interaction with role models in *Twende na Wakati* and *Tinka Tinka Sukh* explained how these radio soap operas influenced audience individuals to change their behavior.

What motivates an individual to develop a parasocial relationship with a fictional character? Perhaps it is to fulfill a basic need for social affiliation with others as a means to understand who we are in relation to the world around us (Cohen & Metzger, 1998). Such social affiliation is achieved through interpersonal communication with peers who help us give meaning to the events in our lives, or by means of parasocial interaction with media characters when we perceive that they can provide us with such understanding (Rubin & Rubin, 1985). Entertainment-education is inherently involving of audience individuals, leading them to wonder how positive char-

---

[14]An early attempt to measure parasocial interaction in an entertainment-education intervention were studies of a sample of the 400,000 letters written to the Indian television soap opera, *Hum Log* (Singhal & Rogers, 1988; Sood & Rogers, 1996).

[15]Brown and Cody (1991) investigated the role of parasocial interaction as an intervening variable between exposure to *Hum Log* and its effects, for audience individuals.

acters will overcome the difficulties they face, problems that are often similar to those experienced by the audience individuals. Here we see why many individuals seek parasocial interaction with the characters in entertainment-education. One manifestation of such parasocial interaction is the thousands and thousands of letters that are sent by audience individuals to radio or television personalities in entertainment-education programs. These letters provide a valuable type of data about how entertainment-education influences behavior change.

EFFECTS OF *TWENDE NA WAKATI*

University of New Mexico communication scholars collaborated with Population Family Life Education Programme (POFLEP), a research center in Arusha, Tanzania, in conduct of the Tanzania Project. The formative research by POFLEP in 1992 consisted of a literature review, 160 focus-group interviews, and interviews with 4,800 men and women. These data provided the scriptwriters and producers of *Twende na Wakati* with a detailed understanding of the educational issues to be addressed, and with the nature of message content that would be appropriate for the audience. For example, the formative evaluation survey found that many Tanzanians believed the HIV virus had been placed in condom lubricant by European and American countries to reduce the African population. The *Twende na Wakati* scriptwriters attacked this rumor in early episodes, and the use of condoms by listeners increased.

The Dodoma comparison area in central Tanzania received all other elements of the national family planning program, including several other radio programs, except for the broadcasts of *Twende na Wakati*, which were not broadcast by the Dodoma radio station (see Fig. 7.1). Ideally, the effects of all other communication influences that occurred contemporaneously in Tanzania were removed by this experimental design. Changes in the knowledge, attitudes, and practice (KAP) dependent variables that occurred in the treatment area but not in the comparison area were thus due to the effects of *Twende na Wakati*. After two years, in September 1995, Radio Tanzania began broadcasting the first 204 episodes of *Twende na Wakati* in the Dodoma comparison area, where the strong effects of the radio soap opera were then reproduced from 1995 to 1997. Meanwhile, additional episodes of the radio soap opera were broadcast throughout the nation.[16]

The effects were measured by a multiple-method triangulation approach. Previous evaluations of entertainment-education soap operas had not included a pre–post measurement of behavioral effects, a comparison area in

---

[16] *Twende na Wakati* was planned for only two years, but in 1995, given the great popularity, Radio Tanzania decided to continue the broadcasts through 1999.

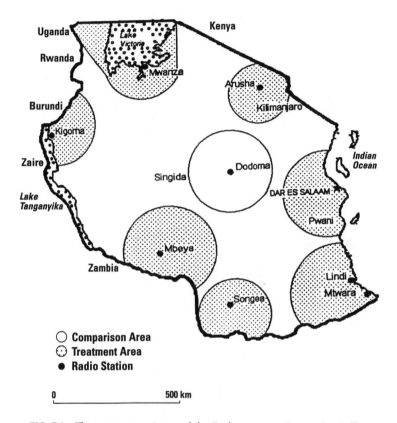

O Comparison Area
⊙ Treatment Area
● Radio Station

0   500 km

FIG. 7.1. The treatment regions and the Dodoma comparison region in Tanzania, which were part of the field experiment to evaluate the effects of *Twende na Wakati*. (*Source:* Rogers et al., 1997).

which the soap opera was not broadcast and effects data from survey, clinic, and other sources in a triangulation approach. The Tanzania Project may be the first evaluation of an entertainment-education project that incorporates these three methodological aspects on a nationwide basis.[17]

Data were gathered in five sample surveys, each of about 3,000 households, conducted annually from 1993 (before the broadcasts began), through 1997; from a 20% sample of the new family planning adopters in 79 Ministry of Health clinics; in three nationwide Demographic and Health Surveys in

---

[17]One other investigation that may also have followed these three methodologies is Valente et al. (1994) in The Gambia. A similar research design, daringly pioneering for its day, was an evaluation of the effects of entertainment-education television dramas in three Nigerian cities (Piotrow et al., 1990). Unlike the Tanzanian project, however, the Nigerian study was not a nationwide investigation. This distinction may not be a crucial factor, other than logistically.

1991–1992, 1994, and 1996; and in an analysis of the radio scripts and of letters written to Radio Tanzania.

Exposure to the Soap Opera Broadcasts. If a communication intervention does not attract the attention of audience individuals, it cannot have effects. One of the presumed advantages of the entertainment-education approach is that such programs achieve a high degree of audience exposure.[18] The Tanzania soap opera was no exception, with the percentage of the exposed treatment audience increasing each year from 46% in 1994, to 52% in 1995, to 56% in 1996, to 57% in 1998.

From 54 to 63% of listeners were exposed to the program regularly, at least once each week. The average listener was exposed to more than half of all the episodes broadcast. We feel that an individual who listens at least half of the time is able to follow the storyline and to be influenced by the educational message content.

Annual surveys in the broadcast areas[19] showed that *Twende na Wakati* reached less than two thirds of adult Tanzanians. This level of popularity is no small accomplishment and speaks well of the ability of the scriptwriters at Radio Tanzania. Furthermore, it is another demonstration of the ability of entertainment-education programs to attract a large audience while at the same time carrying out an educational objective.

Who were the listeners to *Twende na Wakati*? Are they males as well as females? In Tanzania, as in many other countries, men are not as amenable to family planning methods as women are. One reason is that they have not been reached by family planning communication efforts, which center on female outreach workers and contacts with potential adopters in health clinics. Furthermore, an entertainment-education intervention should ideally reach rural and lower socioeconomic individuals, who have the highest fertility and the highest risk of HIV infection.

Of the 67% of adult Tanzanians in the treatment area who listened to radio, 78% were reached by *Twende na Wakati*. Individuals who owned a radio were three times as likely to listen as non-owners, who listened on the radio set of a neighbor or friend, or in a store. During the five years of *Twende na Wakati* broadcasts in Tanzania, radio ownership increased each year, perhaps in part due to the popularity of the radio program.[20] In the

---

[18]On the basis of his review of 20 entertainment-education soap operas, Sherry (1997) concluded that these radio and television interventions have been very successful in attracting large audiences.

[19]In the Dodoma comparison area after 1995, when the radio program was also broadcast in that area, listenership to *Twende na Wakati* surpassed the level of listenership in the original treatment area: 50% of the Dodoma respondents reported exposure in 1996; 75% in 1997.

[20]Evidence of public desire *Twende na Wakati* lies in the 1993–1995 surveys: 2 to 13% of the audience in Dodoma reported exposure to the radio program, mainly through shortwave radios.

Photo 7.1. A restaurant at one of the main truck stops on the Trans-African Highway near Dar es Salaam, Tanzania changed its name to *Twende na Wakati* Café in 1993, soon after the broadcasts of the radio soap opera began. The restaurant owner reported that his sales jumped as a result. Shown here is the director of Radio Tanzania and the actor whose voice is that of Mkwaju, the truck driver in *Twende na Wakati*. (*Source:* Personal files of the authors.)

treatment area, radio ownership increased from 48% in 1993, to 55% in 1995, and 64% in 1997. In the Dodoma control area, radio listenership increased from 61% in 1993, to 69% in 1995, and 80% in 1997.

The higher exposure by radio owners suggests that listeners were of higher socioeconomic status.[21] Indeed, listeners (when compared to non-listeners) were characterized by higher annual incomes, more years of formal education, and higher status occupations. Listening was more likely for urban people (65%) than rural people (47%), and for males (57%) than for females (46%). Despite the tendency for higher exposure by individuals of higher socioeconomic status, *Twende na Wakati* reached a large audience (almost two thirds of the adult population) which included less educated, lower income males, a priority audience for the family planning and HIV prevention message content (see Photo 7.1).

---

[21]This may have been due to who owns radio receivers in an extremely poor country like Tanzania. In nations with radio and television broadcasting systems, like India, radio is more likely to reach lower socioeconomic families (who have higher fertility, greater risk of contracting AIDS, and poorer health).

Infrastructural Factors Mediate Exposure. Exposure to *Twende na Wakati* varied widely within Tanzania. For instance, 78% of the sample households in Mtwara Region were exposed to the radio soap opera from 1993 to 1995, but only 21% in Kigoma Region (see Fig. 7.1). These differences in exposure may have been due to regional differences in individual characteristics like education and income, but the main explanation seems to have been the relative strength and reliability of the broadcasting signal from each of the radio stations (Rogers et al., 1998). Certain of the transmitters were very old and did not provide a strong signal. In a nation like Tanzania, this variable is an important infrastructural factor.[22]

Identification with Characters. Listeners to *Twende na Wakati* were highly involved with the main characters. Mkwaju, the truck driver, was the most widely recognized character, with 49% of all listeners in 1995 identifying him in unaided recall, and 89% identifying him in response to an aided recall question.[23] However, few male listeners thought Mkwaju was a good role model to emulate in their own life (see Fig. 7.2) and female listeners abandoned him even more dramatically than men, as the negative consequences of his behavior became increasingly apparent.[24]

Fundi Mitindo, a tailor, and Mama Waridi, his businesswoman wife, were positive role models and widely recognized (by 70% and 68% of listeners in aided recall in 1995, respectively). More women than men perceived Mama Waridi as a good model to emulate, whereas more male listeners than female listeners thought Fundi Mitindo was a good role model to emulate.

Tunu, Mkwaju's long-suffering wife, was a transitional role model who became assertive, separated from her philandering husband, and became economically self-sufficient. Tunu was identified by 88% of listeners in aided

---

[22]Further evidence of the importance of infrastructural factors in determining audience effects of entertainment-education is provided by the radio program *Apwe Plezi* in Saint Lucia in 1996–1997. The episodes were broadcast daily at 5:15 p.m. However, 25 of the first 260 could not be broadcast due to technical problems, holidays, and national cricket matches (Vaughan, 1997).

[23]Unaided recall was obtained by asking which characters respondents remembered, without prompting by the interviewer. After a respondent recalled characters without assistance—two on average—the interviewer asked, for example, "Do you remember the character Mkwaju?" Aided recall occurred when a respondent remembered a character when provided with the name.

[24]Thus the Archie Bunker effect was not a serious problem in Tanzania. However, audience identification with negative role models, perhaps by a sizable number of audience individuals, has often been reported in other entertainment-education researches. After one year of broadcasts of *Apwe Plezi* (After the Pleasure), 30% of listeners perceived the negative character Tony as morally good and 17% thought the wife-beating, incestuous date-rapist Chester was morally good (Vaughan, 1997). However, only 4% of the respondents identified Tony as the best character to emulate in their life, and only 2% so identified Chester (Regis & Butler, 1997; Vaughan, 1997).

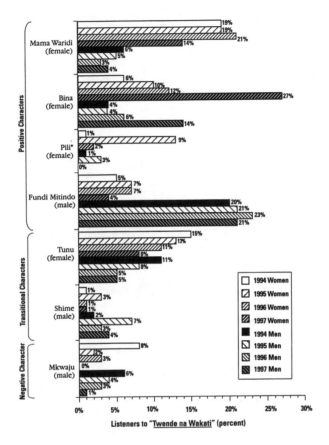

FIG. 7.2. The characters in *Twende na Wakati* that listeners thought were the best to emulate in real life. (*Source:* Personal interviews conducted by POFLEP researchers with 995 listeners in 1994, 1,018 listeners in 1995, 1,483 listeners in 1996, and 1,607 listeners in 1997 in the Dodoma comparison area and in the treatment areas in Tanzania.)
*1996 figures for Pili are unavailable.

recall in the 1995 survey (45% in unaided recall), and 13% of women perceived her as someone to emulate.

The listeners of an entertainment-education program mainly identify with positive role models as the best to emulate in real life (see Fig. 7.2). Furthermore, identification with positive role models increases with further exposure, while identification with negative role models decreases.

The Archie Bunker Effect. Sherry (1997) criticized entertainment-education interventions because certain audience individuals identify with negative role models, through what is commonly called the *Archie Bunker ef-*

fect—the degree to which certain audience individuals identify with negative role models in the media. This effect has been observed in many entertainment-education programs, although it often is characteristic of a relatively small percentage of the audience. For instance, some women who watched *Hum Log* identified Bhagwanti, a negative role model for gender equality, as the character most worthy of emulation (see Chap. 4, this volume). Some Jamaican men admired the sexual exploits of Scattershot, the promiscuous skirt-chaser in the radio series *Naseberry Street* (see Chap. 6, this volume).

Archie Bunker was the central character in the popular CBS sitcom *All in the Family*, which, in 1971, was watched by a record-breaking 50 million Americans (Vidmar & Rokeach, 1974). Played by Hollywood actor Carroll O'Connor, Archie Bunker was a highly prejudiced, working-class American who browbeat his wife Edith, and scorned his long-haired, liberal son-in-law of Polish ancestry, Mike (played by actor Rob Reiner). Archie was adept at employing racial slurs, commonly referring to his wife as "Dingbat" and son-in-law as "Meathead Polack" (Vidmar & Rokeach, 1974). The intention of the show's producer, Norman Lear, was to use humor to raise the consciousness of viewers about ethnic prejudice. By bringing bigotry "out in the open and having people talk about it," according to Lear, children "will ask questions about bigotry . . . and parents will have the answer" (cited in Vidmar & Rokeach, 1974, p. 36).

However, Vidmar and Rokeach (1974) found that *All in the Family* reinforced, rather than reduced, racial and ethnic prejudice among certain highly prejudiced viewers. Highly prejudiced persons, as compared to low prejudiced viewers, were more likely to watch the program. They also admired Archie more than his son-in-law Mike and found support for their existing prejudices. These viewers perceived Archie as a "lovable, down-to-earth, honest, and predictable" person, and were more likely to condone his use of racial slurs than were low prejudiced viewers (Vidmar & Rokeach, 1974, p. 37). Vidmar and Rokeach helped raise the consciousness of media scholars regarding the gap between a message producer's intentions and the viewers' selective interpretations of the message.

The size of the Archie Bunker effect in entertainment-education programs is relatively small, usually only a few percent of the audience. In the fifth year of *Twende na Wakati* only 1% of male listeners and 0% of female listeners perceived Mkwaju as a character to emulate in their life.[25]

---

[25]Here we see an important advantage of gathering data on long-term effects of entertainment-education. After one year of broadcasts, 7% of Tanzanian listeners perceived Mkwaju as a good character to emulate. Three years later, this Archie Bunker effect dropped to only 1%.

One strategy to reduce the Archie Bunker effect is to make the lovable bigot not so lovable. A character, however endearing, who engages in undesirable behaviors, should be heavily and consistently punished so the audience clearly understands the consequences of such negative behaviors. Epilogues can clarify and reinforce what constitutes acceptable versus unacceptable behavior, as in Sabido's soap operas in Mexico (see Chap. 3, this volume) and in the India's television soap opera *Hum Log* (see Chap. 4, this volume).

Formative research and pretesting of entertainment-education messages should be conducted, especially with audience segments who are similar to, and hence more likely to identify with, Archie Bunker-type characters. Are individuals who identify with negative role models characterized by lower socioeconomic status and less formal education, as Sherry (1997) suggests? Are individuals who identify with Mkwaju indeed "Mkwajus" in their own behavior? Ideally, a negative role model should come to regret the behavior, show remorse, and link the negative consequences to negative behaviors, as Bandura's social learning theory would suggest. Such personal conversion by negative role models helps individuals decode the intended educational message. Mkwajus must still die of AIDS, but they should recognize the error of their ways and feel sorry about the consequences of their negative behaviors for themselves and their loved ones before they die.

This change in audience identification indicates a form of learning from negative models, just as much as people trying to copy the positive models. Ceasing to copy the negative models may be just as important (perhaps even more important), since many of the people who identify with Mkwaju initially will perhaps be the ones most in need of the educational intervention (such as by being at a high risk for contracting HIV or AIDS).

Women listeners to *Twende na Wakati* identified more strongly with female role models like Tunu, Bina, and Mama Waridi, while male listeners identified more strongly with male characters.[26] Listeners to entertainment-education programs tend to identify with characters of their same gender.

Role modeling is illustrated in letters to Radio Tanzania, such as a 1995 letter: "By listening to *Twende na Wakati*, I have been able to emulate the good behaviors of some of the characters. Indeed, I am now involved in a tailoring project, and have attracted fellow girls in this economic venture to form our cooperative society. In addition, we are finalizing a vegetable garden project in the near future" (Swalehe et al., 1995). This letter writer and her friends emulated the income-generating activities of Tunu and Mama Waridi, positive role models in *Twende na Wakati*. Another letter writer

---

[26]A similar pattern for same-gender identification was found for *Hum Log* in India (Singhal & Rogers, 1989a).

stated: "We have benefited a lot from the education through your program. Indeed, me and my husband are now actively participating in the use of family planning methods, and we see its advantages" (Swalehe et al., 1995).

Some listeners' letters indicated a recognition that *Twende na Wakati* was entertainment-education: "I have been impressed by this type of radio drama, which keeps us entertained and at the same time educated." This letter also shows that listeners perceived that the fate of characters is a consequence of their behavior: "I request that Mkwaju's behavior be changed to a positive role model as he has suffered a lot, and let another character assume the negative role" (Swalehe et al., 1995).

In Tanzania, positive, negative, and transitional role models for family planning and HIV prevention were perceived as such by the soap opera's listeners. Furthermore, the characters that appeared most frequently in the 204 episodes were most likely to be recognized by listeners. We conclude that the radio soap opera in Tanzania successfully carried out the entertainment-education strategy.

Effects in Closing the Family Planning KAP Gap

Knowledge of family planning methods was high on the part of adult Tanzanians before the radio soap opera broadcasts began in mid-1993. In our 1993 survey, 71% of respondents (67% in the treatment area and 79% in the Dodoma comparison area) could name at least one family planning method on an unprompted basis, and family planning knowledge increased approximately equally in both the comparison and treatment areas from 1993 to 1997 (see Table 7.3). In the treatment area, 80% of respondents had favorable attitudes toward family planning (always approved). Favorable attitudes toward family planning increased to 85% in the treatment area by 1997, while these favorable attitudes varied somewhat from year to year, but were 90% in 1997 as they had been in 1993 in the Dodoma comparison area (see Table 7.3).

The expected effect was to motivate listeners to adopt family planning methods and HIV prevention methods, and thus to convert existing knowledge and favorable attitudes into overt behavior change, thus closing the KAP-gap (see Table 7.3). Did exposure to *Twende na Wakati* indeed lead to adoption?

Twenty-four percent of listeners in the 1997 survey said they adopted family planning as a result of listening to *Twende na Wakati* (see Fig. 7.3). Most adopted oral contraceptives or condoms. The percentage of married female respondents who reported using a family planning method increased from 26% in 1993 to 33% in 1995 and 37% in 1997, in the treatment area, while the percentage decreased from 51% in 1993 to 46% in 1995 in the Dodoma comparison area, but then increased (by 18%) to 64% in 1997 after

TABLE 7.3
How *Twende na Wakati* Closed the KAP Gap for Family Planning

Effect	Annual Surveys	Treatment		Comparison	
1. Knowledge: Percentage of respondents who know at least one modern method of family planning (unprompted)	1993	67%		79%	
	1994	71%	+ 7%	83%	+ 7%
	1995	74%		86%	
	1996	78%	+ 7%	86%	+ 6%
	1997	81%		92%	
2. Attitudes: Percentage of respondents who "always approve" of the use of family planning methods.	1993	80%		90%	
	1994	79%	+ 3%	84%	– 6%
	1995	83%		84%	
	1996	88%	+ 2%	85%	+ 6%
	1997	85%		90%	
3. Practice: Percentage of married women that always use family planning.	1993	26%		51%	
	1994	30%	+ 7%	48%	– 5%
	1995	33%		46%	
	1996	40%	+ 4%	44%	+18%
	1997	37%		64%	
4. Self-efficacy: Percentage of respondents who believe that it is possible to determine their family size.	1993	52%		60%	
	1994	61%	+11%	70%	+ 6%
	1995	63%		66%	
	1996	73%	+ 7%	71%	+18%
	1997	70%		84%	
5. Peer Communication: Percent of married respondents who talked to their spouses about family planning "many times."	1993	42%		62%	
	1994	45%	+ 9%	54%	– 5%
	1995	51%		57%	
	1996	57%	+ 1%	62%	– 5%
	1997	52%		52%	

Source: 2,652 interviews in 1993; 2,785 in 1994; 2,801 in 1995; 2,750 in 1996; and 2,618 in 1997.

the radio program was broadcast in Dodoma (see Table 7.3). Similarly, the percentage of sexually active men who reported using a family planning method increased from 14% in 1993, to 21% in 1995 in our treatment area. This percentage decreased from 29% to 19% in the Dodoma comparison area during the same 2-year period.

These data on the adoption of family planning methods as an effect of exposure to *Twende na Wakati* are self-reports. The respondents who adopted contraceptives were asked whether this behavior change was due to listening to the radio soap opera, whose content, we know, strongly encouraged such behavior change. In essence, the survey respondents were asked to assess the cause of their adoption of family planning methods (as is done in most KAP surveys). We expect such self-report data may over-estimate the actual influence of *Twende na Wakati*. Several other measures of family planning adoption, however, support the self-reports by our Tan-

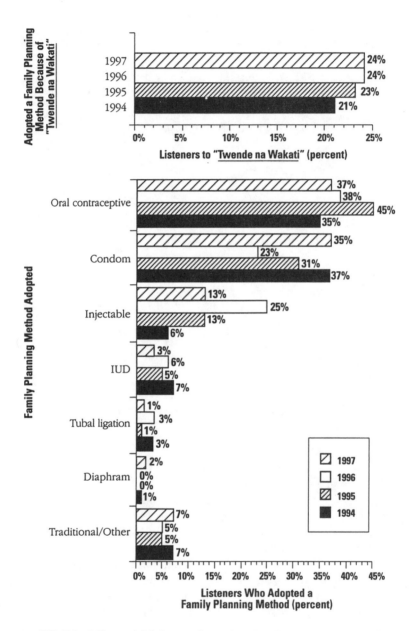

FIG. 7.3. Self-reported behavior change by *Twende na Wakati* listeners. (*Source:* Interviews conducted by POFLEP researchers with 995 listeners in 1994, 1,018 in 1995, 1,483 in 1996, and 1,607 in 1997 in the Dodoma comparison area and in the treatment areas in Tanzania.)

zania respondents. Table 7.3 shows the generally consistent increase in the rate of adoption of family planning methods by married women in the treatment area from 1993 to 1997, and in the former Dodoma comparison area when *Twende na Wakati* was broadcast there from 1995 to 1997. Clinic data were also obtained in Tanzania: 25% of the new adopters of family planning methods attributed their conduct to *Twende na Wakati.* Figure 7.4 shows the average number of new family planning adopters at 27 clinics in the Dodoma comparison area and at 43 clinics in the treatment area from 1990 through 1996. The trend lines for the comparison and treatment areas increased at approximately the same rate until mid-1993, when the radio broadcasts began in the treatment area. Until mid-1995, the number of new adopters increased sharply in the treatment area clinics, but not in the Dodoma comparison area (shown in the boxed area in Fig. 7.4). After September 1995, the trend line in the treatment area plateaus, while the slope of the trendline increases somewhat in the Dodoma comparison area.

These various types of data on the effects of *Twende na Wakati* all reinforce the self-report data.[27]

Spousal Communication and Family Planning Adoption

One of the main processes through which the radio soap opera changed the family planning behavior of its listeners in Tanzania was in stimulating interpersonal communication about its educational content.[28] Past research on the diffusion of innovations shows that exposure to mass media messages mainly results in creating awareness-knowledge of an innovation. Seldom do the media change attitudes or overt behavior (Rogers, 1995). When mass media messages stimulate peer communication about the message content, the media-stimulated interpersonal communication can change audience behavior (Chaffee, 1986; Gumpert & Cathcart, 1986; Katz & Lazarsfeld, 1955; Rogers, 1997; Valente, Poppe, & Merritt, 1996). So while the direct effects of most mass media messages is modest (Klapper, 1960), the indirect effects via the encouragement of peer communication can be substantial. *The entertainment-education strategy is particularly important in stimulating interpersonal communication about the educational content of the messages.*

Content analysis of the radio soap opera showed that spousal communication was stressed in 63% of the 204 episodes of *Twende na Wakati* (Swahele et al., 1995). Sixty-one percent of listeners reported telling someone else about *Twende na Wakati* (see Fig. 7.5). Fifty-five percent of the listeners in our 1995

---

[27]Multivariate regression analysis also provides evidence for the strong effects of *Twende na Wakati* (Rogers et al., 1998).

[28]Research generally indicates that interpersonal communication is important in the diffusion and adoption of family planning (Barker & Rich, 1992; Entwisle et al., 1996; Kohler, 1997; Montgomery & Casterline, 1993; Rosero-Bixby & Casterline, 1993, 1994; Rutenberg & Watkins, 1997; Valente & Saba, 1998; Valente et al., 1997).

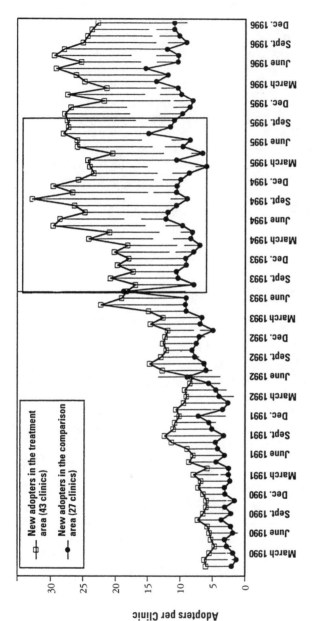

FIG. 7.4. Mean number of new family planning adopters per clinic at 27 clinics in the comparison area and 43 clinics in the treatment area. (*Source*: New adopter reports from 27 clinics in the comparison area and 43 clinics in the treatment area from which we have continuous records from January 1990 to December 1996. The figure shows 3 time periods (1) left of the shaded area is prior to broadcast of *Tuende na Wakati*, (2) the shaded area is the period during which *Tuende na Wakati* was broadcast in the treatment area but not in the comparison area, and (3) right of the shaded area is when *Tuende na Wakati* was broadcast in both the treatment and comparison area. The 95 percent confidence bars do not overlap for 6 out of the 42 months (14%) from Manury 1990 to June 1993, 15 of the 28 months (54%) from July 1993 to October 1995, and 9 out of the 14 months (64%) from November 1995 to December 1996.)

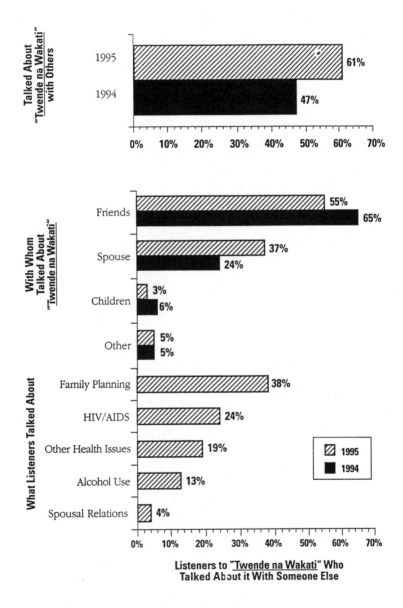

Talked About "Twende na Wakati" with Others

1995 — 61%
1994 — 47%

0% 10% 20% 30% 40% 50% 60% 70%

With Whom Talked About "Twende na Wakati"

Friends — 55% / 65%
Spouse — 37% / 24%
Children — 3% / 6%
Other — 5% / 5%

What Listeners Talked About

Family Planning — 38%
HIV/AIDS — 24%
Other Health Issues — 19%
Alcohol Use — 13%
Spousal Relations — 4%

1995
1994

0% 10% 20% 30% 40% 50% 60% 70%

Listeners to "Twende na Wakati" Who Talked About it With Someone Else

FIG. 7.5. Interpersonal communication about *Twende na Wakati*. (*Source:* Interviews with 995 listeners in 1994 and 1,018 listeners in 1995.)

165

survey talked with a friend, and 37% talked with their spouses. The percentage of married respondents who talked with spouses about family planning "many times" increased from 42% in 1993 to 52% in 1997 in the treatment area. This increase did not occur in the Dodoma comparison area, after 1995, as we had expected (see Table 7.3).

Thirty-eight percent of the listeners talked with their peers about the family planning content, rather than about some other aspect of the radio soap opera (see Fig. 7.5). *Twende na Wakati* both stimulated peer communication about the radio soap opera and directed this interpersonal communication to deal with family planning, HIV prevention, and alcoholism.

Married women in the 1995 survey who listened to *Twende na Wakati* were more likely to adopt family planning (49%) than were those who did not listen (19%). Furthermore, the non-listeners were only half as likely to talk with their spouse about family planning "many times" (32%) as were listeners to *Twende na Wakati* (66%). Exposure to the radio soap opera led to spousal communication about family planning, which in turn was related to the adoption of family planning methods.

Figure 7.6 shows that married respondents who talked with their spouses about family planning were much more likely to adopt family planning methods (about 60%) than were respondents who did not discuss this topic (6%). Married female respondents who talked with their spouses about family planning also had a more accurate perception of their spouses' attitudes toward family planning (Rogers et al., 1998; Yount, 1996). Couples who never discussed family planning were likely to have an inaccurate perception of their spouses' attitudes toward family planning, and to perceive that their spouses were opposed to family planning.

We conclude that *spousal communication about family planning, stimulated by exposure to an entertainment-education program, played an important role in the adoption of family planning methods.* A decision to adopt contraception in Tanzania often must be negotiated with a sexual partner. It is understandable why spousal communication plays a major role in explaining the process through which *Twende na Wakati* had its effects on overt behavior change regarding family planning.[29]

Data from both the annual surveys and from new adopters at health clinics showed that exposure to the entertainment-education radio soap opera had relatively strong effects on the adoption of family planning.[30]

---

[29]In numerous KAP studies, husband–wife communication is the variable most highly related to the adoption of family planning methods (Rogers, 1973). Accordingly, many programs seek to encourage spousal communication.

[30]Further evidence of the effects of *Twende na Wakati* on family planning behavior is provided by the ward-by-ward analysis of our 1993/1994/1995 survey data, using the 35 wards of study as units of analysis, rather than the 3,000 individual respondents (Vaughan & Rogers, 1997a, 1997b).

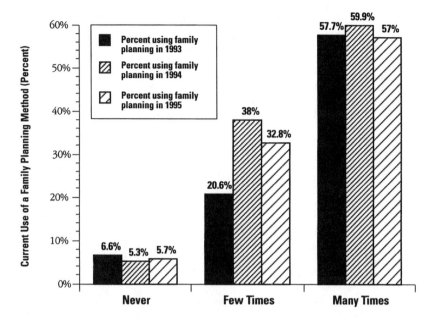

FIG. 7.6. Relationship between the frequency of discussion about family planning with one's spouse and the likelihood of the couple being current users of a family planning method. (*Source:* Interviews with 1,823 married respondents in 1993, 1,953 married respondents in 1994, and 1,899 married respondents in 1995 in Tanzania.)

Media-stimulated interpersonal communication was one main reason why the cost per family planning adopter achieved was relatively low.

Effects on HIV Prevention

When broadcasts of *Twende na Wakati* began in 1993, nearly everyone in Tanzania had heard of AIDS, and many people perceived they were at risk (see Table 7.4). The desired effect of the radio soap opera was to close the KAP gap by encouraging the adoption of HIV prevention methods.

Exposure to *Twende na Wakati* had strong effects in changing HIV prevention behavior. In 1994, 72% of the listeners said they had adopted a preventative measure because of listening to *Twende na Wakati* (see Fig. 7.7).[31] Advances were indicated in reducing the number of sexual partners, using condoms, and the sharing of razors and needles. The number of

---

[31]This self-report seems to have been an overestimate, as indicated by cross-classifying these data with answers to another question in which we asked which specific method of HIV prevention the respondent had adopted.

TABLE 7.4

How *Twende na Wakati* Closed the KAP Gap for HIV Prevention

Effect	Annual Surveys	Treatment		Comparison	
1. Knowledge: Percentage of survey	1993	97%		95%	
respondents who had heard of AIDS	1994	99%	+ 1%	98%	+4%
	1995	99%		99%	
	1996	98%	0%	99%	−1%
	1997	98%		98%	
2. Attitudes: Percentage of survey	1993	55%		72%	
respondents who believed they were at	1994	58%	+ 6%	67%	−17%
risk for AIDS.	1995	61%		55%	
	1996	65%	+ 8%	72%	+21%
	1997	69%		76%	
3. Practice: Average number of sexual	1993	2.3		2.2	
partners in the past year for male	1994	1.7	−0.6	1.5	−0.3
respondents.	1995	1.7		1.9	
	1996	1.6	−0.3	1.5	−0.6
	1997	1.4		1.3	
Average number of sexual partners in the	1993	1.9		1.8	
past year for female respondents.	1994	1.3	−0.7	1.2	−0.5
	1995	1.2		1.3	
	1996	1.2	0	1.2	−0.3
	1997	1.2		1.0	

Source: 2,652 interviews in 1993; 2,785 in 1994; 2,801 in 1995; 2,750 in 1996; and 2,618 in 1997.

listeners who believed they could prevent HIV by using insect repellents decreased from 24% in 1993 to 14% in 1995 in the treatment area, while it remained at 9% in the comparison area from 1993 to 1995 (the incorrect belief that the virus could be transmitted by mosquitoes was debunked in *Twende na Wakati*).[32]

The dominant influence on individuals to adopt safer sex practices was by stimulating interpersonal communication about HIV (as also occurred in the case of family planning). Of the 61% of 1,018 listeners in 1995 who talked with others, 55% reported talking to friends; 37% to spouses; and 8% to other individuals. Those who talked with others were much more likely to adopt an AIDS prevention method (92%) than listeners who did not talk with others (69%).

Male respondents with multiple sexual partners, who perceived they were at higher risk for AIDS, were much more likely to use condoms from 1993 to 1995 than were monogamous men. Of the 204 episodes of *Twende na Wakati* broadcast from 1993 to 1995, 21% (and especially during the second

[32]The Values Grid included this element: "It is good that people are educated to understand that mosquitoes cannot spread AIDS. The AIDS virus cannot survive in mosquitoes."

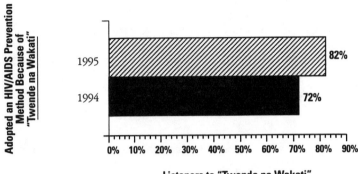

Listeners to "Twende na Wakati"

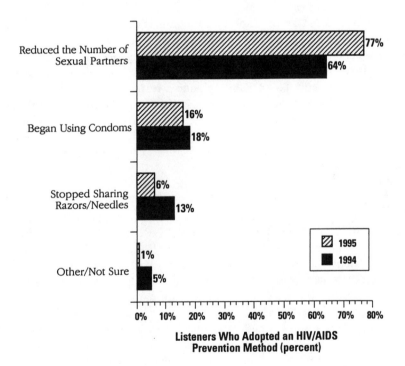

Listeners Who Adopted an HIV/AIDS
Prevention Method (percent)

FIG. 7.7. Self-reported HIV/AIDS behavior change by *Twende na Wakati* listeners. (*Source:* Interviews with 995 listeners in 1994, and 1,018 listeners in 1995.)

year) emphasized this element in the Values Grid: "It is good that people are educated to understand that condoms of whatever brand do not spread AIDS. Condoms serve both as contraceptives and protection against STDs (sexually-transmitted diseases) and AIDS. People should be taught the proper storage and use of condoms." This was stressed because the POFLEP formative evaluation found that many Tanzanians (in November 1992) believed that foreign brands of condoms contained the AIDS virus in the lubricant.

Cost per Adopter of Family Planning and HIV Prevention

For a policymaker with a limited budget, the important consideration is not just whether entertainment-education has an effect, but the cost of each individual behavior change compared to alternative approaches. For this reason, several projects have been evaluated in terms of their cost per adopter. A national family planning communication campaign in Turkey that included the entertainment-education television soap opera *Sparrows Don't Migrate* achieved 344,736 new adopters of family planning methods. The total cost per adopter of the campaign was $6.76 (Kincaid et al., 1993).

The cost per adopter of family planning resulting from the first 2 years of broadcasting *Twende na Wakati* in Tanzania ranged from 29 to 79 cents (depending on the estimate of adopters—1,175,800 versus 440,400). In terms of HIV prevention, the cost per adopter was only 8 cents, which is relatively low because a very large number of individuals reported adopting HIV prevention (4,192,000).

Why were the costs per adopter so modest in Tanzania as compared to the Turkish family planning campaign? Radio, of course, is much cheaper than television. Furthermore, the timing of the Tanzania radio soap opera resulted in a large number of adopters. The actual cost per adopter in Tanzania was even less that estimated here because Radio Tanzania sold advertisements, at $50 per episode, to Ply Foam (Tanzania) Ltd., a company that sells foam mattresses. By 1996, however, Ply Foam discontinued advertising on *Twende na Wakati* because the company could not meet demand.

A degree of insight can be achieved through survey research on entertainment-education at the aggregate level of a nation like Tanzania. But the nuances of how entertainment-education has its effects can best be understood at the community level, where qualitative research methodologies provide deeper understandings of how entertainment-education empowers. Most past research on entertainment-education has used highly quantitative and aggregated research methods, which allow the results to be generalized to the entire nation or at least to a large area. Such research cannot provide the insights and understandings that can be obtained from qualitative studies of highly involved listeners, as we conducted in India.

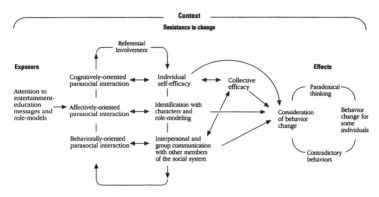

FIG. 7.8.   How entertainment-education effects may occur.

HOW DO ENTERTAINMENT–EDUCATION
EFFECTS OCCUR?[33]

With a few exceptions (Brown & Cody, 1991; Lozano, 1992; Lozano & Singhal, 1993; Storey, 1995; Svenkerud, Rahoi, & Singhal, 1995; Udornpim & Singhal, in press; and perhaps some others) past studies of entertainment-education programs concentrated on determining whether effects occurred, rather than providing theoretical explanations of how audience members change their perceptions, attitudes, or behaviors as a result of exposure to entertainment-education programs. These studies report aggregate changes in audience members' knowledge, attitudes, and behaviors but do not explain exactly how such changes in audience behaviors occur. In fact, determining the "how" of entertainment-education effects is a complicated research process.

Here we investigate how the radio soap opera, *Tinka Tinka Sukh* (Happiness Lies in Small Things), affected its audience in India. An entertainment-education program can spark the process of social change by focusing attention on socially desirable behaviors (see Fig. 7.8). When listeners develop parasocial relationships with characters, they may be motivated to consider changes in their own behavior. The mass media alone seldom effect social change, but media programs can stimulate conversations among listeners that lead to change (as we noted previously in the Tanzania study). These conversations can create opportunities for social learning as people consider new patterns of thought and behavior.

The Radio Soap Opera in India

As discussed in Chap. 6 of this volume, we collected various types of data in a multi-method triangulation to understand the processes through which

---

[33]This section draws on Papa et al. (1998).

the Indian radio soap opera, *Tinka Tinka Sukh*, influenced certain audience effects. Our data set was based on the following:

1. Personal interviews with key officials involved in the production, including executive producer-director, scriptwriters, and actors.
2. Content analysis of educational themes and character portrayals in the 104 episodes.
3. A before–after sample survey in Gonda District (the treatment area), which yielded 88 listeners (representing a listenership of 6%) and Allahabad District (the control area) in the State of Uttar Pradesh in India.
4. Content analysis of a sample of 237 listener letters.
5. An in-depth case study in Village Lutsaan, where the radio program was especially influential (see Chap. 1, this volume).

In the following section, we focus mostly on qualitative insights gleaned from highly involved listeners to *Tinka Tinka Sukh* to understand how entertainment-education has its effects.

Parasocial Interaction With *Tinka Tinka Sukh*

The existence of parasocial relationships between media consumers and different types of performers (for example, newscasters or actors) has been described in a number of research studies over the past 20 years (Auter, 1992; Avery & Ellis, 1979; Babrow, 1987; Conway & Rubin, 1991; Gans, 1977; Grant, Guthrie, & Ball-Rokeach, 1991; Levy, 1979; Houlberg, 1984; McGuire & LeRoy, 1977; Perse & Rubin, 1989; Rubin & McHugh, 1987; Rubin & Perse, 1987; Rubin, Perse, & Powell, 1985; Sood & Rogers, 1996; Turner, 1992, 1993).

What is the role of parasocial interaction in bringing about the effects of entertainment-education? Horton and Wohl (1956), in their initial description of parasocial interaction, argued that this type of relationship can be extremely influential for the media consumer. Once a parasocial relationship is established, the media consumer comes to appreciate the values and motives of the media character, often viewing him or her as a counselor, comforter, and model. Rubin and Perse (1987) argued that parasocial interaction consists of three audience dimensions: cognitive, affective, and behavioral.

1. *Cognitively oriented parasocial interaction* is the degree to which audience members pay careful attention to the characters in a media message and think about its educational content after their exposure (Papa et al., 1998; Sood & Rogers, 1996). Reflecting on the educational themes can help viewers recognize they have behavioral choices. There is little evidence to

date, however, that cognitively oriented interaction within a parasocial context can initiate a process of social change.

Despite the lack of research evidence that cognitively oriented parasocial interaction is part of the social change process, theoretical arguments and other research findings shed light on this issue. For example, the concept of self-efficacy (Bandura, 1988, 1991, 1992a, 1992b, 1995, 1997; Gecas, 1989; Schwarzer, 1992) is linked to behavior change that a person considers or enacts. Self-efficacy is an individual's perceptions of his or her capacity "to deal effectively with a situation and to control this situation. Efficacy beliefs influence how people think, feel, motivate themselves, and act" (Bandura, 1995). For example, after receiving messages from an entertainment-education program, is a person persuaded that they have the ability to change their behavior in a socially desirable way? Bandura (1995) views cognitive parasocial interaction as leading to perceptions of self-efficacy, which then influences behavioral change. We expect that the effects of an entertainment-education program are linked to its ability (through character portrayals) to promote perceptions of self-efficacy among its audience members.

2. *Affectively oriented parasocial interaction* is the degree to which audience members identify with a particular media character (Papa et al., 1998; Sood & Rogers, 1996). When an audience member feels close to a character, he or she believes that their interests are joined (Burke, 1950). The stronger the level of identification, the more likely that the character's behavior will impact the audience member's thinking and behavior.

3. *Behaviorally oriented parasocial interaction* is the degree to which individuals talk with other audience members or with the media characters (Papa et al., 1998; Sood & Rogers, 1996). Such conversations may influence audience thinking about an issue and motivate them to change behavior accordingly. Katz, Liebes, and Berko (1992) argued that parasocial interaction can prompt referential involvement on the part of audience members. *Referential involvement* is the degree to which an individual relates a media message to his or her personal experiences (Papa et al., 1998; Sood & Rogers, 1996). Before audience members consider behavior change, they must be able to relate the experiences of the character to their own personal lives. If a connection cannot be made, behavior change would certainly seem less likely for that individual.

Cognitively oriented parasocial interaction was measured by one survey question in India. Fifty-nine percent of the 88 listeners said they felt like giving advice to particular characters in *Tinka Tinka Sukh* about the major educational themes of the radio program. These listeners thought critically about the contents of the program.

Affectively oriented parasocial interaction was displayed by three distinct responses in our survey: 49% reported they adjusted their daily schedules to listen to the radio program and maintain an ongoing relationship with their favorite characters; 81% felt they knew these characters as close friends; 81% reported becoming emotionally upset when certain characters faced difficult personal situations. These responses reflect close identification between the listeners and the characters, an indicator of affectively oriented parasocial interaction.

Behaviorally oriented parasocial interaction was indexed by two survey questions: 50% of the listeners reported talking back to the characters while the radio program was being broadcast; 9% wrote letters to these characters at AIR expressing their ideas about the program.

The 237 letters also offered evidence of different dimensions of parasocial interaction. Content analysis yielded 11 indicators of parasocial interaction between the letter writers and the soap opera's characters (see Table 7.5). A close reading also provided examples of how listeners display cognitive, affective, behavioral, and referential parasocial relationships with the characters of *Tinka Tinka Sukh*. Here are four letters:

> Poonam's suicide, Kusum's death at child-birth, Sushma's struggle to stand on her own two feet, and Rukhsana's life and problems have shaken up my world and filled my heart with emotions. Nandini has taught me to stick to my ideals and fight against injustice, Champa has inspired me to realize my inner potential, and Suraj has taught me to be proud of my heritage and culture.

> Nandini and Sushma are ideal role models for women. In this day and age it is necessary for women to stand on their feet. I feel you should not have shown Poonam commit suicide. Instead, she should have empowered herself like Sushma and thus provided inspiration for other young women to do the same.

> I can relate completely to Champa since my family life is very similar to hers. I had decided to quit school, but after listening to the soap opera, I have started school again.

> Nandini is my favorite character. She is my role model and my inspiration. The women of the world should unite with the motto that we will not tolerate abuse nor will we be abusive towards other women. Once we women take this stand, men will have to tow the line.

These four quotations show each writer identified with one or more characters in the radio soap opera. Referential parasocial interaction is suggested by the degree to which the writers relate the experiences of *Tinka Tinka Sukh*'s characters to their lives, as in the third quotation listed previously.

Exposure to *Tinka Tinka Sukh* led to parasocial interaction between audience members and characters in the soap opera. How did these parasocial relationships prompt conversations among listeners?

TABLE 7.5
Letter Writers' Parasocial Interaction with
Tinka Tinka Sukh and Its Characters

Indicators	Percent of Letter Writers (N = 237)
I. *Cognitively oriented parasocial interaction*	
1. Letter writer compares personal ideas with *Tinka Tinka Sukh* and its characters when listening.	30
2. Character's opinion helps letter writer decide.	19
II. *Affectively oriented parasocial interaction*	
3. Letter writer looks forward to listening to *Tinka Tinka Sukh* when the program is broadcast.	55
4. Letter writer rearranges schedule to develop a regular relationship with *Tinka Tinka Sukh*.	33
5. *Tinka Tinka Sukh's* character keeps the letter writer company when the program is broadcast.	22
6. Writer feels sorry for the characters when something bad happens to them.	21
7. Letter writer likes listening to the voices of the characters at home.	21
8. Writer feels comfortable when listening to *Tinka Tinka Sukh* as if with friends.	18
9. The letter writer's favorite character is a natural and down-to-earth person.	17
10. Letter writer feels like part of a group when listening to *Tinka Tinka Sukh*.	14
III. *Referential oriented parasocial interaction*	
11. *Tinka Tinka Sukh* understands and covers issues of concern to the letter writer.	29

Source: Papa et al. (1998).

Social Learning Through Peer Conversations

Social learning is particularly important in entertainment-education because the goal is to change perceptions and behaviors through socially desirable or undesirable role models (Bandura, 1973, 1974, 1977, 1997). Characters are designed to be appealing or unappealing with the hope of prompting discussions among audience members concerning the socially desirable behaviors promoted. These conversations can produce a social learning environment in which participants consider options for change.

Audience members can share their similar and different perceptions of the information presented in the program. They can talk about considering or adopting the behaviors highlighted in the program, which creates an environment in which people learn from one another. Collective efficacy emerges when people share ideas about the social problems facing their system and discuss ways of confronting resistance to their plans for social change.

Of the 88 listeners who reported listening to *Tinka Tinka Sukh*, 49% did so with other household members or friends. Forty percent actively discussed aspects of the program with others, especially spouses and same-sex friends. These survey responses provide evidence that *Tinka Tinka Sukh* promoted conversations that initiated a process of social learning for some listeners. For example, 50% said they talked to their spouses about family planning after listening. In addition, 58% reported talking to a same-sex friend about issues of gender equality.

Our interviews in Village Lutsaan show how social learning occurs in conversations among listeners to a radio soap opera:

> Kusum dies at childbirth and we discussed that incident. We work together in the fields, and when we took a break we discussed if we marry off our young daughters we might lose them.

> We had all listened to the [radio] serial and we would hold discussions afterwards. For example, when we listened in the afternoon in the evening when we returned home we would talk about it with others. They would also say that they would not give dowry and tell me that I would not have to give dowry. We would advise each other how we should counsel others not to give or take dowry.

> Of course, I will not marry my daughter before she turns eighteen years. Prior to listening to *Tinka Tinka Sukh*, I had it in my mind that I need to marry off my daughter soon. Now I won't at all and I tell others as well that they should not marry their daughters before the age of eighteen or the girl is ruined. If she marries early, she is bound to get pregnant early and that is ruinous for her. They understand and accept my advice.

Efficacy Stimulated by *Tinka Tinka Sukh*

Our data provided numerous examples of how *Tinka Tinka Sukh* inspired collective efficacy and community aciton to solve social problems. Consider the following two comments taken from in-depth interviews conducted in Village Lutsaan:

> Poonam's suicide in the soap opera resounded with us because we also practice dowry. Now after listening to *Tinka Tinka Sukh*, and after we took the vow that we will not give or take dowry, we have formed a group to end dowry in this village. In this way our sisters and daughters will not suffer.

> In the radio program Chaudhri starts a school. We started a Montessori school because we do not have that much money. We spoke to *Masterji* (village school teacher) and invited him to teach here so that our children might be educated. Chaudhri started a school in the radio program because he had the

funds. All of us here cooperated to start this Montessori school and our children are now being educated.

These examples show how *Tinka Tinka Sukh* inspired people to engage in collective action to address social problems. Importantly, the listeners recognized the role of radio soap opera in motivating collective action. The letters written by radio listeners also provides evidence of collective efficacy:

> Inspired by *Tinka Tinka Sukh*, we have established a youth self-help association for the sole purpose of tackling and eradicating social evils. Superstition and dowry are some of the problems we aim to tackle. We have also started to educate all children in our village about these social evils.

> My brother got married recently and we did not even bring up dowry. Our entire village has collectively decided to neither take nor give dowry. In fact, there have been three weddings in our village in recent months where the issue of dowry never came up. There were some people who previously wanted to take dowry but based on the education we received from the radio program, the discussion on dowry has now ceased.

The evidence shows that exposure to *Tinka Tinka Sukh* stimulated interpersonal discussions about educational issues and motivated some listeners to engage in collective action to solve community problems. However, social change does not always flow directly from exposure to an entertainment-education program in which audience members: engage in parasocial interaction and create a social learning environment. Our case study of Village Lutsaan (see Chap. 1, this volume) showed that social change may proceed in a circuitous manner. What works for a media character does not work so easily in real-life situations where there may be community resistance to the new behavior.

Paradoxes and Contradictions[34]

Paradox and contradiction are part of social change. Since established patterns of thought and behavior are difficult to change, people often engage in an adjustment process until the new behavior patterns are fully internalized. The lessons to be learned from *Tinka Tinka Sukh* are that there is happiness in small families and that married couples should practice family planning. Gender equality is also a prominent theme throughout the episodes. Mukesh, a young male villager in Lutsaan, talked about the importance of small family size and gender equality. He also stated that abortion for sex selection was an acceptable means of limiting the population. Although Mukesh had internalized perceptions about the importance of small family

---

[34]Papa greatly contributed to our understanding of paradoxes and contradictions.

size, he did not recognize that his views on abortion for son preference[35] contradicted his professed support for gender equality.[36]

Gender equality occurred in Village Lutsaan as the result of *Tinka Tinka Sukh*. Dowry was not given or accepted in most marriages. Yet gender equality did not yet exist in many instances, for example, at a musical performance in the village, where approximately 200 men played instruments and sang songs. The women of the village were at the periphery of the crowd. After singing several songs, a woman performed a dance while remaining veiled. One male villager noted that although this woman was veiled, the fact that she danced was one sign of progress. Finally, as the entertainment continued, not a single man left the gathering. Most of the women departed to prepare the evening meal. Also, the percentage of girls who attend school in Lutsaan has increased from 10 to 40%. But Chav, a male villager argued that education was important for girls because it made them more highly "qualified" for marriage.

So paradoxes and contradictions occurred in Lutsaan as people struggle with social change. *Tinka Tinka Sukh* played an important role in stimulating these effects. Conversation that supports behavior change is important, even if that talk is not always supported by subsequent action. As Rushton (1975, 1976) observed, words alone can exert influence on the behavior of others. Thus, a mother who talks to her daughter about gender equality may influence her daughter to further her formal education, even though the mother still acts under the dominance of her husband.

CONCLUSIONS

This chapter explored the process through which entertainment-education has effects, especially behavior changes like the adoption of family planning and HIV prevention. An initial priority for scholars of entertainment-education was to determine *what* effects these interventions cause. By the 1990s this question was largely laid to rest. If an entertainment-education intervention is carried out effectively, it is usually able to attract a large audience of the intended individuals, and to motivate at least some of them to adopt new behaviors.

---

[35]Abortion as a means of son preference, although illegal, has become widespread in the past decade as the equipment needed to perform amniocentesis and ultrasound tests have diffused widely in India (Luthra, 1994; Parikh, 1990).

[36]Weick (1979) argued that this type of paradox emerges when a person does not recognize that their ideas within one system (for example, family planning) contradict one's ideas within another system, such as gender equality.

Then communication scholars set out to better understand *how* entertainment-education has it effects. This research question is a different and more complicated problem. The concepts of parasocial interaction, role modeling, self-efficacy, and media-stimulated peer communication have guided this recent research. We focused particularly on the Tanzania and the India radio soap opera projects to provide insights as to how entertainment-education has its effects.

The Tanzania field experiment provides evidence that one of the main ways in which entertainment-education has its effects is by stimulating interpersonal peer communication about the educational content (family planning and HIV prevention). The behavior change effects of entertainment-education occurred in Tanzania, not through direct exposure to the radio broadcasts, but from such exposure coupled with peer discussion of the episodes. The Tanzania survey respondents were asked whether or not they believed they could determine the size of their family. Self-efficacious married women in our 1995 survey were much more likely (51% vs. 16%) to use a family planning method. This relationship between self-efficacy and family planning adoption may not necessarily be unidirectional, in that adoption may increase self-efficacy as well as vice versa.

The evidence from both the Tanzania and the India projects suggests that effects occur through the social-psychological processes of social modeling, parasocial interaction, and efficacy, which takes place particularly when individuals discuss the content of an entertainment-education message in peer communication.

Studying Entertainment-Education Effects

Summative research has improved from the pre-experimental designs of the Sabido and Hum Log *period to more sophisticated quasi-experimental designs.*

—John Sherry (1997, p. 93)

Observing the village men, who sang passionately about not taking dowry in front of other men and women, is indicative of initiating a process of social change in Lutsaan. Quantitative social science survey research on Tinka Tinka Sukh *would have fallen short in capturing the richness of this experience.*

—Michael J. Papa (personal communication, August 9, 1997)

Conceptual progress in the past decade has been paralleled by improvements in the research tools utilized to evaluate the effects of entertainment-education projects. During the 1980s and 1990s, the rigor of these research methodologies progressed from after-only surveys of audience individuals, to field experiments using multiple measurements of entertainment-education effects. In the late 1990s, scholars also began using more qualitative methods, like community case studies, to understand the effects of entertainment-education (Table 8.1).

EVOLUTION OF RESEARCH METHODOLOGIES

Most research on entertainment-education seeks to determine its effects (see Chap. 7, this volume). Measuring and understanding effects is the general purpose of most mass communication research. However, there are certain

TABLE 8.1
Research Methodologies for Entertainment-Education Interventions

Methodologies	Representative Entertainment-Education Interventions
1. After-only survey	*Hum Log* (*We People*) in India, 1984–85 (Singhal & Rogers, 1989a)—1,170 individuals in 1986.
2. Before–after measurements	*Fakube Jarra* (Wise Man) in The Gambia, 1988–1991 (Valente et al., 1994)—399 individuals in 1990, 402 in 1991.
3. Interrupted time-series	*In a Lighter Mood* in Enugu, Nigeria, 1986–87 (Piotrow et al., 1990)—number of family planning clients at a clinic prior to, and during, the TV broadcasts.
4. Field experiments	*Twende na Wakati* (Let's Go with the Times) in Tanzania, 1993–1998 (Rogers et al., 1998)—broadcasts were blocked from a control area from 1993–95.
5. Multiple methods: triangulation	*Twende na Wakati* in Tanzania—annual surveys, new adopters in clinics, Demographic and Health Survey (DHS) survey, content analysis, letter analysis, and other methods.
6. Content analysis	*Hum Log* in India—videotaped episodes and scripts focusing on educational issues and characters.
7. Semiotic analysis	*Hum Raahi* (*Co-Travelers*) in India, 1992–93 (Ram, 1993)—selected episodes.
8. Case study	*Tinka Tinka Sukh* (Happiness Lies in Small Things) in India, 1996–97 (Papa et al., 1998)—community of Village Lutsaan.
9. Analysis of letters	*Tinka Tinka Sukh* in India—sample of 150,000 letters from listeners.

distinctive aspects of entertainment-education that influence the research methodologies utilized by communication scholars studying entertainment-education. Storey (1998, p. 4) of Johns Hopkins University noted, "Entertainment-education is a point of engagement, a site of discourse, not just another message." This perspective implies that exposure to entertainment-education not only has direct effects on an individual, but, more important, it causes indirect effects on behavior change by stimulating talk with peers about the issues embedded in the entertainment (see Chap. 7, this volume). Hence researchers must investigate both the effects of direct exposure to the intervention itself, and also the effects of the interpersonal communication stimulated by the entertainment-education program.

Further, Storey (1998, p. 7) pointed out, "Entertainment-education encourages less emphasis on the message per se and more emphasis on the audience." This viewpoint explains, in part, why entertainment-education, if it is to be effective, requires extensive formative evaluation. And the results of this formative evaluation research must be used in designing and redesigning the messages to focus on the information needs (and other qualities) of the audience. For example, a 1993 benchmark survey in Tanzania found that many adults did not know the greatest likelihood of pregnancy is midway in the 28-day menstrual cycle. Instead, 66% of respondents believed the greatest likelihood of pregnancy occurred just after menstruation. This misinformation could easily be corrected in an intervention like *Twende na Wakati.*

Formative evaluation can also identify preferences for humor and topics perceived as taboo—too personal and sensitive to discuss. Such issues can be handled only with extreme caution, guided by formative evaluation. An illustration was the issue of clitorectomy in Tanzania. This practice is widespread in most of sub-Sahara Africa as part of the coming-of-age rites for young women and is a strongly held cultural value. In recent years, health authorities have attacked the practice as a possible cause of infection (it is illegal in the United States for this reason). The clitorectomies in Tanzania are often performed by an older woman with a knife or razor blade under conditions that are not antiseptic. The producer of *Twende na Wakati,* Rose Haji, and the scriptwriters at Radio Tanzania, attacked the practice of clitorectomy in the radio soap opera. This educational issue was worked into the episodes during the second year of the broadcasts when Mkwaju's daughter reached puberty. He insisted that she undergo the operation, claiming that no man would marry her otherwise. His daughter did not want to have a clitorectomy, and her mother, Tunu, and other women hid her until her age-cohort in the village had undergone the operation. The topic of clitorectomy was handled in a dignified but forceful manner. Haji and *Twende na Wakati* were presented the Global Media Award at the 1995 International Women's Conference in Beijing for the episodes on clitorectomy. The Award was for the best use of educational radio in bringing about changes in the role of women.

After-Only Surveys of Effects

We investigated the effects of *Hum Log,* in India, broadcast in 1984–1985. Unfortunately, we were unable to study the effects of this important program—the first international transfer of Sabido's strategy—until after its broadcasts were completed. Hence we could only conduct an after-only survey of audience individuals. We established that the degree of exposure to *Hum Log* was related to higher levels of knowledge and attitudes toward gender equality (the main educational issue). But we could not eliminate the possibility that this exposure–effects relationship was because people who already had higher knowledge and more favorable attitudes were more likely to watch the soap opera. The time order of these independent and dependent variables could not be determined with after-only data.

An after-only study cannot determine much about effects, other than that levels of the effects variables are positively related to exposure. The time order cannot be established, nor can alternative explanations be eliminated.

In comparison to alternatives, the after-only research design is a weak means of investigating effects.

Before–After Measurements of Effects

One important advantage of before–after measurements is they allow the investigator to calculate change scores on the effects variables. Thus a sample of individuals exposed to a program is interviewed in first a benchmark and then a follow-up survey as to their knowledge, attitude, and practice of, say, family planning methods. A change score for each variables and each individual can then be calculated to determine whether such scores relate to the degree of exposure to the intervention.

An example of a before–after evaluation research design is the Valente et al. (1994) study of the effects of *Fakube Jarra* (Wise Man) in The Gambia, an Islamic nation in West Africa. Prior to the daily broadcasting of 39 episodes of this radio show in 1991, 19% of survey respondents used family planning methods. Nine months later, 35% of listeners had adopted.

Before–after measurements cannot eliminate the possibility that measured effects result from contemporaneous changes, that is, from other communication activities. In the case of *Fakube Jarra*, some of the increase may have occurred due to exposure to other communication activities about family planning in The Gambia.[1] The best way to eliminate these contemporaneous changes is through a field experiment, although the interrupted-time series can shed light on changes that are due to an intervention.

Interrupted-Time Series

The interrupted-time series collects data about the effects of an entertainment-education project during a number of time periods (typically months): (a) prior to the intervention, (b) during the intervention, and (c) for some time after the intervention (see Fig. 8.1). One would expect the effects indicator, such as the number of family planning adopters, to increase during the intervention and immediately afterwards, and eventually to return to the original rate of increase. This occurred in the case of *In a Lighter Mood* in Enugu, Nigeria (Piotrow et al., 1990).

Previously, Fig. 7.4 showed that a field experiment can be combined with an interrupted-time series, as in the Tanzania Project, and provide both a within-group (the treatment with itself over time) and a between-groups (treatment vs. control) comparison of effects. Essentially, the interrupted-time

---

[1]The JHU evaluation of *Fakube Jarra* had certain aspects of a field experiment when broadcasting in the northern region of the country was halted by a power failure. The results, however, were not reported by Valente et al. (1994).

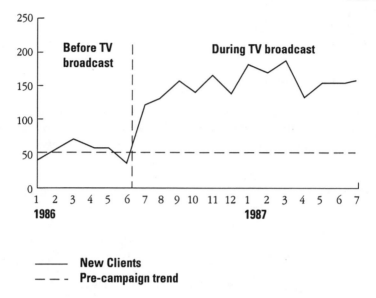

FIG. 8.1. Number of family planning clients at a health clinic in Enugu, Nigeria, prior to and during broadcasts of an entertainment-educations television series, *In a Lighter Mood*. (*Source:* Piotrow et al., 1990; reproduced with the permission of the Population Council.)

series uses the over-time measurements as its control. The result is a within-group comparison of effects over time.

The weakness of the interrupted-time series is also one of its advantages: There is no control group. This absence of a control solves the ethical problem of withholding the possible benefits of the entertainment-education intervention from certain individuals. However, the effects of contemporaneous changes cannot be removed. When broadcasts of *In a Lighter Mood* began in eastern Nigeria (see Fig. 8.1), the health clinic in Enugu, which provided monthly data on the number of family planning adopters, increased its clinic hours from 3 to 6 days per week (Piotrow et al., 1990). Whether the sharp increase in the number of adopters was due to the broadcasts or greater clinic accessibility is unknown.

Field Experiments

In 1960, Berelson and Freedman utilized an experimental research design to measure the impacts of a family planning communication intervention in Taichung, Taiwan. The purpose was to introduce a new family planning method, the intrauterine device (IUD), via posters and print materials, group meetings, and home visits by field workers. Control neighborhoods called *lins*, comprising 30 to 50 families, did not receive one of the three interventions (none was entertainment-education). The control lins and the treatment lins were alternated throughout the city. Benchmark follow-up surveys in Taichung showed that interpersonal communication among network peers influenced the adoption of the IUD in both the treatment and the control neighborhoods (Berelson & Freedman, 1964). This experimental contamination, caused by individuals in the treatment *lins* talking with people in the control *lins*, was the most important finding of the Taichung study. The results convinced policymakers in many countries that family planing communication activities could have a strong effect.

Since the 1960s, few field experiments have evaluated the effects of family planning communication interventions, including entertainment-education programs. One of the first at the national level was the investigation of *Twende na Wakati* in Tanzania. This study was a quasi-experiment, in that the treatment and the control conditions were not randomly assigned to the eight radio broadcasting regions of Tanzania. The assignment of the Dodoma broadcasting area to control was opportunistic, in that this region was cutting away from the national signal of Radio Tanzania for 2 hours of local programs every evening at 5 p.m. By broadcasting *Twende na Wakati* at 6:30 p.m. twice weekly, the Dodoma region became a control, or, more accurately, a comparison (these terms are often used interchangeably, although some scholars prefer "comparison" in field experiments because "control" might imply that no communication activities are underway there and that no contamination exists).

Why is the random assignment of treatment and comparison conditions important in removing the effects of extraneous variables in a true experiment? Random assignment removes unwanted effects, whether or not these variables are measured by the investigators. If the researchers lack the power to randomly assign treatment and comparison conditions, they must determine whether the two areas are matched on the dependent (KAP) variables, and perhaps on independent variables expected to be related to the KAP variables. The Dodoma area was approximately similar to the treatment area in Tanzania, although its population had somewhat higher initial levels of K, A, and P.

The unique advantage of a field experiment is that it can remove the effects of all contemporaneous changes from the treatment effects. This advantage can be gained, of course, only if logistical and other problems can be anticipated and their effects removed. For example, 2% of the respondents in the Dodoma comparison area (see Chap. 7, this volume), who supposedly did not receive broadcasts of the radio soap opera from 1993–1995, somehow managed to listen to the broadcasts, presumably on shortwave radio receivers. While this level of contamination did not threaten the validity of the field experiment, it suggests that an investigator never has complete control over the respondents' behavior. A realistic goal is to minimize the contamination and other logistical threats to experimental design.

One important reason why there are not more field experiments on the effects of entertainment-education on family planning adoption, HIV prevention, and other issues is due to ethical problems. The broadcasts of *Twende na Wakati* were blocked for 2 years (1993–1995) from the 2.4 million people living in the Dodoma comparison area. One fourth of these people would have listened to the radio program, so about 600,000 people were denied access to the broadcasts. They were more likely to have unwanted children and to have contracted HIV/AIDS (because of not adopting HIV prevention methods).[2]

The program was broadcast in the Dodoma region for 3.5 years after mid-1995, where it had similar effects, with a 2-year lag behind the 1993–1995 treatment area in Tanzania. These similar (but lagged) effects represent strong evidence of entertainment-education effects because they were reproduced in the former control area. The ethical problem of withholding the entertainment-education intervention from a control area can be minimized: by shortening the length of time that the treatment intervention is withheld, and limiting the size of the control area. In the Tanzania project, the Dodoma control area was large because it was covered by one of the eight transmitters of Radio Tanzania. In retrospect, given the rather strong effects of exposure to *Twende na Wakati* measured during 1993–1994, it might have been appropriate to begin broadcasting the entertainment-education radio program in the Dodoma area a year sooner. But in mid-1994, the effects of the radio soap opera were not entirely clear. The decision was made to continue blocking the broadcasts in Dodoma for a second year. If a treatment is found to have minimal effects in a field experiment, the ethical problems of withholding the treatment intervention in the control area are less important.

A field experiment requires that the researcher have a high degree of control over the communication treatment. Seldom is this the case, which is one reason why there are so few field experiments on entertainment-education, or, more generally, in any type of communication research. Radio Tanzania officials understandably wanted to broadcast *Twende na Wakati*, their most popular program, from all of their stations, including Dodoma. They agreed not to do so because they were convinced (in 1993) by the University of New Mexico communication scholars of the scientific value of a field experiment with a control area. Officials in Radio Tanzania and the Tanzania Ministry of Health signed agreements about carrying out the field experiment, a type of informed consent. Obtaining such consent from everyone in the treatment and comparison areas was impossible. Although this research carried disadvantages for Radio Tanzania and those in the control area, a field experiment promised definitive evidence of the effects of en-

---

[2]Ethical problems such as these are discussed by Brown and Singhal (1990, 1993, 1995, 1998) in Chapter 9.

tertainment-education. When the Tanzania Project was designed in 1993, officials in the UNFPA, PCI, and the government of Tanzania, as well as the University of New Mexico researchers, felt that such evidence was necessary. The ultimate beneficiaries are policymakers and people in other nations who learn from the Tanzanian findings.

Problems with the ethics of control and with gaining permission to conduct a field experiment are avoided in the interrupted-time series, as explained previously, because there is no control group in the usual sense. The treatment intervention (an entertainment-education program in the present case) is not withheld from anyone.

St. Lucia, Covered Entirely by One Transmitter!

St. Lucia is a small nation of 138,000 people in the Caribbean. In 1995 local officials realized that the national bird, the St. Lucia parrot, was becoming extinct because of habitat loss due to the conversion of forest land to farming. This pressure on the land was due in part to population growth. The strength of the family unit on St. Lucia had declined disastrously, with 85% of births out of wedlock. Only 20% of parents were married, and 62% of pregnancies were unintended. In order to teach family responsibility and to encourage use of family planning, a radio soap opera was designed through collaboration of the RARE Center for Tropical Conservation, St. Lucia Planned Parenthood, the National Population Unit, the Ministry of Health, and Radio St. Lucia, with technical assistance provided by Population Communications International. Dr. Peter Vaughan, who was also involved in evaluating the effects of *Twende na Wakati* in Tanzania, planned the summative evaluation study, and advised on the data analysis. Dr. Kimani Njogu of Twaweza Communications and Tom Kazungu of Top Com Productions, both in Nairobi, who were trained by Miguel Sabido in the entertainment-education strategy, and who was an experienced scriptwriter for radio soap operas in Kenya and Tanzania, advised their St. Lucian counterparts in design and scriptwriting. The entertainment-education program was named after the popular St. Lucian saying (in the local patois), *Apwe plezi c'est la pain* (After the pleasure comes the pain).

A negative role model, Chester, was a popular character in *Apwe Plezi*. He was depicted as a 30-year-old alcoholic who drives heavy construction equipment for a living. Chester is abusive when drunk, and has had a number of children by various women. He does not see nor care for his children. In short, Chester represents what the entertainment-education radio drama is designed to oppose. Chester is a wife-beater, date-rapist, and incestuous. In the soap opera's storyline, Chester is punished in various ways, and listeners gradually realize that his lack of parental responsibility is dysfunctional for his children, their mothers, for society, and for Chester himself. The advantages of stable parental relationships are demonstrated through the lives of positive role-models. Chester's lack of self-efficacy becomes evident as one of his central problems in life. An audience survey of listeners indicated that only

2% perceived Chester as a good character to emulate in their own lives (Vaughan, 1997).

What effects did *Apwe Plezi* have on its listening audience? Some 32% of the adult population of St. Lucia listened to the radio drama, and it became the second most popular radio program on Radio St. Lucia in 1997 (Vaughan, 1997). Some 14% of listeners said that they adopted family planning methods as a result of listening to *Apwe Plezi*, 6% called a telephone hotline for family planning counseling, and 4% went to a family planning clinic. A 5% increase occurred in the number of new family planning adopters at planned parenthood clinics, and a 41% spurt was recorded in the number of continuing clients (Vaughan, 1998). No increase had occurred in 1994–1995, before the broadcasts of *Apwe Plezi* began. This interrupted time-series design for the summative evaluation could not determine how much of these effects were uniquely due to the entertainment-education radio soap opera, and how much should be attributed to other family planning communication activities underway in St. Lucia.

It was not feasible to have a control area without broadcasts of *Apwe Plezi* because the island-nation is so small that it was entirely covered by one radio transmitter (Vaughan, 1997).

Multiple Methods: Triangulation

Triangulation is the use of multiple research methods to measure the same variable or set of variables. The term *triangulation* comes from surveying by civil engineers. Given a point relative to three other spots on the earth's surface, the exact location of the point can be determined. Triangulation eventually was generalized to mean any research study using several types of data. Whereas each method may be a thin reed on which to base conclusions, stronger claims result from the triangulation of multiple measurements (a bundle of reeds). Generally, the more research methods used and the more varied the methods, the more confidence one has in the strength of the research findings.[3]

The leading method of measurement in most field experiments is the audience survey. These self-reports may be overestimates if the respondents believe that they are expected to report strong effects of the entertainment-education intervention. It is reassuring to an investigator to gather other types of data that provide a check on the accuracy of survey self-reports. One approach is to gather data from new adopters of the behavioral change emphasized by the intervention. An example is to gather data from new adopters of family planning methods at clinics or at other service-providing sites. Policymakers regard such point-of-sale service statistics as highly cred-

---

[3]Triangulation can also produce conflicting findings. We discuss later how to address such findings.

ible. One of the advantages of such data is that they are usually gathered at the time the individual adopts, so there is no problem of inaccurate recall. Further, these exit interview data are generated by actual observations of the adoption of family planning methods.

A pioneering entertainment-education project in using a triangulation approach was the Johns Hopkins University study of the effects of television programs in three Nigerian cities (Piotrow et al., 1990).[4] In each city, a soap opera about family planning was inserted in an existing television variety program. Its effects were evaluated by a survey of the city's residents, and by gathering data from new family planning clients at one or more health clinics in each city (see Fig. 8.1). Thus a comparison of two different types of effects data were made in a kind of triangulation.

The JHU study in Enugu, a city in southeastern Nigeria, gathered clinic and survey data on the effects of *In a Lighter Mood.* The number of clients visiting the clinic increased from 50 per month to 120 (Piotrow et al., 1990), as shown in Fig. 8.1.[5] When asked their source of referral in an unprompted manner by clinic staff during the first 6 months of the broadcasts, 55% of the patients said *In a Lighter Mood.* This figure dropped to 33% over the following 6 months. An after-only survey in Enugu found that 54% of respondents watched *In a Lighter Mood,* and 37% could recall the address of the health clinic, which was emphasized in the program. The cost of the 43 episodes was $38,297 (less than $1,000 each), plus the technical assistance on entertainment-education provided by JHU.

In the Tanzania Project mentioned previously, every fifth new family planning adopter ($N = 3,452$) at a national sample of 49 health clinics in the treatment area was asked, in both unaided recall and then in aided recall, whether they adopted family planning because of exposure to *Twende na Wakati.* A similar rate of adoption was measured as due to the entertainment-education radio soap opera: (a) 23% of the 1995 survey respondents, and (b) 25% of the clinic adopters in unaided responses (Rogers et al., 1998). This convergence of effects measurements is reassuring to investigators, although it might be a coincidence, as the data come from different samples of respondents.

What if the multiple measures do *not* agree as to the effects of entertainment-education? Perhaps only two of three measurements agree in showing strong effects, while a third measurement shows no effect. What does one then conclude? In this case, one would look closely at the third measure in order to determine why it diverged from the other two measures. For example, the Tanzania Project also analyzed data from the Demographic and Health Survey

---

[4]At the same time, we were investigating the effects of *Hum Log* using survey interviews, an analysis of audience letters, and content analysis of the episodes in a similar triangulation.

[5]As mentioned previously, the clinic expanded services from 3 to 6 days per week, which confounds the measurements.

in 1996 on the effects of *Twende na Wakati*. The DHS showed somewhat smaller effects of the radio program on family planning adoption, presumably because it used a different sampling frame (all fertile-aged women in Tanzania, including many who did not live in the broadcast areas).

One disadvantage of triangulation is the greater cost and effort of obtaining multiple measurements of the effects variables (usually K, A, and P). Undoubtedly, this greater cost is one main reason why more investigations do not follow a triangulation design.[6] The other main reason is the lack of adequate control by the investigator over the entertainment-education intervention, mentioned previously, which makes it difficult to gather multiple data sets.

More creative research designs are needed in the future to evaluate the effects of entertainment-education interventions in ways that have not yet been tried, as we move gradually toward more rigorous measurement of effects, and improved theoretical understanding of how such effects occur. Examples of such ingenious measurement strategies are[7]:

1. A telephone hotline in St. Lucia for personal advice about family planning, HIV prevention, and other educational content in *Apwe Plezi* (After the Pleasure), an entertainment-education radio soap opera. The hotline received 1,200 calls in a 10-month period from 1996 to 1997, which represents about 1% of the adults in St. Lucia's total population of 138,000 (Vaughan, 1998).[8] This measure of effects was compared with such other measures as a benchmark-follow-up survey, clinic intake data, focus group interviews, and a special "marker" that was featured in the radio program. This marker was a new slang term for condoms, "catapult," which was identified by 28% of the program's listeners, *and* by 13% of the nonlisteners, suggesting that the message was diffusing via interpersonal communication networks from listeners (Vaughan, 1998).

2. The Tanzania Project provided radios and batteries to 30 "satellite" families who agreed to listen regularly to *Twende na Wakati*, fill out a diary

---

[6]One reason for the relatively high cost of the research in Tanzania was the high degree of triangulation. Eight different effects measures were gathered (Rogers et al., 1998).

[7]Another creative research design was put in place to evaluate the effects of several heart health education episodes in a popular hospital drama serial *Medisch Centrum West* in the Netherlands. While the evaluation was designed as an after-only survey effects study (which has certain limitations), three audience sub-samples were interviewed: (a) regular viewers of an *Medisch Centrum West* who saw the specific cardiovascular health episodes, (b) regular viewers of *Medisch Centrum West*, who missed viewing the specific cardiovascular health episodes; and (c) viewers who had not seen any episode of *Medisch Centrum West* (Bouman, Maas, & Kok, 1998). Comparison of Sub-sample 1 and 2 represents a methodological innovation, not common in other entertainment–education research studies conducted to date.

[8]A telephone hotline was also utilized as part of the communication campaign in the Philippines in 1988 featuring the popular song by Lea Salonga and Charlie Masso, "I Still Believe."

on their reactions, and to be personally interviewed by POFLEP researchers at certain intervals. In practice, these data-gathering arrangements were not followed through completely over the 5 years of the project. Nevertheless, the data from the satellite families were useful to the scriptwriters of *Twende na Wakati* as a source of ongoing formative evaluation. Similarly, nine satellite families in St. Lucia provided their reactions to each episode of *Apwe Plezi* (Vaughan, 1998).

3. The establishment of a registered listeners' club of 6,000 individuals by All India Radio (AIR), prior to the broadcasts of *Tinka Tinka Sukh.*[9] While conducting pre-program publicity, AIR invited audiences to register as listeners, who then provided feedback when *Tinka Tinka Sukh* was broadcast. AIR broadcast a separate listeners' interaction program every 2 weeks during the year-long broadcasts of *Tinka Tinka Sukh* to respond to the registered listeners' feedback, and to invite reactions to the educational issues promoted in the radio series. Prizes were awarded for commendable responses. A sample of 500 registered listeners[10] were surveyed through a mailed questionnaire, of which 215 replies were received. While atypical of regular listeners, this highly involved group of listeners, can provide insights on *how* entertainment-education has its effects.

4. Heriberto Lopez, a communication scholar in Mexico, is presently gathering data by means of participant observation techniques and repeated personal interviews each week from a sample of several hundred Mexico City respondents about the effects of Miguel Sabido's television soap opera, *Los Hijos de Nadie* (Children of No One). Data from these satellite viewers about their likes and dislikes (and the effects) of each episode are fed back immediately to the *telenovela*'s scriptwriters.

Content Analysis

One means to determine whether the educational issues planned for an entertainment program are actually incorporated in the message is content analysis. The frequency of negative or positive role models can also be determined by a content analysis of episodes. Such frequency is expected to be related to the strength of effects of each character on audience behavior.

---

[9]All India Radio had used this innovative technique as a way of obtaining listeners' feedback for several of its previous serials (see Bhasin & Singhal, 1998).

[10]Several dozens of these questionnaires were returned due to inadequate mailing address. However, the mailed questionnaire to listeners of *Tinka Tinka Sukh* was the first systematic attempt at conducting an assessment of how highly-involved listeners process entertainment-education messages. Suruchi Sood at Johns Hopkins University's Center for Communication Programs, and a PhD candidate at the University of New Mexico's Department of Communication and Journalism, is analyzing these data for her doctoral dissertation.

The usual approach to content analysis is to define categories and count the frequency with which they appear. For instance, the University of New Mexico/POFLEP scholars counted the number and percentage of the 205 episodes of *Twende na Wakati* that were broadcast in 1993 to 1995 in which family planning, HIV prevention, and alcoholism appeared.

An entertainment-education soap opera typically is planned around a values grid that specifies the elements to be featured in the program. *Twende na Wakati* was expected to convey 57 specific elements, such as: mosquito bites could not transmit HIV; exchanging needles or razors could. The scripts were analyzed to determine the frequency of the 57 elements in the episodes.

Similarly, content analysis identified the frequency of negative, positive, and transitional characters. For example, content analysis determined that Mkwaju was initially depicted as a positive character when the truck driver married and became a father. Once his character was well-established with the audience, however, Mkwaju became a negative role model for family planning and HIV prevention and was punished accordingly in the storyline. The issue of HIV prevention received increasing attention in *Twende na Wakati* after the first year (1993–1994), as the audience received increasing hints that Mkwaju was HIV positive.

In general, the character and script analyses show the entertainment-education strategy had been implemented effectively. The effects of the content could be traced in annual surveys and from other data. Listener exposure was expected to have increasing effects in changing the HIV prevention behavior during the second year of the broadcasts (compared to the first) as it was emphasized more heavily in the 1994–1995 episodes, which it did.

Semiotic Analysis

Semiotic analysis is one type of qualitative[11] content analysis. Ram (1993), a communication scholar from India studying at Ohio University, analyzed

---

[11]*Qualitative research methods* are those means of gathering data that are not expressed in numerical form. Such methods are generally less structured by the investigator and hence are more open to measuring respondents' experiences, or understanding the nuances of a particular situation. In-depth interviews, focus-group interviews, and textual analysis are examples of qualitative data-gathering. An example of how qualitative research methods like focus group interviews allow an investigator to understand a respondent's definition of the situation, even though it is not what the researcher expected, occurred in India. A low-income, older male respondent in a focus group interview in Delhi, when asked to view and then discuss a key episode of *Hum Raahi* (Co-Travelers), insisted that a beloved young girl (Anguri) died in childbirth, *not* because she was married and impregnated as a 14-year-old teenager, but because she ate too much junk food! This traditional male respondent was strongly supportive of child marriage and dowry (both practices are illegal in India), which the designers of the soap opera had intended to attack with the death of Anguri (Rogers, Hirata, Chandran, & Robinson, 1994). Nevertheless, the older man insisted that the problem was junk food.

the text of selected episodes of the Indian television soap opera *Hum Raahi* (Co-Travelers) broadcast in 1992–1993. The purpose of *Hum Raahi* was to promote equal status for women, through gaining formal education and economic independence (Engineer, 1992). A more subtle purpose was to promote smaller family-size norms through opposition to child marriage, female feticide, and preference for male children (Ram, 1993). *Hum Raahi* commanded audience ratings of 78% in Hindi-speaking North India, an audience of more than 100 million (Rogers et al., 1994).

Ram's (1993) semiotic analysis (a) examined the garment, proxemic (spatial), and kinesic (body language) codes that positioned women in *Hum Raahi*, based on the first 26 episodes, and (b) included in-depth interviews with female viewers in 1992 in Pune, India. The garment codes provide useful insights about how women were positioned in the soap opera. For instance, garment codes positioned Manorama and Prema as opposites in terms of gender equality (Ram, 1993). Manorama, the all-suffering mother, usually covered her head with her sari. In the presence of men, she pulled her sari even more closely around her head to cover her face. This garment code "reinforced her status as a passive, self-effacing, subjugated woman" (Ram, 1993, p. 58). On the other hand, Prema, an independent career woman and a positive role model for female equality, did not use her sari to cover her head or shoulders. Instead, she pinned her sari across her left shoulder, signifying she rejected the "ritual of gender subordination" (Ram, 1993, p. 58).

Proxemics is another dimension of nonverbal communication, focusing on how space affects communication behavior (Hall, 1966). Proxemic codes convey power, distance, hierarchy, intimacy, and other factors (Ram, 1993). In the first episode of *Hum Raahi*, Manorama was shown cooking in a smoke-filled kitchen, sighing and coughing in the absence of adequate ventilation. The proxemic codes in Manorama's kitchen, which represented a "gendered space," reinforced her plight as the "all-suffering oppressed mother" (Ram, 1993, p. 63). Men were rarely shown in the kitchen. The text thus helped to maintain the dominance of patriarchal social structures (Ram, 1993).

Kinesics is body language, another type of nonverbal communication indicated by gestures and behaviors (Birdwhistell, 1952; Rogers & Steinfatt, 1999). Ram (1993, pp. 69–70) argued that in *Hum Raahi*, the village gossip, Devaki, was characterized by kinesic codes that signified "manipulation and seduction": She rolled her eyes, tossed her head loosely, gyrated her shoulders, let her sari's *pallav* (the part that covers the head) fall, chewed beetle leaves (which lends a deep red color to the teeth and mouth), and fluttered her eyelids. Further, Devaki was often depicted talking on a mobile telephone, which was a status symbol at the time of the broadcasts in the early 1990s.

Manorama, on the other hand, exhibited kinesic behavior that connoted "passivity and subjugation" (Ram, 1993, p. 70): Her head was bowed and her face was covered with her sari's *pallav*. She walked in jerky, nervous steps, talked softly, and avoided direct eye contact with others. Her body language conveyed subservience. Ram also conducted several in-depth interviews with female viewers of *Hum Raahi* in India, to gauge their perceptions of gender portrayals. She found respondents felt *Hum Raahi* portrayed the following:

- Women against other women, especially by depicting the anti-woman stance of Devaki (Ram, 1993).
- The manipulative woman versus the women liberationist (Ram, 1993). While Devaki was viewed as someone who had "men dance around her," Prema was viewed as being "always against men" (Ram, 1993).
- Certain women characters as too passive, especially Manorama and her daughter Kusum. Many respondents expressed impatience with these characters, urging them to be more assertive.
- The need for women to have social support (Ram, 1993), not only from other women but also from men.

Based on semiotic analysis and in-depth interviews, Ram (1993) argued that the *Hum Raahi* text did not challenge the "patrilineal, patrilocal, and patriarchal" structure of the Indian family, but instead worked "subtly to preserve it" (Ram, 1993, p. 109). Ram commended *Hum Raahi* for promoting women's education and rights, and for opposing child marriage, female feticide, and male child preference. But she questioned the ideological underpinnings of the text, which, she claimed, were steeped in patriarchy. Ram (1993) cited numerous ways in which *Hum Raahi* inadvertently subverted, blunted, or deflected the progressive aims of the text. Devaki, for instance, who epitomizes female sexuality, is depicted as a gossipy villain who disrupts the peace and harmony of her village. "By making Devaki bear the burden of guilt, the text neatly managed to reinforce the patriarchal norm of female sexual oppression" (Ram, 1993, p. 109).

Case Study

A *case study* is a descriptive type of research in which individuals, groups, or systems are interviewed or observed, or various types of archival records are examined, to search for underlying patterns and insights into a phenomena (Williams et al., 1988). Case studies are valuable when the phenomena are contemporary and not under the control of the researcher, yet there is a desire to answer questions of *how*, *why*, or *when* (Yin, 1984). As explained in Chapter 7, researchers have mainly utilized quantitative methods to determine whether entertainment-education interventions had educational effects. In the late 1990s when the main question shifted to how entertainment-education had effects, researchers turned to case study.

The opportunity presented itself in Village Lutsaan of India, where *Tinka Tinka Sukh* engendered strong audience effects (see Chap. 1, this volume). The case study involved gathering data in unstructured interviews, focus-group interviews, participant observations, and examinations of archival records to understand the context of the program's reception, including the role of key opinion leaders—like the village tailor and postmaster—in engendering strong audience effects (Papa et al., 1998). The Lutsaan case study also helped explain previous actions that had occurred in the village, such as founding the Shyam Club,[12] that contributed to the effects of the radio broadcasts.

One of the disadvantages of the case study is the data require more time and skill to analyze. Expressed as verbal impressions rather than numerical quantities, case study data are more difficult to reduce during analysis. Also, results of a case study are not generalizable to a larger population, which may not be a problem when the main purpose is to gain insight about a phenomena, rather than to generalize the results.

Analysis of Letters

Entertainment-education radio and television programs in India attracted a huge number of audience letters. An estimated 400,000 letters were written to *Hum Log*, and 150,000 to *Tinka Tinka Sukh*. This outpouring was encouraged in the epilogues by inviting audience members to write and providing an address. These letters did more than express admiration (Singhal & Rogers, 1989a). Most commented on characters and storylines, often suggesting future directions, and provided examples of how entertainment-education had affected the letter writers' lives (Singhal & Rogers, 1989c; Sood & Rogers, 1996). For example, one writer to *Hum Log* explained he had organized several hundred people in his small city to sign organ donation pledge cards, in response to an episode in which a positive role model received an eye transplant.

Letters can provide rich data for analysis. For example, we obtained 20,000 letters mailed to *Hum Log*, which had been left in two large mailbags on a rooftop in Delhi and selected a random sample of 500 for content analysis. A questionnaire was then mailed to these viewers. The 92% response rate suggested a high degree of parasocial interaction with the characters and with the actor Ashok Kumar, who delivered the epilogues. The analysis of letters was important, in that it represented an early attempt by communi-

---

[12]This Shyam Club was a village self-development organization that fixed broken water pumps, promoted theater and music, and that settled disputes in Village Lutsaan. The club members listened to *Tinka Tinka Sukh*, and then promoted female equality, opposed dowry, and child marriages, and other educational themes of the radio soap opera.

cation scholars to study parasocial interaction by highly involved audience individuals with an entertainment-education program.[13]

Audience letters can provide a low-cost and extremely valuable type of data for qualitative analysis of the effects of entertainment-education (Law & Singhal, 1998). They represent highly detailed personalized narratives and unbiased self-reports, as the writers are usually unaware of the general research design. The letters can also be rich in local idioms and metaphors and provide input for the program's melodramatic plot. However, one should never forget that the individuals who send letters to an entertainment-education program are atypical. Many are young (often teenagers), who are well-educated (students), and highly involved with the program. Nevertheless, their letters, in part because of these characteristics, provide insight into the process through which individuals are influenced by entertainment-education.

You Need a Post Office

The Japanese animated entertainment-education television series, *Superbook*, based on stories of the Old Testament, evoked an unusually high degree of letter-writing from viewers in several of the 50 countries where it has been broadcast. In Russia, an estimated 400,000 viewers responded, including one day in 1991 when the Moscow central post office, where a post office box was established for the television series, received 30,000 letters (Fraser & Brown, 1997). When the program sponsors decided to assess the effects of *Superbook* by holding a nationwide Bible quiz, a whopping 1.2 million replies were received, easily the largest volume of letters stimulated by a media program. Post office officials told the sponsors, "You do not need a post office box. . . . You need a post office" (Fraser & Brown, 1997, p. 15).

COSTS OF STUDYING EFFECTS

Research on entertainment-education effects should look at the investment as a matter of costs and benefits. JHU/PCS devotes approximately 10% of the cost of an entertainment-education project to its evaluation, a reasonable proportion.

One payoff is better informed decisions about whether to continue or discontinue (or expand or contract) an entertainment-education project. Most evaluations have indicated positive effects, particularly during the 1990s (see Table 7.1, Chap. 7, this volume). However, there have been failures due to various factors.

---

[13]Previous research on parasocial interaction focused on audience members' perceived relationships with news broadcasters and others.

A popular song in Latin America in 1988, performed by Karina and Charlie, promoted teenage sexual responsibility and the use of contraception—like Tatiana and Johnny's "*Cuando Estemos Juntos*" (see Chap. 5, this volume). Methods of designing and implementing the song project, similar to those utilized by JHU in producing Tatiana and Johnny's hit song, were followed. But the song by Karina and Charlie did not attract many listeners, and the lack of exposure lessened the effects.

A 1987 entertainment-education television soap opera in Kenya was canceled after the first broadcast, on orders of President Daniel Arap Moi. The first episode showed an explicit sexual scene involving a sugar daddy,[14] which set off a strong protest by Kenya's Parliament. The television producers implemented their show in a rush, without conducting formative evaluation research. The result was a setback for entertainment-education.

In 1994, the South African Ministry of Health commissioned the award-winning producer of *Sarafina*, a musical that was a worldwide hit, to produce a similar program on HIV/AIDS prevention. The resulting $2.5 million musical production scored highly on its musical content, but contained several pieces of inaccurate (and even dangerous) public health information. Subject-matter specialists on HIV/AIDS were not consulted, and the production's elements were not pretested, leading to this public debacle. The ensuing scandal, prominently featured on the South African mass media, came close to unseating the Minister of Health.

These three projects seem to be the notable entertainment-education failures to date, which is rather amazing given the sizable number of projects that have been attempted.[15] Most interventions have been successful (several extremely so) in attracting large audiences, usually because they are highly entertaining. The educational content is effectively infused into these messages, so the audience is not turned off. However, most professionals who have been involved in entertainment-education projects acknowledge that they require more time and resources for planning and production than do comparable programs that are purely entertainment. Sabido estimates that an extra 6 to 12 months of planning are needed for an effective entertainment-education *telenovela*.

---

[14]A *sugar daddy* is a wealthy, powerful man who supports a younger woman in exchange for sexual favors.

[15]There may, of course, be other entertainment-education failures that have not been documented. The authors are aware of some entertainment-education projects, which despite several years of design and planning, did not take off. They represent "failures" of another kind. For example, in the late 1980s, Miguel Sabido in Mexico was planning *Sangre Joven* (Young Blood), an entertainment-education soap opera, focusing on teenage sexuality, which was eventually shelved. Also, officials of Johns Hopkins University's PCS planned a research evaluation of an Ecuadorian entertainment-education soap opera in the 1990s, but the soap opera was never produced.

Given that most entertainment-education projects are evaluated, the important questions are: How much should be spent for evaluation research? How should funding be divided between formative and summative research? What balance of quantitative and qualitative research methodologies should be employed? There are no set answers to these questions, but past experience suggests certain guidelines.

Formative Evaluation Overkill

Formative evaluation is conducted while an activity, process, or system is being developed or is ongoing to improve its effectiveness.[16] The core meaning of the term is "to form" the communication message. Any message producer operates on perceptions and assumptions about the intended audience, such as how much knowledge about the message content the audience already possesses. Formative evaluation can sharpen the accuracy of the message producer's premise. For example, *Twende na Wakati* was initially expected to focus only on family planning. But during the planning workshop, held in Dar es Salaam in February 1993, participants stressed the importance of the AIDS epidemic in Tanzania. Especially influential were two studies: an AMREF (1992) study of the high rate of HIV infection among commercial sex workers and truckdrivers at 7 truck stops on the Trans-African Highway, and a POFLEP survey of 4,800 respondents showing many individuals perceived themselves at risk for HIV infection. The Workshop decided HIV prevention should become an equally important educational issue in *Twende na Wakati*. This decision was implemented, in part, by characterizing Mkwaju the truckdriver as one of the main negative role models in the radio soap opera.

In retrospect, the 1992 POFLEP evaluation for the design of *Twende na Wakati* in Tanzania was overkill. In addition to interviews with 4,800 respondents, POFLEP conducted 160 focus-group interviews and a review of literature on family planning, sexual attitudes, and related topics. These data were gathered in November and POFLEP researchers presented preliminary findings at a February 1993 workshop. POFLEP argued the huge sample was needed to adequately represent the 16 cultures (tribes) in Tanzania. *Twende na Wakati* was meant to match the cultural values of the main tribes. The cost of the formative evaluation was about $30,000, a modest expenditure by most standards. From the vantage point of hindsight, the

---

[16]The idea of conducting formative evaluation comes primarily from the field of *social marketing*, the application of commercial marketing strategies to the diffusion of nonprofit products and services (Kotler & Roberto, 1989; Kotler & Zaltman, 1971; Wiebe, 1952). Entertainment-education and social marketing have many common elements. There may be an increased cross-fertilization of ideas between these two fields in the future.

formative evaluation in Tanzania seems much larger than necessary. Perhaps a sample of 1,000 would have been sufficient.

What is needed is a model of formative evaluation that is affordable in time and money, and justifiable in terms of cost–benefits. One way to identify such a model is to look at elements of more expensive formative evaluations utilized by the creative team in designing an entertainment-education project.

In Tanzania, the number of focus-group interviews ($N = 160$) was excessive, because the qualitative data could not be analyzed in time to be used in designing the radio soap opera.[17] A dozen focus groups analyzed and available to the designers of the radio soap opera would have been more useful and economical. Similarly, a personal interview survey of several hundred respondents might have been more satisfactory in forming the storyline and characters than a survey of 4,800 respondents requiring 1 year to analyze.

A crucial quality of formative evaluation is that it be fast. A key difference between researchers and designers is time orientation. A formative evaluation costing over $100,000 (U.S.) was conducted in China in 1996 to design a television soap opera about family planning and HIV prevention, *Zhonggou Baixing* (Ordinary Chinese People). The results were still not published[18] in 1998. Meanwhile, design and production went forward with limited inputs from the formative evaluation.

How should a budget for evaluation research be allocated? No rule of thumb exists. It depends on the uncertainty over forming the entertainment-education message, versus the effects of the intervention. Usually, more funding is allocated for the summative evaluation, which is likely to be more quantitative and larger scale, than for the formative research. Table 8.2 compares approximate costs of formative and summative research for several entertainment-education projects.

The chief benefit from formative evaluation is improved effectiveness in bringing about behavior change. Disasters like the Kenyan program on sugar daddies could be avoided, and misinformation, like HIV being spread by condom use in Tanzania, can be attacked, suggesting formative evaluation can focus an entertainment-education intervention in ways it could not otherwise.

If formative evaluation is to be useful, two different types of individuals must collaborate: evaluation researchers and creative professionals, like scriptwriters, producers, and actors. These two professions have different

---

[17]While there is room to scale back investments in formative research (by reducing or eliminating large-scale personal interview surveys), more attention needs to be given to program monitoring research (using focus groups and in-depth interviews) to provide ongoing feedback to creative teams, especially to address oppositional readings (such as the Archie Bunker effect) in a timely manner.

[18]The lesson from the formative evaluation research of China is the importance of identifying reliable research collaborators before beginning an entertainment-education project.

TABLE 8.2
Formative Versus Summative Evaluation Research Costs

Project	Formative Research (U.S. dollars)	Summative Research (U.S. dollars)
1. *Twende na Wakati* in Tanzania, 1993–98.	$30,000	$267,000
2. *Tinka Tinka Sukh* in India, 1996–1997.	$20,000	$129,000
3. *Zhongguo Baixing* in China*	$100,000	$156,500

*Due to begin broadcasts in 1999.

values and often disagree about the role each should play in message design and production. The creative people may resent researchers dictating what to do. The evaluators are likely to perceive message producers as mavericks. But collaboration is necessary if entertainment-education is to be effective.

Sugar Daddies Are the Problem

In 1991, Corinne Shefner-Rogers, a JHU/PCS employee, was assigned to provide technical assistance to a project with the Ministry of Health in the Ivory Coast intended to reduce teenage pregnancy. A formative evaluation survey showed only a small percentage of Ivorian teenagers knew about contraceptives or where they could be obtained. Based on quantitative needs assessment, a youth project was designed in which high school students wrote and performed skits that would increase contraceptive knowledge. A half dozen theater groups were selected to participate in a workshop to improve their theatrical skills.

During the workshop, Shefner-Rogers found herself talking informally with about 20 students. To her great surprise, they insisted the real cause of pregnancy was "sugar daddies," powerful older men who exploited school girls, demanding sexual intercourse in exchange for gifts and other favors. The workshop participants insisted that many school principals were sugar daddies. The qualitative data from this informal discussion, something like a focus group, defined the situation quite differently from the formative evaluation. The real problem was sugar daddies, not adolescents' lack of contraceptive knowledge.

A panel of local judges awarded first prize to a play depicting the problems of an adolescent girl impregnated by a sugar daddy. The play was video-taped and broadcast on national television in the Ivory Coast and other Francophone African nations, and later subtitled in English and distributed throughout Africa.

Here is a case in which the quantitative data from the formative evaluation survey did not disclose the full problem, which could only be tapped via more open-ended, qualitative data gathering.

Summative Evaluation

Summative evaluation is defined as research conducted to form a judgment about the effectiveness of a communication intervention in reaching its objectives. In contrast to formative research, a summative evaluation is usually conducted after the intervention is completed, when its effects can be measured. The root word *sum* denotes measuring the bottom line of effects.

The nature of summative evaluation can be threatening to message producers, as it shapes the decisions of policymakers about whether a communication program should be continued. Thus message producers resist summative evaluations, and tend not to cooperate with them.

Cost Recovery

The entertainment part of an education project usually earns an income, and sometimes returns a profit. This aspect of entertainment-education is all the more unusual when we remember that most educational activities require a considerable investment that is not returned.

The cost of broadcasting each episode of *Twende na Wakati* was about $50. Three advertisements were sold by Radio Tanzania for $50 per episode. Radio Tanzania is a government broadcasting network, and its officials had not previously sold advertising. They were initially pessimistic about being able to do so. However, when the second annual survey (in 1994) showed half the adult population was listening, Radio Tanzania was able to sell advertising to Ply Foam Limited, a company that marketed foam mattresses.

The JHU/PCS budget for Tatiana and Johnny songs was $300,000 (U.S.). An estimated $50 million (U.S.) was contributed in airtime by radio and TV stations across Latin America.[19] The sales as records, tapes, and videotapes netted an additional $2 million (U.S.); $30,000 was returned to Johns Hopkins University, with the remainder going to the production company and the singers.

Hum Log was a big commercial success, represented a turning point for the government television network, Doordarshan, in becoming commercialized. The show was very popular, which attracted advertisers in large numbers.

PUTTING RESEARCH FINDINGS INTO PRACTICE

A research study on the effects of entertainment-education is incomplete until findings are put into use. Who benefits from entertainment-education research? Message producers and scriptwriters can benefit from formative

---

[19]These estimates are provided by Patrick L. Coleman, Deputy Director of Johns Hopkins University's Center for Communication Programs, who spearheaded the Tatiana and Johnny project (Coleman, personal communication, September 1, 1998).

evaluation if they use the findings to produce an effective program. Unfortunately, the results are not always used.

Physical distance may impede the use of formative evaluation research. POFLEP was located in Arusha, several hundred miles from the headquarters of Radio Tanzania in Dar es Salaam. Thus contact between formative evaluators and the creative team for *Twende na Wakati* was sporadic and infrequent.

The results of summative evaluation on entertainment-education are not always put into use either, although on some occasions, the findings have influenced important decisions. The summative evaluation of *Fakube Jarra* (Valente et al., 1994) led to a decision to continue the radio soap opera in 1992 and to extend the broadcasts to three additional languages in The Gambia.

Bill Musoke and the Woodcarver

In fall 1994, the second annual survey of approximately 3,000 households in Tanzania showed that *Twende na Wakati* had reached a very large audience in the treatment (broadcast) area, and that exposure to the radio soap opera was having rather strong effects on its listeners. These summative research findings were presented to policymakers at Radio Tanzania, the Ministry of Health, and the United Nations Population Fund (UNFPA), the organization providing the major funding. Particularly important as a supporter of the radio soap opera was Dr. Bill Musoke, the country mission director for the UNFPA in Tanzania. The data-based findings about the effectiveness of *Twende na Wakati* were influential in the decision to continue its broadcasts for another year, but what really clinched Musoke's decision was a village woodcarver.

Musoke visited this elderly man to look at his carvings. The woodcarver worked on a bench under a tree. His transistor radio, tuned to Radio Tanzania, sat beside him on the bench. Musoke asked the woodcarver if he had a favorite program. "Yes, I listen regularly to *Twende na Wakati*." Musoke inquired, "What do you learn from this program?" The woodcarver replied: "If there had been a radio program like this one when I was young, I would be a rich man today. I would not have so many children, and I would have been able to save my money." This accidental and unplanned testimonial clinched the UNFPA official's full support for the entertainment-education radio program. Musoke continued funding the production of *Twende na Wakati*, and its evaluation. He also recommended the entertainment-education strategy to UNFPA officials for other nations.

PROBLEMS IN STUDYING
ENTERTAINMENT-EDUCATION EFFECTS

Insider Bias. One useful distinction in understanding any investigation is between insiders and outsiders. In the case of entertainment-education, insiders are the individuals and organizations directly involved in, and identified with, the production of the program. For example, Sabido found strong effects of his *telenovelas* broadcast in Mexico in the late 1970s. These summative evaluation results were achieved by using aggregate data and various ingenious research methodologies (Nariman, 1993). But the *credibility*—the degree to which a source is perceived as unbiased and trustworthy—of the results was questioned by some observers because Sabido directed not only the television soap operas but also the evaluation research. When an insider conducts research on effects, the results are likely to be questioned. A bias may be unknowingly and unintentionally injected in the evaluation.

JHU entertainment-education projects are evaluated by the university's evaluation research unit. The problem here is that the research is not entirely independent of the organization in charge of producing the message; or at least that is the appearance. Conversely, an insider can often have more control over the communication intervention that is being evaluated and may understand it better. So there are trade-offs in the insider–outsider dimension.

Center Versus Field Relationships. Another problem in some entertainment-education projects is the potential for disconnects between field and center. The success of the Tanzania Project rested on frequent communication between the University of New Mexico scholars and their counterparts at POFLEP. Mail service between Albuquerque and Arusha required three weeks (one way), and long distance telephone service was erratic. Access to e-mail could not be arranged by POFLEP until the final 6 months of this 5-year project. Furthermore, innumerable problems occurred due to computer incompatibility. Diskettes could not be accessed for several months. Data analysis slowed and the publication schedule was disrupted.

Funding. The research component of a project, if funded separately from the production of the communication intervention—to maintain outsider status—must occur at the appropriate time. We were fortunate in obtaining funding in time to study projects in Tanzania, India, and China. But the timing has sometimes been problematic. We could not begin the evaluation of *Hum Log* until a year after the broadcasts, which restricted us to an after-only design.

This timing problem is solved by JHU researchers, who are insiders in charge of the interventions. This affiliation solves one problem, but poses another, previously mentioned.

CONCLUSIONS

This chapter reviewed the use of research methods like field experimentation, interrupted-time series, and others that in the 1990s have sharpened our ability to evaluate the effects of entertainment-education projects. During the past decade, scholars have accumulated evidence that the entertainment-education strategy can have strong effects in changing audience behavior.

Evaluation research methods have evolved from (a) Sabido's early 1970s measures of television ratings and such aggregate effects as the national rate of family planning adoption, to (b) measuring such individual effects as the adoption of a behavior change in audience surveys and in field experiments, to (c) investigating the process of individual behavioral change and the mechanisms through which they occur. Today, the primary research question is not whether entertainment-education can change behavior, but how such effects take place. This watershed in the field of entertainment-education means future research will utilize more qualitative methods to probe the process through which entertainment-education has effects.

Lessons Learned About Entertainment-Education[1]

Easy learning is naturally pleasant to all.
—Aristotle (cited in Cooper, 1932)

You can be Goebbels who had a method for propaganda. Or you can use commercial television for social use.
—Miguel Sabido (personal communication, December 13, 1997)

The eight previous chapters of this book generally chronicle the development of entertainment-education projects. The accidental use of entertainment-education in the Peruvian *telenovela Simplemente María* in 1969–1970 led Miguel Sabido to formulate a strategy that he applied to eight *telenovelas* in Mexico. Sabido's work also inspired other entertainment-education projects in developing countries. This chapter summarizes lessons learned about the entertainment-education strategy and identifies contingencies that determine the effectiveness of such programs, as well as ethical dilemmas.

FACTORS DETERMINING THE EFFECTIVENESS OF ENTERTAINMENT-EDUCATION

Six factors determine the effectiveness of entertainment-education: audience characteristics, organizational factors, media environment, audience research, program-specific factors, and infrastructural factors (see Fig. 9.1).

---

[1]This chapter draws on Brown and Singhal (1990, 1993a, 1995, 1998); Singhal (1990); Singhal, Rogers, and Brown (1993); Singhal and Rogers (1994). Also, we acknowledge the extensive suggestions provided by our colleague Dr. Peter Vaughan.

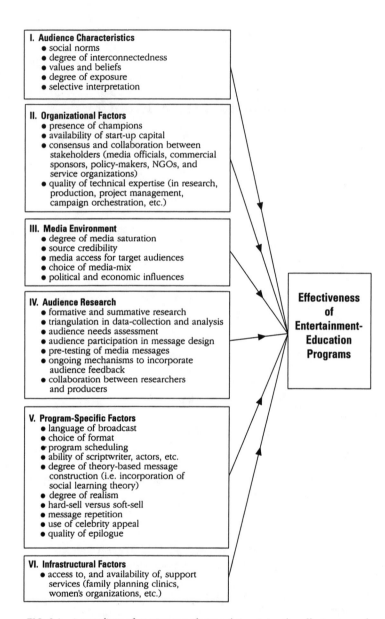

I. Audience Characteristics
- social norms
- degree of interconnectedness
- values and beliefs
- degree of exposure
- selective interpretation

II. Organizational Factors
- presence of champions
- availability of start-up capital
- consensus and collaboration between stakeholders (media officials, commercial sponsors, policy-makers, NGOs, and service organizations)
- quality of technical expertise (in research, production, project management, campaign orchestration, etc.)

III. Media Environment
- degree of media saturation
- source credibility
- media access for target audiences
- choice of media-mix
- political and economic influences

IV. Audience Research
- formative and summative research
- triangulation in data-collection and analysis
- audience needs assessment
- audience participation in message design
- pre-testing of media messages
- ongoing mechanisms to incorporate audience feedback
- collaboration between researchers and producers

V. Program-Specific Factors
- language of broadcast
- choice of format
- program scheduling
- ability of scriptwriter, actors, etc.
- degree of theory-based message construction (i.e. incorporation of social learning theory)
- degree of realism
- hard-sell versus soft-sell
- message repetition
- use of celebrity appeal
- quality of epilogue

VI. Infrastructural Factors
- access to, and availability of, support services (family planning clinics, women's organizations, etc.)

Effectiveness of Entertainment-Education Programs

FIG. 9.1. A paradigm of contingency factors determining the effectiveness of entertainment-education programs.

Audience Characteristics

The following lessons have been learned about how audience characteristics—norms, values, beliefs, degree of interpersonal interconnectedness, and selective interpretation—determine the effectiveness of entertainment-education.

1. *Audience members actively negotiate the meanings they perceive when processing an entertainment-education text.* Entertainment-education program designers cannot ensure that everyone will "read" the text exactly as intended. Some viewers make an oppositional or unintentional reading (Malwade-Rangarajan, 1992; Rogers et al., 1994; Ram, 1993; Sherry, 1997). The Archie Bunker effect is an oppositional reading of negative role models. However, both formative and summative audience research (including the pretesting of messages) can facilitate a dominant reading of entertainment-education (Rogers et al., 1998; Singhal & Brown, 1996).

2. *Audience selectivity processes and the hierarchy-of-effects model suggest that entertainment-education is more effective in creating knowledge of an educational issue than in changing overt behavior.* Entertainment-education messages are interpreted selectively by audience members through the processes of exposure, perception, and retention. Usually a message in rock music, a soap opera, or a comic book informs a considerable portion of the intended audience about the educational issue. But only a fraction of the target audience—a select segment—actually changes overtly. This select segment still may constitute a large number of people. For example, 2% of *Hum Log*'s viewing audience numbered 1.2 million. In Tanzania, 25% of *Twende na Wakati* listeners adopted family planning—more than 440,000 adults (Rogers et al., 1997).

Organizational Factors

Various organizational factors, such as the presence of champions, the availability of start-up funding, collaboration among stakeholders, available technical expertise, and others, determine the effectiveness of entertainment-education. We have learned the following lessons:

3. *Several champions in a nation must become interested in an entertainment-education project and put the weight of their influence[2] behind the idea. An entertainment-education project depends on committed leadership. The strategy is still perceived as daring today by media professionals and government officials. Hum Log* was implemented in India because PCI's Poindexter convinced India's Prime Minister and Secretary of Ministry of Information and Broadcasting to champion the project.

---

[2]The effective implementation of entertainment-education often depends on the ability to leverage status, power, and resources.

4. *Although start-up funding may be high, and considerable time is required, entertainment-education programs are cost-effective and may yield a profit.* PCS investigators pioneered cost analyses and found that an entertainment-education television project in Turkey was economical (Kincaid et al., 1993). Tanzania changed family planning and HIV prevention behavior for less than $1 U.S. per individual (Rogers et al., 1997).

5. *Entertainment-education projects are more effective when the stakeholders—health officials, broadcast officials, development planners, religious leaders, commercial sponsors, and others—collaborate.* Sabido insisted that stakeholders sign-off on the Values Grid before he began producing his *telenovela* in Mexico. Such agreements mitigate dependency relationships that often exist between producers and funders.[3] The behavior change effects of Sabido's *Acompáñame* can be attributed in part to this consensus-building between Mexican government officials, the national family planning program, the Roman Catholic Church, Televisa, and the infrastructure of government health clinics. We have learned that most effective entertainment-education projects require collaboration (Bouman, 1997, 1998; Bouman & Wieberdink, 1993), especially among creators and researchers.

6. *Technical expertise in communication research, message production, project management, and campaign implementation is needed to conduct an effective entertainment-education communication project.* This expertise may be developed or available locally, or it might be provided by an external organization, like JHU/PCS, PCI, or Top Comm (a Nairobi-based company headed by Tom Kazungu, who was trained by Sabido). External training or consultation by experts has been involved in most of the effective projects described in this volume.

Media Environment

Various characteristics of a media environment—the degree of media saturation, media credibility, penetration of the target audience, and others—influence the effectiveness of entertainment-education.

7. *Exposure to an entertainment-education message competes for audience attention with other media messages.* The degree of media saturation and diversity in a country strongly impacts the degree of audience exposure to a project. *Hum Log* attracted a huge audience, in part, because it was India's first long-running television soap opera. Similarly, *Twende na Wakati* achieved high exposure on Radio Tanzania, in part, because there were no

---

[3]If such agreements are not in place, producers of entertainment-education can be subject to direct censorship by commercial sponsors, or may exercise self-censorship (see Cambridge, McLaughlin, & Rota, 1995).

competing television or radio networks in Tanzania.[4] The high degree of media saturation in the United States is one main reason why entertainment-education is not more widely used in America.

8. *The perceived credibility of the mass medium transmitting an entertainment-education message influences the effectiveness of the project.* If the media system of a country is government-run, censored, and perceived as a propaganda arm of those in power, its credibility will be low.

9. *Choosing the most appropriate channel for entertainment-education is important.* For instance, if the intended audience lives in rural, remote areas where television penetration is low, radio or folk theater will be more appropriate than television as a channel for entertainment-education. *Tinka Tinka Sukh* was broadcast on radio, rather than on television, in the late 1990s to reach the high-fertility, less-educated audience of north Indian villagers. It is also important to choose the most suitable genre for entertainment-education, such as drama, music, or game show.

10. *The effects of entertainment-education are greater when accompanied by supplementary messages to form an integrated communication campaign.* A communication campaign (a) intends to achieve specific effects, (b) in a large number of individuals, (c) within a specified time period, and (d) through an organized set of communication activities (Atkin & Wallack, 1990; Backer, Rogers, & Sopory, 1992; Bradac, 1989; Rice & Atkin, 1989; Rogers & Singhal, 1990; Rogers & Storey, 1987; Salmon, 1989). The rock songs promoting sexual responsibility among teenagers in the Philippines were accompanied by print and broadcast advertisements, personal appearances by the singers, label buttons urging "Say No to Sex," posters, and a telephone hotline ("Dial-A-Friend"). These messages constituted a coordinated communication campaign, rather than just a popular song featuring lyrics with an educational message. While the cost and effort is greater, the synergy enhances effects in changing behavior.

11. *The effects of entertainment-education are shaped by economic and political factors* (Montgomery, 1989). The discontinuance of the family planning television soap opera *Tushauriane* in Kenya in 1988 is an example of how economic and political factors can affect a popular television program. The first entertainment-education television program on India's national network, *Hum Log*, was broadcast because the government had built 200 TV ground stations by the early 1980s and needed popular programming to justify the cost.

---

[4]As more private stations are established in developing countries, government stations are likely to lose market share. So government entertainment-education programs will face tougher competition for ratings from alternative media channels.

Audience Research

The degree and quality of audience research—formative and summative evaluations, needs assessment, audience participation in message design, pretesting, and collaboration between communication researchers and message producers—influence the effectiveness of entertainment-education.

12. *Formative evaluation research contributes to the design of an effective entertainment-education message.* Research about the characteristics, needs, and preferences of a target audience can sharpen the design of entertainment-education. Sometimes the evaluation represents overkill, as in Tanzania. The funding for formative evaluation should equate to its potential for improving the effectiveness of the project.

13. *Triangulated data collection, using both qualitative and quantitative methods, can provide in-depth information for designing an effective entertainment-education message and evaluating its effects.* It requires more funding but also provides more accurate and useful data than any single research method (Papa, Auwal, & Singhal, 1995).

14. *Formative evaluation can bridge important differences between researchers and producers, easing the usual tension in their relationship.* Collaboration between the JHU/PCS program staff and communication researchers, the creative professionals of Fuentes y Fomento Intercontinentales (FFI), a Mexican music marketing and production company, and the artists Tatiana and Johnny was essential in the success of "*Cuando Estemos Juntos.*" *Hum Log* was created in such a rush that formative evaluation of the target audience was skipped, and early episodes were ineffective (Singhal & Rogers, 1989a).

15. *A summative evaluation can determine the effectiveness of a program relative to stated goals.* Different research methods are appropriate for determining individual changes at each level in the hierarchy-of-effects model. An audience survey can measure the degree to which individuals are exposed to a message, but point-of-referral monitoring data (such as service statistics gathered from new adopters in family planning clinics) are more effective in measuring actual behavioral change. These hard data are more convincing to policymakers involved in decisions about entertainment-education.

16. *The evaluation of entertainment-education programs should guard against research overkill.* Using research to scrutinize every minute element of a message could be analogous to analyzing each component of a joke, only to find there is nothing to laugh about (Mielke & Swinehart, 1976). Formative and summative evaluation are crucial in an effective strategy, but they cost money and demand heavy time commitments of professionals and respondents (often many person-years). The point at which evaluation costs outweigh advantages should be determined.

Program-Specific Factors

The language used in an entertainment-education message, the degree of situational realism depicted, the use of celebrity appeals, program scheduling, and the degree of repetition can influence the effectiveness of entertainment-education.

17. *The use of colloquial, conversational language (which the target audience can understand and with which they identify), the depiction of real-life characters in realistic situations, and the use of celebrity actors and epilogue-providers can increase the audience effects of entertainment-education programs.*

18. *A balanced mix of entertainment and education content is essential to create effective messages.* Most educational messages are dull, although they need not be. The instructional content in entertainment-education can be too blatant or hard sell, and the audience will reject such messages. The educational theme must be woven into the entertainment message in a subtle way through positive, negative, and transitional role models, without seeking to indoctrinate or dogmatize.

19. *Audience size is a function of time of day and week, so the effects of entertainment-education can be increased by appropriate pre-program publicity and by program scheduling.* To prevent its broadcast in the Dodoma control area during 1993–1995, *Twende na Wakati* was scheduled at 6:30 p.m. twice each week. After mid-1995, the program was broadcast at 8:30 p.m., a more convenient hour for women. Audience exposure increased accordingly.

20. *The theory-based nature of entertainment-education increases the audience effects of this strategy.* Seldom are human communication theories used in designing media messages. Bandura's social learning theory lies at the heart of understanding the process of entertainment-education: learning can occur through observing media role models, and this vicarious learning usually is more effective and efficient than direct experiential learning. Why should a couple produce more children than they can afford and suffer economic hardship, to realize eventually that not adopting a family planning method was a mistake? This lesson could be learned by observing the rewards and punishments that accrue to positive and negative role models in a television soap opera.

21. *Repetition of the educational content in an entertainment-educational message increases its educational effects.* The effects of one-shot exposure to a communication message are typically minimal. Yet research on entertainment-education messages shows they have considerable effects. Why? One main reason is repetition. A television soap opera that is broadcast 1 hour per day, 5 days a week, for a year or more, represents massive exposure for a regular viewer. Also, the message is repeated in multiple forms through various positive and negative role models who find themselves in different situations, and not in a singularly repetitive way. This extends

the "wear-out threshold" for the message, avoiding annoyance and boredom on the part of the audience (Bettinghaus & Cody, 1994). *"Cuando Estemos Juntos"* was played by Mexican radio stations 14 times per day during the song's peak popularity. Not surprisingly, the intended message of the song was correctly identified by the target audience, who could remember the lyrics months later (Kincaid et al., 1988).

The effects produced by a single-shot message are vastly different from effects produced by repeated persuasive messages (Bettinghaus & Cody, 1994; Bradac et al., 1989; Fishbein & Ajzen, 1975; Hovland et al., 1949; Petty & Cacioppo, 1981). Repetition stores a message in an individual's long-term memory. Thus an entertainment-educational message is more likely to induce overt behavior change incrementally over time and to maintain the changed behavior.

Infrastructural Factors

22. *An entertainment-education intervention must be accompanied by an adequate infrastructure for providing services or it will not have strong effects in changing audience behavior.* When an episode of *Ven Conmigo* announced free literacy booklets were available at a government warehouse in Mexico City, the demand exceeded availability and a huge traffic jam resulted. When the same *telenovela* was rebroadcast in Peru the next year, it still contained the street address of the warehouse in Mexico City. The result was frustration. In the Philippines, thousands of young people called a telephone hot line for advice on sexual behavior (advertised in television spots), but reached a busy signal.

On certain occasions, however, a mass media message may help create the needed infrastructure.[5] *Hum Log* encouraged the signing of eye-donation cards in India, when, in 1985, an episode showed a police officer who needed an operation to restore his eyesight. One viewer, the president of a youth club, was motivated to sign up several thousand eye donors.

Soul City: Entertainment-Education Exemplar[6]

Soul City is an exemplary entertainment-education project in South Africa that has incorporated most of the lessons distilled in this book (Goldstein, 1998;

---

[5]In Nigeria, for instance, clinic hours were extended from 3 to 6 days a week, sparked in part by audience effects of *In a Lighter Mood.*

[6]This case draws on Japhet and Goldstein (1997a), which represents an audiotape recording of a presentation by Dr. Garth Japhet and Dr. Sue Goldstein on Soul City at the Second International Conference on Entertainment-Education and Social Change in Athens, Ohio, on May 7, 1997. This audiotape was produced and distributed by RoSu Productions, Inc. in Columbus, Ohio. We also thank Ms. Sue Goldstein for clarifying various aspects of Soul City with us (Goldstein, personal correspondence, September 3, 1998).

Japhet & Goldstein, 1997a). What is remarkable about Soul City is that it is a homegrown entertainment-education project developed independently of the key principals involved in projects reviewed in this book.

The story of Soul City begins in the late 1980s, when Dr. Garth Japhet, a young medical doctor, was assigned to a rural health clinic in South Africa's Natal Province. While treating poor, rural patients, Japhet realized that South Africa harbored "developing" country health problems in a "developed" country environment. Eight percent of South African adults were HIV positive. For children under 5 years of age, the leading cause of death is diarrhea. This dismal health record existed despite a highly developed mass media system: 65% of South Africans regularly watch television, 93% regularly listen to radio, and 50% regularly read newspapers and magazines.

Japhet noticed that health promotion activities in the media were inadequate and mainly slogan based. There was a Tuberculosis Day, an AIDS Day, a Malaria Day, and so on. Such health promotional efforts lacked sustainability. Also, research did not play much role in health promotion. Although South Africa had a robust advertising industry, lessons from advertising and social marketing were not being applied in health communication campaigns. Institutional partnerships among the media, the government, and the private sector did not exist for health promotion. The health ministry usually implemented programs in a top-down manner. Japhet also realized that despite a wealth of mass media talent and resources, there was no good indigenous drama on South African television or radio.

Japhet knocked on many doors, recruiting partners from the entertainment and media industries, professionals, professors, medical doctors, and international agencies (Lesson 5). In 1992, with the help of another medical doctor, Shereen Usdin, he established Soul City, a non-governmental organization whose mission was to harness mass media for promoting health. Intuitively, he realized that for media-based health promotion interventions to be sustainable, they had to be popular, attract the largest possible prime-time audience, and be of top-notch quality. He also knew that the institutional partnerships had to be forged among government, media, private corporations, and donor agencies so commercial and social interests could both be honored. From day one, entertainment-education was at the core of Soul City's health promotion strategy. Research, both formative and summative, would undergird this focus (Lesson 12): "It is research that distinguishes 'edu-tainment' from pure entertainment" (cited in Japhet & Goldstein, 1997a).

Soul City is a unique example of entertainment-education that represents a series of integrated, ongoing mass media activities, year after year[7] (Lesson 10). Each year a series of mass media interventions are implemented, including the flagship *Soul City*, a 13-part prime-time (Lesson 19) television drama that runs for 3 months promoting specific health education issues. Simultaneously,

---

[7]Three *Soul City* television series have been broadcast to date (in 1994, 1996, and 1997) and one is slated for broadcast in 1999. The eventual aim is to broadcast one new 13-episode TV series *each* year. In past years, when the television series have not been broadcast, for instance, in 1995 and 1998, other health campaign activities were still underway.

Dr. Garth Japhet, founder of Soul City in South Africa. (*Source:* Garth Japhet, used with permission.)

a 60-episode radio drama series is broadcast daily (Monday through Friday) at prime time in eight South African languages. While the story in the radio drama is different, the health issues and topics addressed are the same as in the TV series. While the television and radio series are broadcast, 2.25 million health education booklets, designed around the popularity of the TV characters, are distributed free to select target audience groups. The booklets are serialized by 10 major newspapers.

The first *Soul City* television series in 1994 focused on maternal and child health and HIV prevention and control. The second, in 1996, focused on HIV and tuberculosis prevention and control, housing and urban reform, alcohol abuse, and domestic violence. The third dealt with HIV prevention and control, alcohol and tobacco abuse, and domestic violence, in 1997. The series slated for broadcast in May 1999 will focus on violence against women, AIDS and youth sexuality, and hypertension. Other issues of national priority, for instance, housing and urban reform and small business management, are also woven into the *Soul City* storyline.

How popular are these mass media interventions? In past years, the *Soul City* television series emerged as the number-1 rated drama in South Africa (Japhet & Goldstein, 1997a). The radio series also earned very high ratings. The Soul City year-long health campaign reaches an estimated half (more than 20 million) of South Africa's population, including 8 million adults.

By using a multimedia approach, Soul City sustains a campaign atmosphere throughout the year. Each medium reinforces the popularity of the *Soul City* television series while appealing to a different target audience. Television reaches urban viewers while radio broadcasts reach rural listeners. Furthermore, each medium reinforces the health education messages of the others (Lesson 21), while carrying different aspects of the educational message. Booklets[8] and newspapers provide detailed information on a health topic, not possible on television or radio. Such a multimedia strategy facilitates the brokering of media partnerships: "Print wants to be involved because television is involved; radio wants to come aboard because print is on board," said Japhet (cited in Japhet & Goldstein, 1997a [tape]).

Soul City recognizes that overt behavior change is facilitated when audience members talk to one another. Each year, after the television and radio broadcasts, several campaign activities keep people talking. Education packets, produced cooperatively by curriculum specialists and creative designers, are targeted to adult and youth populations nationwide. The adult packet includes the health booklet, comic books based on the storyline, audiotapes of the comic books, *Soul City* posters, and a facilitator's guide to maximize impact.

The youth packets, in keeping with the audience needs, are geared toward building life skills and consist of a comic book based on the television series, and 4 workbooks that address personal responsibility, self-identity, personal relationships, and so forth. They also include a facilitator's guide for use in high schools (and by other non-governmental organizations). The credibility of the brand name and popularity of mass media programs are harnessed in additional initiatives, such as the "Soul City Search for Stars" (to recruit talent for next year's television and radio series), the "Soul City Health Care Worker of the Year" (to recognize outstanding outreach workers), and "Soul Citizens" (recognizing outstanding youth who engage in community development activities). Additionally, Soul City has struck a partnership with 12 journalists, representing the most influential South African newspapers, who regularly publish health education features derived from Soul City's activities. By carrying out these multiple health promotion activities, Soul City has emerged as a highly credible brand name in South Africa, an honor they use to their advantage.

The cornerstone of the Soul City health promotion strategy rests on producing high-quality media materials. The best scriptwriters, actors, cartoonists, and producers are hired (Lesson 6) and paid at market rate or better. The *Soul City* television series is broadcast at 8 p.m., a prime-time slot

---

[8]Audiences are encouraged to keep the printed booklets and to refer to them when needed. Each booklet has comic sections and activity-inserts, helping the audience members integrate health improvement into their daily lives.

when one third of South Africa's population is tuned in.[9] "So our media materials have to not just compete with the best ... They have to be the best," Japhet said (cited in Japhet & Goldstein, 1997a).

The ongoing nature of Soul City's health promotion activities provides several advantages. Soul City's media interventions serve as a resource for various health and development groups in South Africa to piggyback issues of national priority, without re-inventing the research-production-partnership wheel, as happens when a new health-development initiative is launched. More important, by broadcasting a recurrent television and radio series, Soul City avoids the problem of *audience lag*, the time taken to build a sizable and dedicated audience for a new media program. A highly watched *Soul City* television series in a previous year ensures a large audience at the beginning of the next season.

Formative and summative research are key to designing and evaluating the mass media interventions at Soul City (Lessons 13, 14, and 15). Formative research is conducted to identify health issues of national priority and to ensure that mass media interventions can be backed at the ground level by needed infrastructure (Lesson 22).[10]

Formative research activities include focus-group and in-depth interviews, participatory rural appraisals, archival research, and pretesting. Summative research includes gathering ratings and viewership data, and conducting before–after national and regional sample surveys to determine the effects of the television, radio, and print interventions. Summative evaluation reports show that Soul City mass media interventions have increased knowledge about health issues, promoted more positive attitudes toward them, and contributed to behavior change on the part of certain audience members (CASE, 1995; Japhet & Goldstein, 1997b).

The cost incurred by Soul City for one year of multimedia materials, including the 13-episode television series, the 60-episode radio series in nine languages, 2.25 million booklets, plus marketing, advertising, and public relations activities, is $3.5 million (U.S.). How is this money raised? Twenty-five percent is provided by the South African government, 25% by international donor agencies, such as the European Union and UNICEF, 25% by corporations like British Petroleum and Old Mutual, and the remaining 25% by the broadcast media.[11] Japhet emphasizes the key reason for Soul City's effectiveness is these partnerships with government, media, corporate, and donor agencies:

---

[9]In contrast, the educational slots on South African television earn dismal ratings of 2 to 3%.

[10]If the health issue is not a national priority, it is not addressed in the television series but instead is treated in local radio broadcasts, with booklets, educational packets for adults and youths, and serialized newspaper pages. Before addressing any health education issue, whether nationally or locally, field research is carried out to ensure the local infrastructure can support the message.

[11]The national television network covers the cost of producing the *Soul City* TV series. The national and regional radio stations carry out the production and translations of the eight-language radio series (from a common script) at no cost to Soul City. Newspapers provide the space for serializing the booklets at no cost.

"Partnerships make this intervention possible. . . . The more you work together, the more people understand the intervention, and the stronger the partnership gets. . . . Also the expertise of the technical production staff improves" (Japhet & Goldstein, 1997a [tape]). Japhet aptly calls this process the "The cycle of positive reinforcement."

Interestingly, Soul City is mostly a research and management organization. It coordinates the activities of its various corporate, government, media, and donor partners. Its employees do not directly produce, direct, or publish its health communication materials. They commission them from professionals, and through research, ensure their high quality. Soul City owns the media product that is produced, and they pay the bills. This role gives them veto power if a product does not meet high standards.

The reach of Soul City extends beyond South Africa, thus multiplying its impact. In partnership with UNICEF—which considers the Soul City experience as a "best practice"—Soul City materials are distributed in neighboring Botswana, Zimbabwe, Lesotho, Swaziland, Namibia, and Zambia. Research evaluations show the materials are highly popular in these countries and audiences find these materials to be culturally shareable (Japhet & Goldstein, 1997a; Singhal & Svenkerud, 1994). African countries like Nigeria, Ghana, and Malawi have also requested Soul City materials for local use.[12]

Entertainment-education practitioners and researchers will undoubtedly hear more about Soul City in the future and learn from its innovative initiatives in improving public health in South Africa.

RESOLVING ETHICAL DILEMMAS

The entertainment-education strategy involves several ethical dilemmas (Brown & Singhal, 1990, 1993a, 1995, 1998; Cambridge et al., 1995). *Ethics* is a branch of philosophy that studies the principles of right or wrong in human conduct. Entertainment-education implementers are unique in the development organizing community in that they have from the start questioned whether what they are doing is ethical. Rarely do agricultural extension agents worry about the ethics of introducing new strains of rice. Equally rare is for health care workers to worry about the ethics of promoting immunizations. Most implementers of development projects assume their work is good; the ethical criticisms typically come from the outside (Goulet, 1995).

Entertainment-education implementers have taken several proactive steps to be ethical. Sabido establishes a moral framework to ensure the values

---

[12]This is not geared as much to promote South Africa-made media materials in other countries, as much as it is to share the on-going, partnership-brokered, multi-media model of Soul City with other nations and organizations.

promoted are enshrined in the country's constitution and legal statutes. The signed agreement on the program's Values Grid by the various stakeholders—government officials, commercial sponsors, religious leaders, and broadcast media officials—guides the scriptwriters about the program's educational content. The use of local writers and creative teams ensures the program is culturally sensitive and incorporates local language. The use of subject-matter specialists to review program scripts ensures that technical information in the program is accurate. The systematic depiction of positive and negative role models of behaviors, and realistic consequences of these behaviors, allows the audience to draw their own conclusions[13]—reinforced in the epilogues—rather than being preached to in a didactic manner. Furthermore, formative and summative evaluation research helps (a) analyze the target audience's needs and aspirations, (b) produce relevant and user-friendly media materials, and (c) understand the intended and unintended effects of the intervention.

However, entertainment-education practitioners must be mindful of at least seven important ethical dilemmas (see Fig. 9.2): (1) the development dilemma of using media as a persuasive tool for prosocial change; (2) distinguishing prosocial from antisocial content; (3) the source-centered dilemma of who should determine the prosocial content for others; (4) the audience segmentation dilemma of who among the audience should receive the prosocial content; (5) the oblique persuasion dilemma of justifying the embedding of educational messages in entertainment; (6) the sociocultural equality dilemma of ensuring the prosocial media uphold socioeconomic equality among viewers; and (7) the dilemma of preventing unintended consequences of prosocial media (Brown & Singhal, 1990, 1993a, 1995, 1998).

The Prosocial Development Dilemma. The foremost ethical problem in the entertainment-education strategy centers around a fundamental question: Is it right to use the mass media as a persuasive tool to foster social change? It is virtually impossible to produce value-free or socially innocuous entertainment messages (Bettinghaus & Cody, 1994; Day, 1991; Thoman, 1989). The idea that persuasive communication is unethical and therefore should be avoided denies reality. Persuasive communication cannot be eliminated in a democratic society (Bettinghaus & Cody, 1994). Therefore, arguing that it is unethical to use television, radio, or another channel to promote prosocial behavior seems unreasonable and inconsistent with democratic freedom.

However, prosocial to some may not be to others. Whether it is ethical to produce an entertainment-education message depends on the nature of the behavior being promoted, on who decides whether a behavior is prosocial,

---

[13]Reinforced in the epilogue.

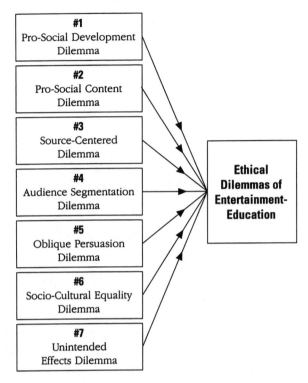

FIG. 9.2. Ethical dilemmas associated with entertainment-education programming. (*Source:* Based on Brown and Singhal, 1990, 1993a, 1995, 1998.)

and on the effects the promotion is likely to have on an audience. The
educational issues promoted by past entertainment-education are of unques-
tionable value, such as HIV prevention. Who would want individuals to
contract HIV/AIDS?

The Prosocial Content Dilemma.   The prosocial content dilemma centers around the problems of distinguishing between prosocial and antisocial
content. What is construed as prosocial by certain audience members might
be perceived as antisocial by other individuals. Pro-abortion groups, which
support a woman's choice in controlling her reproductive behavior, consider
a media message about abortion to be prosocial. Anti-abortion groups, which
support the rights of the unborn fetus, consider such messages to be antisocial.
Labeling an issue obviously involves a value judgment on the part of the
message source, which may be perceived different from the receiver's value
judgment.

The Source-Centered Dilemma.   This dilemma deals with who decides
about entertainment-education. In most developing countries in which entertainment-education programs are broadcast, the decision-maker is typically

the national government, which decides what is prosocial, which audience is targeted, and with what message. But what assurance is there that government leaders will use entertainment-education appropriately? How can one forget Hitler's skillful use of mass media to spread anti-Semitic propaganda in Nazi Germany?

Assurance that media will be used for prosocial purposes is no greater in nations where the responsibility is left to television producers and commercial advertisers, rather than to national governments. Producers and advertisers usually avoid controversial social issues (Montgomery, 1989). Until recent years, U.S. television networks opposed the broadcast of condom advertisements, even though their programming depicted numerous sexual acts every day (Lowry & Towles, 1989). The reconciliation of prosocial media messages in free market economies like the United States (where television systems are commercially driven) is an ethical dilemma (Brown & Singhal, 1990).

The Audience Segmentation Dilemma. A fourth ethical issue concerning the use of entertainment-education programs is associated with targeting educational messages to a particular audience segment (Brown & Singhal, 1993a). *Audience segmentation* fine-tunes messages to fit the needs of a relatively homogeneous group to maximize outcomes. For instance, media messages about family planning in developing countries are usually targeted to fertile-aged couples, a key audience segment for the educational issue of family planning. However, such segmentation may alienate other important audience segments, like adolescents, sexually active singles, and others who feel they could benefit from contraceptive messages.

Another ethical dilemma associated with audience segmentation centers around the effects of entertainment-education messages. In the field experiment for *Twende na Wakati*, blocking radio broadcasts for two years in the Dodoma region may have resulted in unwanted pregnancies and HIV infections, which otherwise could have been prevented (Rogers et al., 1998).

The Oblique Persuasion Dilemma. The entertainment-education strategy takes an oblique route to persuasion by sugarcoating the lessons, in part to break down individuals' learning defenses to the educational message. Audiences might think they are being entertained, while being educated subtly about a prosocial issue. However, most audiences realize the messages are both educational and entertaining (Rogers et al., 1998).

The Sociocultural Equality Dilemma. How can one insure sociocultural equality by providing equal treatment to various audience segments? Equality means regarding each social and cultural group with the same importance (Gudykunst & Kim, 1984). Achieving sociocultural equality through entertainment-education is especially important in a diverse country like India. *Hum Log*, within the limits of the patriarchal social system of India, confronted viewers' traditional beliefs about women's status. But the viewers' ethnicity, linguistic background, and gender were found to be important determinants of beliefs about gender equality (Brown, 1988, 1992a, 1992b; Singhal, 1990; Singhal & Rogers, 1989a). Subservience of women is still considered acceptable in many Indian households. However, such is not the case throughout India. When an entertainment-education message does not give equal play to different voices, it presents an ethical dilemma for certain viewpoints who may feel their views are not represented.

The Unintended-Effects Dilemma. A seventh ethical dilemma of entertainment-education is unintended effects. Development is a complex phenomenon whose consequences are not always predictable. Undesirable, unintended consequences sometimes result from the diffusion of prosocial messages. Reluctance to broadcast condom ads on U.S. television in the 1980s demonstrated how a fear of unintended consequences can discourage the broadcast of prosocial content. Network officials feared that messages intending to promote sexual responsibility might encourage sexual promiscuity instead, for which they would be criticized (Brown & Singhal, 1990).

The entertainment-education strategy can improve the quality of people's lives. Decisions about it should not be made solely by commercial advertisers or by government officials. Such decisions should take into consideration people's freedom, equality, dignity, and well-being. The ethical dilemmas ultimately are decided by the audience, as they choose whether to expose themselves to an entertainment-education message.

LOOKING FORWARD

What is the future of the entertainment-education strategy? *If implemented in a systematic manner, with theory-based message design, formative research, and other necessary elements (see Fig. 9.1), the entertainment-education strategy can be a powerful influence in changing audience knowledge, attitudes, and behavior regarding an educational issue.* The entertainment-education strategy can also be commercially viable and socially responsible. On the other hand, if implemented in a haphazard manner, the outcomes can be disappointing. Entertainment-education projects require a high level of technical expertise in research and production and relatively high start-up costs.

We expect that the application of entertainment-education will increase greatly in the future.[14] Here we outline the new directions in which the field might be headed.

1. *Moving from a "production-centered" approach to a more "audience-centered" approach.* Entertainment-education programs have often come under criticism for their seemingly top-down nature, as when message producers determine what the audience members need. Entertainment-education has also been criticized for allowing commercial (advertiser-centered) interests to override social (audience-centered) interests.

As discussed previously, formative research can bridge the gap between producers and audience goals. Producers of entertainment-education programs should try to more actively involve target audiences in the production of media messages (Bhasin & Singhal, 1998; Mody, 1986). Such a participatory form of entertainment-education message development occurred in the 1970s and 1980s in the Kheda Communication Project (KCP) in Gujarat, India, where target audiences (the villagers in Kheda District) regularly participated in designing and acting in entertainment-education television serials (Mody, 1991). Several KCP television serials, including *Chatur Mota* (Wise Elder) and *Nari Tu Narayani* (Women You Are Powerful) can be considered exemplars of participatory forms of entertainment-education programming (Mody, 1991). The Office of Latino Affairs in Washington, D.C., also utilizes such a participatory type of message design in their entertainment-education television series, *Linea Directa* (Direct Line), broadcast on Spanish-language channels in the United States.

2. *Incorporation of more cultural, humanistic, and literary traditions in both designing and researching entertainment-education programs.* In recent years, insights were gleaned from the cultural, humanistic, and literary traditions (Law & Singhal, 1998; Lozano, 1992; Lozano & Singhal, 1993; Malwade-Rangarajan, 1992; Papa et al., 1998; Ram, 1993; Singhal & Udornpim, 1997; Storey, 1995, 1998; Svenkerud et al., 1995). A further integration of cross-disciplinary theoretical viewpoints in designing and researching entertainment-education is expected.

3. *Integration of traditional and modern media channels of entertainment to more widely disseminate educational messages.* Folk theater, dance, puppetry, storytelling, and other traditional forms of communication can play an important role in entertainment-education (Sujan, 1993; Valente &

---

[14]The Second International Conference on Entertainment-Education and Social Change, held in Athens, Ohio in 1997, was attended by 300 participants from 50 countries, a fourfold increase from the first conference held in Los Angeles in 1989. In 1994, the United Nations Population Conference in Cairo recognized entertainment-education as a viable communication strategy for population communication, and in recent years, the U.S. Centers for Disease Control and Prevention in Atlanta has adopted this strategy, especially to target adolescents at high risk for drug abuse and HIV/AIDS.

Bharath, in press). A comprehensive entertainment-education strategy should utilize such pre-existing local, traditional media forms. Local folk channels of recreation and education can be adopted for wider dissemination of entertainment-education messages. JHU/PCS used a traditional theatrical art form, *Koteba*, to address family planning in Mali. *Koteba* was then videotaped and broadcast on national network television, achieving strong audience effects (Schubert, 1988).

4. *Moving from a focus on family planning and public health issues to other educational needs.* Most of the past programming efforts have focused on family planning, its proximate determinants like status of women and maternal and child health, and public health topics like HIV/AIDS prevention, alcohol and tobacco abuse, and others. This emphasis on family size and related public health issues is understandable given the two institutional leaders in implementing entertainment-education efforts worldwide are Johns Hopkins University's Population Communication Services and Population Communications International of New York. Both emphasize population and health issues. In the future, the scope of the entertainment-education strategy is likely to include environmental conservation, human rights, ethnic and racial tolerance,[15] and world peace, as more organizations (such as Soul City) embrace the entertainment-education approach.

5. *Going beyond applications in mass communication to include classroom instruction, distance learning, and other educational interventions.* In recent years, a growing trend in instructional settings is for teachers to supplement lectures with audiovisual aids, classroom activities, and participatory games to enhance student involvement and learning (Lieberman, 1997, 1998). Incorporating entertainment-education in formal instructional practices will grow in the future (Adams, 1982), especially, perhaps, as part of multimedia technology in classrooms.

Future Needs

In addition, we see the following areas of need with respect to the future of the entertainment-education strategy.

---

[15]In 1988, Israeli Television (ITV) broadcast *Neighbors*, a situation comedy about two families, one Arab and one Jewish, who live in a Jerusalem apartment building as next-door neighbors. Both Arabic and Hebrew were spoken with subtitles for each language. *Neighbors* had a regular audience of 10 million viewers, more than half of whom lived in Egypt, Jordan, Lebanon, and Syria (Warburg, 1988). Similarly, a popular Venezuelan *telenovela*, *Kassandra*, centering around a Gypsy character, has reportedly indirectly furthered peace in Bosnia Herzegovina in the mid-1990s. The potential for promoting tolerance through entertainment-education has been demonstrated (Rogers & Steinfatt, 1999).

1. *The need to provide training and instruction in the entertainment education strategy will increase for both the creative and scholarly community.* Few scriptwriters or radio, television, and film producers have formal training in implementing the entertainment-education strategy. A recent survey of international media producers of religious programs indicated more than 80% requested formal training in entertainment-education (Henrich, 1997). As the demand for this programming increases, so will the need for training and instruction, especially in universities.

2. *The need to spur media advocacy for entertainment-education messages will increase in the future. Media advocacy* is the strategic use of mass media to advance social or public policy initiatives (Wallack, 1990). Media advocates recognize that mass media, in addition to influencing attitudes, beliefs, and behaviors, are effective in setting the policy agenda and stimulating public discussion of an issue (Dearing & Rogers, 1996). For instance, certain Hollywood lobbyists question the excessive depictions of alcohol, smoking, and drug use, poor dietary habits (eating junk food), reckless driving, and unprotected sex in prime-time television programs (Resnick, 1990). By spurring public debate on these issues, health advocates have been able, on a limited basis, to persuade the entertainment community to exercise more responsibility in handling such antisocial behaviors[16] (Montgomery, 1989). Such media advocacy in the United States involves a special type of entertainment-education and will likely spur more community participation.

3. *The need to produce more culturally shareable entertainment-education programs,*[17] *which are not limited by local or national boundaries, will increase in the future* (Singhal & Svenkerud, 1994; Singhal & Udornpim, 1997; Sthapitanonda-Sarabol & Singhal, 1998; Straubhaar, 1991; Svenkerud et al., 1995; Udornpim & Singhal, in press). Such programs can address common regional problems (for instance, HIV prevention in Latin America) in a cost-effective way by pooling creative talent and resources.[18]

Examples[19] of cultural sharing include Sabido's *telenovelas* and the Tatiana and Johnny songs, which were popular in dozens of Spanish-speaking countries.

---

[16]Media advocacy for entertainment-education will likely spur local community groups like parents, churches, and schools to be more involved in demanding entertainment-education.

[17]Cambridge (1992) and Svenkerud (1995) liken the concept to global advertising, in which an advertisement is produced in one nation for broadcast in several countries. Multinational companies, such as Coca Cola and McDonalds, use this strategy in Latin American countries.

[18]See Singhal and Svenkerud (1994) for the pros and cons of culturally shareable programs.

[19]Others are Sesame Street; the popular Japanese television soap opera *Oshin*, broadcast in more than 55 countries (Mowlana & Rad, 1992; Singhal & Udornpim, 1997; Udornpim & Singhal, in press); the animated series *Meena*, produced by UNICEF to promote children's

4. *More scholarly research is needed on entertainment-education to better understand how, why, and when entertainment-education programs are more or less effective.* This future research is crucial as more entertainment-education projects are launched worldwide through the initiatives of JHU/PCS, PCI, Soul City, and other organizations. During the past decade, scholarly publications about entertainment-education increasingly appeared in mainstream of communication studies, a trend which will intensify in the future.

Research evidence for the effectiveness of the entertainment-education strategy has been strengthened in recent years, aided by improved evaluation designs. Today there is little doubt that entertainment-education has effects, at least if it is implemented correctly. Also, several useful lessons have been learned about the conditions that determine the effectiveness of entertainment-education. However, important questions remain about entertainment-education.[20]

- What are the relative merits of different vehicles? Do soap operas and music videos operate in the same manner while reaching different target audiences, or do they affect their audiences differently? Which vehicles are better in meeting educational goals? Which vehicles are cost-effective?
- Within the soap opera format, what are the merits of broadcasting (a) different lengths of melodramatic series (13, 26, 52, 104, 208, or more episodes), (b) different lengths of episodes (15-, 30-, or 60-minute episodes), and (c) episodes with different broadcast frequencies (once a week vs. several times a week)? Also what are the merits and demerits of repeating or not repeating episodes?
- Which broadcast vehicle is best: commercial, broadcast on private stations, publicly funded and broadcast on government stations, or a combination of both?
- What are the merits and demerits of sharing entertainment-education programs across cultures and of *transcreation*, the process of adapting an existing program's plot, characters, and context to suit the needs of

---

causes; "Karate Kids," produced by Street Kids International to reduce incidence of HIV among street children (Sthapitanonda-Sarabol & Singhal, 1998); *Superbook*, a collection of Bible stories, produced by the Christian Broadcasting Network and broadcast in 50 countries (Fraser & Brown, 1997); *Soul City*; and feature films like *Consequences, More Time, Neria*, and others produced by Zimbabwean filmmaker John Riber (Hill, 1993; Singhal & Svenkerud, 1994; Smith, 1989; Wray, 1991).

[20]We thank our colleague Dr. Peter Vaughan for his important inputs in defining a future research agenda for entertainment-education.

a local audience? Can scripts, storylines, and characters of entertainment-education programs be shared across cultures by just changing names, locales, and situations?[21] Should such culturally shareable, transcreation programming models be increasingly adopted by organizations that implement entertainment-education on a global or regional basis?

- What kind of support programs do entertainment-education programs need to enhance their effectiveness? Are interactive "Ask the Doctor" types of media programs useful to answer audience questions? Or are telephone hot lines more personal and effective? Should the program be serialized in other media (newspapers, comic books, or posters) as in Soul City? Can popular media role models effectively train professionals? For instance, can Bina from *Twende na Wakati* create a tape to train nurses about family planning? Is merchandising (T-shirts, toys, etc.) a worthwhile investment, as is practiced by *Sesame Street* and *Soul City*?

Furthermore, there are several theoretical questions about entertainment-education that need further investigation.

- How does individual versus collective efficacy influence the effects of entertainment-education messages?
- Is the entertainment-education strategy more effective for certain educational issues than for others?
- Are entertainment-education programs designed with a theoretical framework more effective than non-theory based programs?
- What are the short-term versus long-term effects of entertainment-education? The latter have scarcely been investigated.
- What is the most effective balance of education versus entertainment?
- What role do entertainment-education programs play in developing an individual's sense of what represents normal behavior in their communities?, and in making the individual feel the depicted problems are relevant to him or her?
- Do entertainment-education programs increase polarization in societies by hardening the positions of both the "Archie Bunkers" and the "Meatheads" in the audience, or do they promote social cohesion by promoting dialogue across these gulfs?

---

[21]AIR has effectively transcreated several radio dramas for wider dissemination within India. The original Hindi-language serial *Dehleez* (Threshold) was transcreated and broadcast in various regional languages. The Soul City radio drama series in South Africa is also similarly transcreated in eight local languages.

Entertainment-education is a flexible, adaptable, and versatile mass media strategy. If implemented correctly, it works in a wide variety of situations. To date, it has been applied in various mass media (radio, television, film, music, theater, and print), their various genres (soap operas, talk shows, game shows, variety magazine shows, cartoons, rock, rap, or folk music, and comics), to address a variety of problems in various development sectors (agriculture, family planning, gender equality, adult literacy, HIV prevention, environment, and others). As a communication strategy, entertainment-education holds promise not just for the hundreds of millions of students in the world's classrooms, but for the billions of audience members who each day tune in their radio sets, rev-up their stereos, and flip open a comic book.

Glossary

Archie Bunker effect is the degree to which certain audience individuals identify with negative media role models.

Affectively oriented parasocial interaction is the degree to which audience members identify with a particular media character.

Antisocial behaviors are undesirable or detrimental to other individuals and society at large.

Attentional involvement uses emotional appeals to sustain parasocial interaction between the audience and the media role model.

Audience lag is the time taken to build a sizable and dedicated audience for a media program.

Audience segmentation is fine-tuning messages to fit a relatively homogeneous audience segment in order to maximize communication effects.

Behaviorally oriented parasocial interaction is the degree to which individuals talk with other audience members or with the media characters.

Boredom-education programs emphasize educational content to the point that audience members are put off.

Case study is a descriptive type of research in which individuals, groups, or systems are interviewed or observed, or various types of archival records are examined, to search for patterns and insights into a phenomenon.

Cognitively oriented parasocial interaction is the degree to which audience members pay careful attention to the characters of a media program and think about its educational content after viewing it.

Collective efficacy is the degree to which individuals in a system believe they can organize and execute courses of action required to achieve collective goals.

Collectivistic cultures are those in which the collectivity's goals are more important than the individual's.

Credibility is the degree to which a source or channel is perceived as unbiased and trustworthy.

Culturally shareable media products are those that appeal to audiences in a broader sociocultural context, outside the local or national boundary.

Education is a formal or informal program of instruction and training with potential to develop an individual's skill to achieve a particular end by boosting his or her mental, moral, or physical powers.

Entertainment is a performance or spectacle that captures interest or attention, giving pleasure or amusement.

Entertainment-degradation programs are those that consciously degrade (morally or culturally) a media message to increase its attractiveness.

Entertainment-education is the process of purposely designing and implementing a media message to both entertain and educate, in order to increase knowledge about an issue, create favorable attitudes, and change overt behavior.

Epilogue is a short final note added to a dramatic (or literary) message.

Ethics is a branch of philosophy that studies the principles of right or wrong in human conduct.

Formative evaluation is a type of research conducted while an activity, process, or system is being developed or is ongoing to improve effectiveness.

Homophily is the degree to which two or more individuals who communicate are similar.

Identification is the process through which an individual takes on a model's behavior or personality.

Imitation is the process by which one individual matches the actions of another, usually closely in time.

Individualistic cultures are those in which the individual's goals are more important than the collectivity's.

Kinesics is body language, a type of nonverbal communication indicated by gestures and behaviors.

Media advocacy is the strategic use of the mass media for advancing social or public policy initiatives.

Meta-communication is communication about communication (epilogues are an example of meta-communication).

Modeling is the psychological processes in which one individual matches the actions of another, not necessarily closely in time.

Myths are legendary stories that express the beliefs of a people, often serving to explain natural phenomena or the origins of a people.

Parasocial interaction is the seemingly face-to-face interpersonal relationships that develop between a viewer and a mass media personality like a television performer.

Prestige modeling is the use of model media characters who exhibit culturally admired behaviors.

Prosocial behaviors are those that are desirable and beneficial to other individuals or to society at large.

Proxemics is a dimension of nonverbal communication focusing on how space affects communication behavior.

Pseudo-gemeinschaft implies feigning personal concern to manipulate an individual more effectively.

Qualitative research methods are means of gathering data not expressed in numerical form.

Referential involvement is the degree to which an individual relates a media message to his or her personal experiences.

Self-efficacy is an individual's perception of his or her capability to deal effectively with a situation, and one's sense of perceived control over a situation.

Similarity modeling is the incorporation of a variety of media characters each of which appeal to different audience segments.

Social change is the process by which an alteration occurs in the structure and function of a social system.

Summative evaluation is research that is conducted in order to form a judgment about the effectiveness of the communication intervention in reaching its objectives.

Transcreation is the process of adapting an existing program's plot, characters, and context to suit the needs of a local audience.

Transitional modeling is the portrayal of media characters that exhibit positive (socially desirable) behaviors, negative (socially detrimental) behaviors, or transitional behaviors, in which a negative role model adopts a prosocial behavior.

Triangulation is the use of multiple research methods to measure the same variable or set of variables.

Vicarious motivation involves presenting behavior change as a cost-beneficial decision.

References

Abt, D. (1987). Music video: Impact of the visual dimension. In J. Lull (Ed.), *Popular music and communication* (pp. 96–111). Newbury Park, CA: Sage.

Actriz Peruana: Saby Kamalich filma en Buenos Aires. (1970, May 4). *El Comercio,* p. 1.

Adams, D. S. (Ed.). (1982). *Teaching sociology through humor.* Washington, DC: American Sociological Association.

Alexander, A. (1985). Adolescent's soap opera viewing and relational perceptions. *Journal of Broadcasting and Electronic Media, 29*(3), 295–308.

Allen, P. G. (1979). *Spider woman's grand daughters: Traditional tales and contemporary writing by native American women.* New York: Fawcett-Columbine.

Allen, R. C. (Ed.). (1995). *To be continued: Soap operas around the world.* New York: Routledge.

Amato, P. P., & Malatesta, A. (1987, May). *Effects of prosocial elements in family situation comedies.* Paper presented to the International Communication Association, Montreal.

AMREF (1992). *Tanzania: AIDS education and condom promotion for transportation workers: Strengthening STD services.* Dar-es-Salaam, Tanzania: African Medical and Research Foundation.

Andere, A. (1987, May 17). 'Tushauriane' takes off tonight. *Standard* (Nairobi, Kenya), 4.

Andison, F. S. (1980). Television violence and viewer aggression. In G. C. Wilhoit & H. de Bock (Eds.), *Mass communication review yearbook 1* (pp. 555–572). Newbury Park, CA: Sage.

Aristotle (1961). *Poetics.* Translated by S. H. Butcher. New York: Hill and Wang.

Ashraf, M. (1975). *Political verse and song.* Berlin: Seven Seas.

Atkin, C., & Wallack, L. (Eds.). (1990). *Mass communication and public health.* Newbury Park, CA: Sage.

Aufderheide, P. (1990). Let's talk. *Foundation News, 31*(6), 45–47.

Auter, P. J. (1992). TV that talks back: An experimental validation of a parasocial interaction scale. *Journal of Broadcasting & Electronic Media, 36,* 173–181.

Avery, R. (1979). Adolescents use of the mass media. *American Behavioral Scientist, 23,* 53–70.

Avery, R. K., & Ellis, D. G. (1979). Talk radio as an interpersonal phenomenon. In G. Gumpert & R. Cathcart (Eds.), *Inter/media: Interpersonal communication in a media world* (pp. 108–115). New York: Oxford University Press.

Babrow, A. S. (1987). Student motives for watching soap operas. *Journal of Broadcasting & Electronic Media, 31,* 309–321.

Backer, T. E., & Rogers, E. M. (Eds.). (1993). *Impact of organizations on mass media health behavior campaigns.* Newbury Park, CA: Sage.

Backer, T. E., Rogers, E. M., & Sopory, P. (1992). *Designing health communication campaigns: What works?* Newbury Park, CA: Sage.

Bakshi, P. K. (1989). Jagran: Theater for education and development. *New Theater Quarterly, 5*(18), 124–139.

Ball, S., & Bogatz, G. A. (1970). *The first year of Sesame Street: An evaluation.* Princeton, NJ: Educational Testing Service.

Ball-Rokeach, S. J., Rokeach, M., & Grube, J. W. (1984). *The great American values test: Influencing behavior and belief through television.* New York: The Free Press.

Ball-Rokeach, S., Grube, J., & Rokeach, M. (1981). Roots: The next generation—who watched and with what effect. *Public Opinion Quarterly, 45,* 58–68.

Bandura, A. (1962). Social learning through imitation. In M. R. Jones (Ed.), *Nebraska Symposium on Motivation* (pp. 211–269). Lincoln: University of Nebraska Press.

Bandura, A. (1965). Influence of model's reinforcement contingencies on the acquisition of imitative responses. *Journal of Personality and Social Psychology, 1,* 589–595.

Bandura, A. (1973). *Aggression: A social learning analysis.* Englewood Cliffs, NJ: Prentice-Hall.

Bandura, A. (1974). Analysis of modeling processes. In A. Bandura (Ed.), *Modeling: Conflicting theories* (pp. 178–211). New York: Lieber-Atherton.

Bandura, A. (1977). *Social learning theory.* Englewood Cliffs, NJ: Prentice-Hall.

Bandura, A. (1986). *Social foundations of thought and action: A social cognitive theory.* Englewood Cliffs, NJ: Prentice-Hall.

Bandura, A. (1988). Perceived self-efficacy: Exercise of control through self-belief. In J. P. Dauwalder, M. Perrez, & V. Hobi (Eds.), *Annual series of European research in behavior therapy* (Vol. 2, pp. 27–59). Amsterdam/Lisse: Swets & Zeitlinger.

Bandura, A. (1991). Self-efficacy conception of anxiety. In R. Schwarzer & R. A. Wicklund (Eds.), *Anxiety and self-focused attention* (pp. 89–110). New York: Harwood.

Bandura, A. (1992a). Exercise of personal agency through the self-efficacy mechanism. In R. Schwarzer (Ed.), *Self-efficacy: Thought control of action* (pp. 3–38). Washington, DC: Hemisphere.

Bandura, A. (1992b). Self-efficacy mechanism in psychobiologic functioning. In R. Schwarzer (Ed.), *Self-efficacy: Thought control of action* (pp. 355–394). Washington, DC: Hemisphere.

Bandura, A. (1995). Exercise of personal and collective efficacy in changing societies. In A. Bandura (Ed.), *Self-efficacy in changing societies* (pp. 1–45). New York: Cambridge University Press.

Bandura, A. (1997). *Self-efficacy: The exercise of control.* New York: Freeman.

Bandura, A., Grusec, J. A., & Menlove, F. L. (1966). Observational learning as a function of symbolization and incentive set. *Child Development, 37,* 499–506.

Barker, G. K., & Rich, S. (1992). Influences on adolescent sexuality in Nigeria and Kenya: Findings from recent focus-group discussions. *Studies in Family Planning, 23*(3), 199–210.

Barnouw, E., & Kirkland, C. (1989). Entertainment. In E. Barnouw (Ed.), *International encyclopedia of communications* (pp. 101–104). New York: Oxford University Press.

Barnum, H. J., Jr. (1975). Mass media and health communications. *Journal of Medical Education, 50,* 25–36.

Barron, J. (1993, November 9). There's nothing comic in subway strip's warning. *The New York Times,* pp. B1, B4.

Batra, N. D. (1982). *The hour of television: Critical approach.* Methuen, NJ: Scarecrow Press.

Bentley, E. (1967). *The life of drama.* New York: Atheneum.

Berelson, B., & Freedman, R. (1964). A study in fertility control. *Scientific American, 210*(5), 29–37.

Bernstein, C. (1990, December 24). The leisure empire. *Time*, 56–59.

Berrueta, M. (1986). *The soap opera as a reinforcer of social values*. Unpublished master's thesis, Iberoamericano University, Mexico City.

Bettelheim, B. (1977). *The uses of enchantment: The meaning and importance of fairy tales*. New York: Alfred Knopf.

Bettinghaus, E. P., & Cody, M. J. (1994). *Persuasive communication* (5th ed.). New York: Harcourt Brace.

Bhargava, S. (1987, April 30). Ramayan: Divine sensation. *India Today*, 170–171.

Bhasin, U., & Singhal, A. (1998). Participatory approaches to message design: 'Jeevan Saurabh,' a pioneering radio serial in India for adolescents. *Media Asia*, 25(1), 12–18.

Bhatia, S. (1988, February 4). An epic goes electronic and India gets hooked. *Far Eastern Economic Review*, 70–73.

Bineham, J. L. (1988). A historical account of the hypodermic model in mass communication. *Communication Monographs*, 55, 230–246.

Birdwhistell, R. (1952). *Introduction to kinesics*. Louisville, KY: University of Louisville Press.

Boal, A. (1985). *Theater of the oppressed*. New York: Theatre Communications Group.

Bogatz, G. A., & Ball, S. (1971). *The second year of Sesame Street: An evaluation*. Princeton: Educational Testing Service.

Bouman, M. P. A. (1989). Gezondheidsvoorlichting en amusement: Een strategie voor het bereiken van niet spontane informatezoekers. *Tijdschrift voor Gezondheidsbevordering*, 10(3), 113–130.

Bouman, M. P. A. (1997, May). *Health communication and television entertainment: Collaboration aspects*. Paper presented at the Second International Conference on Entertainment-Education and Social Change, Athens, Ohio.

Bouman, M. P. A. (1998). *The turtle and the peacock: Collaboration for prosocial change*. Wageningen, The Netherlands: Wageningen Agricultural University.

Bouman, M. P. A., & Wieberdink, E. (1993, May). Villa Borghese: A soap-series on heart health. *Canadian Journal of Cardiology*, 9, Supplement D.

Bouman, M. P. A., Mass, C., & Kok, G. (1998). Health education in television entertainment: A Dutch drama serial. *Health Education Research*, 13(4), 503–518.

Bradac, J. (Ed.). (1989). *Message effects in communication science*. Newbury Park, CA: Sage.

Bradac, J. J., Hopper, R., & Wiemann, J. M. (1989). Message effects: Retrospect and prospect. In J. Bradac (Ed.), *Message effects in communication science* (pp. 294–317). Newbury Park, CA: Sage.

Breed, W., & De Foe, J. R. (1982). Effecting media change: The role of cooperative consultation on alcohol topics. *Journal of Communication*, 32(2), 88–99.

Brown, L. (1978, January 28). 'Que Pasa, USA?' succeeds, cheaply. *Buffalo Courier Express*, 6.

Brown, W. J. (1988). Effects of *Hum Log*, a television soap opera, on pro-social beliefs in India. *Dissertation Abstracts International*, 50(01A), 20.

Brown, W. J. (1991). Prosocial effects of entertainment television in India. *Asian Journal of Communication*, 1(1), 113–135.

Brown, W. J. (1992a). Effects of entertainment television on development. *Howard Journal of Communications*, 3(4), 253–266.

Brown, W. J. (1992b). Socio-cultural influences of pro-development soap operas in the Third World. *Journal of Popular Film and Television*, 19, 157–164.

Brown, W. J., & Cody, M. J. (1991). Effects of pro-social television soap opera in promoting women's status. *Human Communication Research* 18(1), 114–142.

Brown, W. J., & Singhal, A. (1990). Ethical dilemmas of prosocial television. *Communication Quarterly*, 38(3), 268–280.

Brown, W. J., & Singhal, A. (1993a). Ethical considerations of promoting prosocial messages through the popular media. *Journal of Popular Film and Television*, 21, 92–99.

Brown, W. J., & Singhal, A. (1993b). Entertainment-education media: An opportunity for enhancing Japan's leadership role in Third World development. *Keio Communication Review, 15*, 81–101.

Brown, W. J., & Singhal, A. (1995). Influencing the character of entertainment television: Ethical dilemmas of pro-social programming. In D. E. Eberly (Ed.), *The content of America's character: Recovering civic virtue* (pp. 333–346). New York: Madison Books.

Brown, W. J., & Singhal, A. (1998). Ethical guidelines for promoting prosocial messages through the popular media. In G. Edgerton, M. T. Marsden, & J. Nachbar (Eds.), *In the eye of the beholder: Critical perspectives in popular film and television* (pp. 207–223). Bowling Green, OH: Bowling Green State University Popular Press.

Brown, W. J., Singhal, A., & Rogers, E. M. (1988). Pro-development soap operas: A novel approach to development communication. *Media Development, 4*, 43–47.

Browne, D. (1983). Media entertainment in the Western world. In L. J. Martin & A. G. Chaudhary (Eds.), *Comparative mass media systems* (pp. 187–208). New York: Longman.

Bryan, J. H., & Walbek, N. (1970). Preaching and practicing generosity: Children's actions and reactions. *Child Development, 3*, 329–353.

Bryant, J., & Zillmann, D. (Eds.). (1986). *Perspectives on media effects.* Hillsdale, NJ: Lawrence Erlbaum Associates.

Bryant, J., & Zillmann, D. (Eds.). (1994). *Media effects: Advances in theory and research.* Hillsdale, NJ: Lawrence Erlbaum Associates.

Buerkel-Rothfuss, N. L., & Mayes, S. (1981). Soap opera viewing: The cultivation effect. *Journal of Communication, 31*(3), 108–115.

Burke, K. (1950). *A grammar of motives.* Berkeley, CA: University of California Press.

Cambridge, V. (1989). *Mass media entertainment and human resources development: Radio serials in Jamaica from 1962.* Unpublished doctoral dissertation, Ohio University, School of Telecommunications, Athens.

Cambridge, V. (1992). Radio soap operas: The Jamaican experience 1958–1989. *Studies in Latin American Popular Culture, 2*, 93–109.

Cambridge, V., McLaughlin, E., & Rota, J. (1995, May). *Entertainment-education and the ethics of social intervention.* Paper presented at the International Communication Association, Albuquerque, New Mexico.

Campbell, J. (1971). *The essential Jung.* New York: Viking Penguin.

Campbell, J. (1988). *The power of myth.* New York: Doubleday.

Campesi, R. J. (1980). Gratifications of daytime TV serial viewers. *Journalism Quarterly, 57*, 155–158.

Cantor, M., & Pingree, S. (1983). *The soap opera.* Newbury Park, CA: Sage.

Carawan, G., & Carawan, C. (1965). *We shall overcome.* New York: Oak Publications.

Carberry, J. (1975, February 24). A stitch in time? Singer Co., resurgence stopped by recession, faces a critical period. *Wall Street Journal,* p. 1.

CASE (Community Agency for Social Inquiry). (1995). *Let the sky be the limit: Soul City evaluation report.* Johannesburg, South Africa: Jacana Education.

Cassata, M. B., & Skill, T. D. (1983). *Life on daytime television: Tuning-in American serial drama.* Norwood, NJ: Ablex.

Cassata, M. B., Skill, T. D., & Boadu, S. O. (1979). In sickness and in health. *Journal of Communication, 27*(3), 189–198.

Chaffee, S. H. (1986). Mass media and interpersonal channels: Competitive, convergent, or complementary. In G. Gumpert & R. Cathcart (Eds.), *Inter/media: Interpersonal communication in a media world* (3rd ed.). New York: Oxford University Press.

Chaffee, S. H. (1988). Differentiating the hypodermic model in mass communication. *Communication Monographs, 55*, 246–249.

Chesebro, J., & Glenn, J. (1982). The soap opera as a communication system. In G. Gumpert & R. Cathcart (Eds.), *Inter/media: Interpersonal communication in a media world* (2nd ed.). New York: Oxford University Press.

Children's Television Workshop. (1987). *Corporate profile*. New York: Children's Television Workshop.

Children's Television Workshop. (1988). *International adaptations of Sesame Street: Description and evaluation*. New York: Children's Television Workshop.

Children's Television Workshop (1998). Website: *http://www.ctw.org*

Church, C. A., & Geller, J. (1989). Lights! camera! action! Promoting family planning with TV, video, and film. *Population Reports, J-38*, Baltimore: Johns Hopkins University, Population Information Program.

Cohen, J., & Metzger, M. (1998). Social affiliation and the achievement of ontological security through interpersonal and mass communication. *Critical Studies in Mass Communication, 15*, 41–60.

Coleman, P. L. (1988). Enter-educate: New word from Johns Hopkins. *JOICEP Review*, 28–51.

Coleman, P. L., & Meyer, R. C. (Eds.). (1990). *Proceedings from the enter-educate conference: Entertainment for social change*. Baltimore: Johns Hopkins University, Population Communication Services.

Collins, W. A., & Getz, S. K. (1976). Children's social responses following modeled reactions to provocation: Pro-social effects of a television drama. *Journal of Personality, 44*, 488–500.

Comstock, G. (1977). Types of portrayal and aggressive behavior. *Journal of Communication, 27*(3), 189–198.

Comstock, G., Chaffee, S., Katzman, N., McCombs, M., & Roberts, D. (1978). *Television and human behavior*. New York: Columbia University Press.

Conway, J. C., & Rubin, A. M. (1991). Psychological predictors of television viewing motivation. *Communication Research, 18*, 443–463.

Cook, T. D., Appleton, H., Conner, R. F., Shaffer, A., Tamkin, G., & Weber, S. J. (1975). *Sesame Street revisited*. New York: Russell Sage Foundation.

Cooper, L. (1932). *The rhetoric of Aristotle*. New York: Appleton-Century Crofts.

Cooper-Chen, A. (1994). *Games in the global village*. Bowling Green, OH: Bowling Green State University Popular Press.

Day, L. A. (1991). *Ethics in media communications: Cases and controversies*. Belmont, CA: Wadsworth.

Dearing, J. W., & Rogers, E. M. (1996). *Agenda-setting*. Newbury Park, CA: Sage.

De Fossard, E. (1996). *How to write a radio serial drama for social development: A scriptwriter's manual*. Baltimore: Johns Hopkins University, Center for Communication Programs.

De-Goshie, J. (1986). *Mass media and national development: A content analysis of a Nigerian developmental television drama series—"Cock Crow at Dawn."* Unpublished doctoral dissertation, Ohio University, College of Communication, Athens.

DeJong, W., & Winsten, J. A. (1990). *The Harvard alcohol project: A demonstration project to promote the use of the "designated driver."* Cambridge, MA: Harvard School of Public Health, Harvard University.

Denisoff, R. S. (1983). *Sing a song of social significance*. Bowling Green, OH: Bowling Green State University Popular Press.

Dissanayake, W. (1977). New wine in old bottles: Can folk media convey modern messages. *Journal of Communication, 27*(2), 122–124.

Donnerstein, E. (1980). Pornography and violence against women. *Annals of the New York Academy of Sciences, 347*, 227–288.

Donnerstein, E. (1983). Erotica and human aggression. In R. Geen & E. Donnerstein (Eds.), *Aggression: Theoretical and empirical reviews*. New York: Academic Press.

Downing, M. (1974). Heroine of a daytime TV serial. *Journal of Communication, 24*(2), 130–137.

Dunaway, D. K. (1987). Music as political communication in the United States. In J. Lull (Ed.), *Popular music and communication* (pp. 36–52), Newbury Park, CA: Sage.

Engineer, S. (1992, February). *Hum Raahi*: The long road home. *TV & Video World*, 22–26.

Entwistle, B., Rindfuss, R. R., Gulkey, D. K., Chamratrithirong, A., Curran, S., & Sawangdee, Y. (1996). Community and contraceptive choice in rural Thailand: A case study in Nang Rong. *Demography*, *33*(3), 1–11.

Epskamp, K. P. (1985). Radio drama as a learning tool. *Gazette*, *35*, 145–156.

Estep, R., & MacDonald, P. T. (1985). Crime in the afternoon: Murder and robbery on soap operas. *Journal of Broadcasting & Electronic Media*, *29*(3), 323–331.

Evans, R. I. (1980). *The making of social psychology*. New York: Gardener Press.

Federman, J. (1998). *National television violence study (Volume 3): Executive summary*. Santa Barbara, CA: University of California, Center for Communication and Social Policy.

Finke, N. (1988, November 25). TV series join crusade to curb drunk driving. *Los Angeles Times*, p. A-11.

Fischer, H., & Melnik, S. R. (Eds.). (1979). *Entertainment: A cross-cultural examination*. New York: Hastings House Publishers.

Fishbein, M., & Ajzen, I. (1975). *Belief, attitude, intention and behavior*. Reading, MA: Addison-Wesley.

Fiske, J. (1987). *Television culture*. New York: Methuen.

Fiske, J., & Hartley, J. (1978). *Reading television*. London: Methuen.

Food and Agriculture Organization (1987). *"The Archers"—an everyday story of country folk*. Rome: Food and Agriculture Organization.

Fraser, B. P., & Brown, W. J. (1997, May). *The diffusion of Superbook: One of the world's most popular entertainment-education television series*. Paper presented at the International Communication Association, Montreal, Canada.

Gans, H. (1975). *Popular culture and high culture: An analysis and evaluation of taste*. New York: Basic Books.

Gans, H. J. (1977). Audience mail: Letters to an anchorman, *Journal of Communication*, *27*(3), 86–91.

Garavito, H. (1989). Simplemente Saby: Veinte anos despues del gran exito. *Revelacíon*, 8–9.

Gargan, E. A. (1996, August 27). Mere soap opera? It's Mexican magic (in Tagalog). *The New York Times*, p. 4A.

Gecas, V. (1989). The social psychology of self-efficacy. *Annual Review of Sociology*, *15*, 291–316.

Geddes-Gonzalez, H. (1992). Articulating narrative strategies: The Peruvian telenovelas. In A. Fadul (Ed.), *Serial fiction in TV: The Latin American telenovelas* (pp. 47–60). São Paulo: University of São Paulo, School of Communication and Arts.

Gelman, M. (1989, April 17). Drunk driving TV campaign a success. *Variety*, 7.

George, A. (1990, June). *The trickster character in development soap operas: Hero or villain?* Paper presented to the International Communication Association, Dublin, Ireland.

Goldsten, R. K. (1975). Throwaway husbands, wives, and lovers. *Human Behavior*, *4*, 64–69.

Goulet, D. (1995). *Development ethics: A guide to theory and practice*. New York: Apex Press.

Graham, R. (1988). *The Da Capo Guide to Contemporary African Music*. New York: De Capo Press.

Grant, A. E., Guthrie, K. K., & Ball-Rokeach, S. J. (1991). Television shopping: A media system dependency perspective. *Communication Research*, *18*, 773–798.

Greenberg, B. S., Abelman, R., & Neuendorf, K. (1981). Sex on the soap operas: Afternoon delight. *Journal of Communication*, *31*(3), 83–89.

Greenberg, B. S., & Busselle, R. W. (1996). Soap operas and sexual activity: A decade later. *Journal of Communication*, *46*(4), 153–160.

Greenberg, B. S., & D'Alessio, D. (1985). Quantity and quality of sex in the soaps. *Journal of Broadcasting & Electronic Media*, *29*(3), 309–321.

Griswold, F. (1918). *Hindu fairy tales: Retold for children.* Boston: Lothrop, Lee, & Shepard Company.

Gudykunst, W. B., & Kim, Y. Y. (1984). *Communicating with strangers.* Reading, MA: Addison-Wesley.

Gumpert, G., & Cathcart, R. (Eds.). (1986). *Inter/Media: Interpersonal communication in a mass media world* (3rd ed.). New York: Oxford University Press.

Gunther, B. (1984). Television as a facilitator of good behavior amongst children. *Journal of Moral Education, 13,* 69–77.

Hall, E. T. (1966). *The hidden dimension.* New York: Random House.

Harrison, R. (1981). *The cartoon: Communication to the quick.* Newbury Park, CA: Sage.

Hazzard, M., & Cambridge, V. (1988). *Socio-drama as an applied technique for development communication in the Caribbean: Specialized content and narrative structure in the radio drama of Elaine Perkins in Jamaica.* Paper presented at the Caribbean and Latin American Studies Conference, Guadelupe, French West Indies.

Heath, S., & Skirrow, G. (1986). An interview with Raymond Williams. In T. Modleski (Ed.), *Studies in entertainment* (pp. 3–17). Bloomington, IN: Indiana University Press.

Henrich, D. J. (1997). AD2000. *Religious Broadcasting, 29*(2), 92.

Herzog, H. (1944). Daytime serials. In P. F. Lazarsfeld & F. Stanton (Eds.), *Radio Research 1942–43.* New York: Duell, Sloan and Pearce.

Hill, H. (1993). The widow's revenge. *Africa Report, 38*(2), 64–66.

Himmelweit, H. T., Swift, B., & Jaeger, M. E. (1980). The audience as critic: A conceptual analysis of television entertainment. In Percy H. Tannenbaum (Ed.), *The entertainment functions of television* (pp. 67–106). Hillsdale, NJ: Lawrence Erlbaum Associates.

Horton, D., & Wohl, R. R. (1956). Mass communication and para-social interaction: Observation on intimacy at a distance. *Psychiatry, 19*(3), 215–229.

Houlberg, R. (1984). Local television news audience and the parasocial interaction. *Journal of Broadcasting, 28,* 423–429.

Hovland, C., Lumsdaine, A., & Sheffield F. (1949). *Experiments on mass communication.* Princeton. NJ: Princeton University Press.

Huizinga, J. (1950). *Homo ludens.* Boston: Beacon Press.

Hurr, K. K., & Robinson, J. P. (1978). The social impact of 'Roots.' *Journalism Quarterly, 55,* 19–24.

Jain, M. (1985, April 14–20). Be Indian, see Indian. *Sunday,* 24–27.

James, B. (1992, July 18–19). BBC cancels Archers' visa for Europe. *International Herald Tribune,* p. 4.

Japhet, G., & Goldstein, S. (1997a, May 7). *The Soul City experience in South Africa.* Audiotape recording of presentation made at the Second International Conference on Entertainment-Education and Social Change, Athens, Ohio. Columbus, OH: RoSu Productions.

Japhet, G., & Goldstein, S. (1997b). Soul City experience. *Integration, 53,* 10–11.

Joffee, L. (1990, April 16). Teenage star light London stage. *The Christian Science Monitor,* p. 13.

Johns Hopkins University Center for Communication Programs. (1998). *A report on the second international conference on entertainment–education and social change.* Baltimore, MD: Johns Hopkins University Center for Communication Programs.

Jory, T. (1978, January 31). Bilingual barrier falls in Que Pasa? *Los Angeles Times,* p. 11.

Jung, C. G. (1958). *Psychology and religion.* Translated by R. F. C. Hall. New York: Pantheon Books.

Jung, C. G. (1970). *Archetypes and the collective unconscious.* Buenos Aires: Ed. Paidos.

Kalwachwala, D., & Joshi, H. (1990). *Nari tu Narayani: A retrospective look.* Space Application Center, Ahmedabad: Development and Education Communication Unit.

Katz, E., Blumler, J. G., & Gurevitch, M. (1974). Utilization of mass communication by the individual. In J. G. Blumler & E. Katz (Eds.), *The uses of mass communications* (pp. 19–32), Newbury Park: Sage.

Katz, E., Gurevitch, M., & Haas, H. (1973). On the use of mass media for important things. *American Psychological Review, 38,* 164–181.

Katz, E., & Lazarsfeld, P. F. (1955). *Personal influence: The part played by people in the flow of mass communications.* New York: Free Press.

Katz, E., Liebes, T., & Berko, L. (1992). On commuting between television fiction and real life. *Quarterly Review of Film and Video, 14,* 157–178.

Kincaid, D. L., Coleman, P. L., Rimon II, J. G., & Silayan-Go, A. (1991). *The Philippines multimedia campaign for young people project: Summary of evaluation results.* Paper presented to the American Public Health Association.

Kincaid, D. L., Jara, R. Coleman, P., & Segura, F. (1988). *Getting the message: The communication for young people project.* Washington, DC: U.S. Agency for International Development, AID Evaluation Special Study 56.

Kincaid, D. L., Rimon II, J. G., Piotrow, P. T., & Coleman, P. L. (1992, April–May). *The enter-educate approach: Using entertainment to change health behavior.* Paper presented to the Population Association of America, Denver, CO.

Kincaid, D. L., Yun, S. H., Piotrow, P. T., & Yaser, Y. (1993). Turkey's mass media family planning campaign. In T. E. Backer & E. M. Rogers (Eds.), *Organizational aspects of health communication campaigns: What works?* (pp. 68–92). Newbury Park, CA: Sage.

Klapper, J. T. (1960). *The effects of mass communication.* New York: Free Press.

Kohler, H. (1997). Learning in social networks and contraceptive choice. *Demography, 34*(3), 369–383.

Kotler, P., & Zaltman, G. (1971). Social marketing: An approach to planned social change. *Journal of Marketing, 35:* 3–12.

Kotler, P., & Roberto, E. L. (1989). *Social marketing: Strategies for changing public behavior.* New York: Free Press.

Kottak, C. (1991). Television's impact on values and local life in Brazil. *Journal of Communication, 41,* 70–87.

Kristof, N. D. (1990, March 26). A Mongolian rock group fosters democracy. *The New York Times,* p. B-1.

Kunkel, D., Cope, K. M., Colvin, C. (1998, July). *Sexual messages in "family hour" television.* Paper presented at the International Communication Association, Jerusalem, Israel.

Law, S., & Singhal, A. (1998, July). *Efficacious dimensions in the communication of letter-writers to an entertainment-education radio soap opera.* Paper presented at the International Communication Association, Jerusalem, Israel.

Leifer, A. D., Gordon, N. J., & Graves, S. B. (1974). Children's television: More than just entertainment. *Harvard Educational Review, 44,* 213–245.

Lent, J. A. (1995). Comic and cartoons: They are more than just pow! wham! or ha! ha! *The Journal of Development Communication, 6*(2), 1–15.

Lesser, G. S. (1974). *Children and television: Lessons from Sesame Street.* New York: Vintage.

Lettenmaier, C., Krenn, S., Morgan, W., Kols, A., & Piotrow, P. (1993). Africa: Using radio soap operas to promote family planning. *Hygie, 12*(1), 5–10.

Levy, M. R. (1979). Watching TV news as para-social interaction. *Journal of Broadcasting, 23,* 69–80.

Lieberman, D. A. (1997). Interactive video games for health promotion: Effects on knowledge, self-efficacy, social support, and health. In R. L. Street, W. R. Gold, & T. Manning (Eds.), *Health promotion and interactive technology: Theoretical applications and future directions.* Mahwah, NJ: Lawrence Erlbaum Associates.

Lieberman, D. A. (1998, July). *Health education video games for children and adolescents: Theory, design, and research findings.* Paper presented at the International Communication Association, Jerusalem, Israel.

Liebert, R. M., Neale, J. M., & Davidson, E. S. (1973). *The early window: Effects of television on children and youth*. New York: Pergamon.

Livingstone, S. M. (1990). Interpreting a narrative: How different viewers see a story. *Journal of Communication, 40*(1), 72–83.

Long, M. C. (1978). Television: Help or hindrance to health education. *Health Education, 9*(3), 32–34.

Lovelace, V. O., & Huston, A. C. (1982). Can television teach prosocial behavior. *Health Education, 9*(3), 32–34.

Lowry, D. T., Love, G., & Kirby, M. (1981). Sex on the soap operas: Patterns of intimacy. *Journal of Communication, 31*(3), 90–96.

Lowry, D. T., & Towles, D. E. (1989). Soap opera portrayals of sex, contraception, and sexually transmitted diseases. *Journal of Communication, 39*(2), 77–83.

Lozano, E. (1992). The force of myth of popular narratives: The case of melodramatic serials. *Communication Theory, 2*(3), 207–220.

Lozano, E., & Singhal, A. (1993). Melodramatic television serials: Mythical narratives for education. *Communications: The European Journal of Communication, 18*(1), 115–127.

Lull, J. (Ed.). (1992). *Popular music and communication* (2nd ed.). Newbury Park, CA: Sage.

Luthra, R. (1994). A case of problematic dillusion: The use of sex determination techniques in India. *Knowledge, 15*(3), 259–272.

MacLean, P. D. (1973). *A triune concept of the brain and behavior*. Toronto, Canada: University of Toronto Press.

Maggs, J. (1990, November 20). Comic book spread anti-import message. *The Journal of Commerce,* 1 & 3A.

Maibach, E., & Murphy, D. A. (1995). Self-efficacy in health promotion research and practice: Conceptualization and measurement. *Health Education Research, 10*(1), 37–50.

Malwade-Rangarajan, A. (1991). *Television and social identities: Audience interpretations of 'Hum Log,' an Indian soap opera*. Paper presented at the Fourth International Television Studies Conference, London.

Malwade-Rangarajan, A. (1992). *Television and social identity: Audience interpretations of 'Hum Log.'* Unpublished doctoral dissertation, Pennsylvania State University, School of Communications, State College.

Matelski, M. J. (1988). *The soap opera evolution: America's enduring romance with daytime drama*. Jefferson, NC: McFarland & Company.

Mazrui, A., & Kitsao, J. (1988, June). *A formative survey of Ushikwapo Shikimana*. Nairobi, Kenya: National Council for Population and Development.

McAnany, E. G. (1993). The telenovela and social change: Popular culture, public policy, and communication theory. In A. Fadul (Ed.), *Serial fiction in TV: The Latin American telenovelas* (pp. 135–147). São Paulo: University of São Paulo, School of Communication and Arts.

McGuire, B., & LeRoy, D. J. (1977). Audience mail: Letters to a broadcaster. *Journal of Communication, 27* (3), 79–85.

McGuire, W. (1981). Theoretical foundations of campaigns. In R. E. Rice & W. Paisley (Eds.), *Public communication campaigns* (pp. 43–65). Newbury Park, CA: Sage.

Medved, M. (1992). *Hollywood versus America: popular culture and the war on traditional values*. New York: Harper Collin Publishers.

Melkote, S. R. (1991). *Communication for development in the third world: Theory and practice*. Newbury Park, CA: Sage.

Mendelsohn, H. (1966). *Mass entertainment*. New Haven, CT: College and University Press.

Mendelsohn, H. (1969, December). What to say to whom in social amelioration programming. *Educational Broadcasting Review,* 19–26.

Mendelsohn, H. (1971, October). '*Canción de la Raza*' evaluated. *Educational Broadcasting Review,* 45–53.

Mendelsohn, H., Espic, T., & Rogers, G. (1968). Operation Gap-Stop: A study of the application of mass communication technique in reaching the unreachable poor. *Television Quarterly*, Summer, 56–67.

Mendelsohn, H., & Spetnagel, H. T. (1980). Entertainment as a sociological enterprise. In Percy H. Tannenbaum, (Ed.), *The entertainment functions of television* (pp. 13–29). Hillsdale, NJ: Lawrence Erlbaum Associates.

Menon, R. (1993, September 30). Street plays: Drumming for literacy. *India Today*, p. 93.

Merton, R. K., Fiske, M., & Curtis, A. (1971). *Mass persuasion: The social psychology of a war bond drive*. Westport, CT: Greenwood Press.

Mielke, K. W., & Swinehart, J. W. (1976). *Evaluation of the "Feeling Good" television series*. New York: Children's Television Workshop.

Miller, R. (1993, March 25). Sitcoms get serious, tackle serious issues. *The Miami Herald*, pp. 5–6F.

Ministry of Health (1995). *The green star: Lighting the way with lessons learned*. Dar-es-Salaam, Tanzania: Tanzania Family Planning Communication Project. 1991–1994, MOH/HED/FPU-JHU/PCS/PIP: Funded by USAID.

Modleski, T. (1984). *Living with a vengeance: Mass-produced fantasies for women*. New York: Methuen.

Modleski, T. (Ed.). (1986). *Studies in entertainment: Critical approaches to mass culture*. Bloomington, IN: Indiana University Press.

Mody, B. (1986). The receivers as sender: Formative evaluation in Jamaican radio, *Gazette, 38*, 147–160.

Mody, B. (1991). *Designing messages for development communication*. Newbury Park, CA: Sage.

Monaghan, P. (1991, October 23). Alaska professors' comic book helps students in junior high schools grasp economic history. *The Chronicle of Higher Education*, pp. A13–15.

Montgomery, K. C. (1989). *Target: Prime time*. New York: Oxford University Press.

Montogomery, K. C. (1993). The Harvard Alcohol Project: Promoting the designated driver on television. In T. E. Backer & E. M. Rogers (Eds.), *Organizational aspects of health communication campaigns: What works?* (pp. 178–202). Newbury Park, CA: Sage.

Montgomery, M. R., & Casterline, J. B. (1993). The diffusion of fertility control in Taiwan: Evidence from pooled cross-section time-series models. *Population Studies, 47*, 457–479.

Mowlana, H., & Rad, M. H. (1992). International flow of Japanese television programs: The 'Oshin' phenomenon. *Keio Communication Review, 14*, 51–68.

Muchiri, F. (1989, May 18). They must return '*Tushauriane*' to us. *Kenya Times*, p. 3A.

Murdock, G. (1980). Radical drama, radical theater. *Media, Culture, & Society, 2*, 151–168.

Muroki, F. (1989, May 25). '*Tushauriane*': Now actor speaks out. *Standard* (Nairobi, Kenya), p. 3E.

Nariman, H. (1993). *Soap operas for social change*. Westport, CT: Praeger.

Noble, G. (1975). *Children in front of the small screen*. Newbury Park, CA: Sage.

Nordlund, J. (1978). Media interaction. *Communication Research, 5*, 150–175.

O'Connor, J. J. (1990). Cartoons teach children, but is the lesson good? *The New York Times*, p. B-1.

Odindo, J. (1987, May 11). Local soap opera sets new standards. *Daily Nation* (Kenya), p. 1.

Palmer, E. L. (1988). *Television & America's children: A crisis of neglect*. New York: Oxford University Press.

Papa, M. J., Auwal, M. A., & Singhal, A. (1995). Dialectic of control and emancipation in organizing for social change: A multitheoretic study of the Grameen Bank in Bangladesh. *Communication Theory, 5*, 189–223.

Papa, M. J., Singhal, A., Law, S., Sood, S., Rogers, E. M., & Shefner-Rogers, C. L. (1998, July). *Entertainment-education and social change: An analysis of parasocial interaction, social learning, and paradoxical communication.* Paper presented at the International Communication Association, Jerusalem, Israel.

Parikh, M. (1990). Sex-selective abortions in India: Parental choice or sexist discrimination. *Feminist Issues, 10*(2), 19–32.

Parmar, S. (1975). *Traditional folk media in India.* New Delhi: Geka Books.

Parmar, S. (1979). Traditional folk forms in India and their use in national development. In H. Fishcer & S. Melnik (Eds.), *Entertainment: A cross-cultural examination* (pp. 74–82). New York: Hastings House Publishers.

Pekerti, R., & Musa, R. (1989, October). Wait a while my love—An Indonesian popular song with a family planning message. *JOICFP Integration, 21,* 41–43.

Perse, E. M., & Rubin, A. (1987). Audience activity and soap opera involvement: A uses and effects investigation. *Human Communication Research, 14,* 247–268.

Perse, E. M., & Rubin, R. B. (1989). Attribution in social and parasocial relationships. *Communication Research, 16,* 59–77.

Petty, R., & Cacioppo, J. (1981). *Attitudes and persuasion: Classic and contemporary approaches.* Dubuque, IA: Wm. C. Brown.

Phillips, D. P. (1982). The behavioral impact of violence in the mass media: A review of evidence from laboratory and non-laboratory investigations. *Sociology and Social Research, 66,* 386–398.

Piaget, J. (1952). *The origins of intelligence in children.* New York: International Universities Press.

Piotrow, P. T. (1990). Principles of good health communication. In P. L. Coleman & R. C. Meyer (Eds.), *Proceedings from the enter-educate conference: Entertainment for social change* (pp. 13–14). Baltimore: Johns Hopkins University, Population Communication Services.

Piotrow, P. T. (1994, March). Entertainment-education: An idea whose time has come. *Population Today,* 4–5.

Piotrow, P. T., Kincaid, D. L., Rimon II, J., & Rinehart, W. (1997). *Health communication: Lessons from family planning and reproductive health,* Westport, CT: Praeger.

Piotrow, P. T., Meyer, R. C., & Zulu, B. A. (1992). AIDS and mass persuasion. In J. Mann, D. J. M. Tarantola, & T. W. Netter (Eds.), *AIDS in the World* (pp. 733–759). Cambridge, MA: Harvard University Press.

Piotrow, P. T., & Rimon II, J. G. (1988). New directions in family planning communication: 12 predictions for the 1990s. *Asia-Pacific Population Journal, 3*(4), 17–32.

Piotrow, P. T., Rimon II, J. G., Winnard, K., Kincaid, D. L., Huntington, D., & Convisser, J. (1990). Mass media family planning promotion in three Nigerian cities. *Studies in Family Planning, 21*(5), 265–273.

Population Reports. (1986). *Radio spreading the word in family planning,* J(32), pp. 853–887.

Postman, N. (1985). *Amusing ourselves to death.* New York: Viking.

Potter, J. E., Assunção, R. M., Cavenaghi, S. M., & Caetano, A. J. (1998). *The spread of television and fertility decline in Brazil: A spatial temporal analysis.* In National Research Council's Committee on Population (Eds.), *Social processes underlying fertility change in developing countries* (pp. 79–93). Washington, DC: National Research Council.

Prasad, P. (1986, January 13). Ashok Kumar: T.V.'s agony uncle. *Star & Style,* pp. 34–38.

Prochaska, J. O., DiClemente, C. C., & Norcross, J. C. (1992). In search of how people change: Applications to addictive behavior. *American Psychologist, 47,* 1102–1114.

Quiroz, M. T. (1992). La telenovela en el Peru. In A. Fadul (Ed.), *Serial fiction in TV: The Latin American telenovelas* (pp. 33–46). São Paulo: University of São Paulo, School of Communication and Arts.

Quiroz, M. T. (1993). *Historia y conditiones de produciones de la telenovela Peruana.* Nexus: Coleccíon Interfacultades.

Quiroz, M. T., & Cano, A. (1988). Antecedentes y condiciones de la producaoa de telenovelas en Peru. *Estudios Sobre las Culturas Contemporaneas, 2*(4), 128–159.

Ram, A. (1993). *Women as sign: A semiotic analysis of gender portrayal in Hum Raahi.* Unpublished master's thesis, Ohio University, School of Interpersonal Communication, Athens.

Reckert, C. M. (1970, February 13). Singer Co. sets profit record; Northwest industries net dips. *The New York Times,* p. 53.

Regís, A., & Butler, P. (1997). *A summary report of RARE Center's family planning initiative for St. Lucia.* St. Lucia: Rare Center for Tropical Conservation, Report 6.

Reinarman, C. (1988). The social construction of an alcohol problem: The case of mothers against drunk drivers and social control in the 1980s. *Theory and Society, 17,* 91–120.

Resnick, H. (Ed.). (1990). *Youth and drugs: Society's mixed messages.* Rockville, MD: Office for Substance Abuse Prevention.

Rice, R. E., & Atkin, C. (Eds.). (1989). *Public communication campaigns* (2nd ed.). Newbury Park, CA: Sage.

Rimon, J. G., II. (1989, December). Leveraging messages and corporations: The Philippine experience. *Integration, 22,* 37–44.

Rimon, J. G., II. (1990). Sing and the world sings with you. *Development Communication Report, 71,* 7–8.

Risopatron, F., & Spain, P. L. (1980). Reaching the poor: Human sexuality education in Costa Rica. *Journal of Communication, 30,* 81–89.

Roe, K. (1987). The school and music in adult socialization. In J. Lull (Ed.), *Popular Music and Communication* (pp. 212–230). Newbury Park, CA: Sage.

Rogers, E. M. (1973). *Communication strategies for family planning.* New York: Free Press.

Rogers, E. M. (1976). Communication and development: The passing of the dominant paradigm. In E. M. Rogers (Ed.), *Communication and development: Critical perspectives.* Newbury Park, CA: Sage.

Rogers, E. M. (1986). *Communication technology.* New York: Free Press.

Rogers, E. M. (1995). *Diffusion of innovations* (4th ed.). New York: Free Press.

Rogers, E. M. (1997). When the mass media have strong effects: Intermedia processes. In J. Trent (Ed.), *Communication: Views from the helm for the twenty-first century* (pp. 125–137). Boston: Allyn & Bacon.

Rogers, E. M., Aikat, S., Chang, S., Poppe, P., & Sopory, P. (1989). *Proceedings from the conference on entertainment-education for social change.* Los Angeles, CA: University of Southern California, Annenberg School for Communication.

Rogers, E. M., & Antola, L. (1985). *Telenovelas* in Latin America: A success story. *Journal of Communication, 35,* 24–35.

Rogers, E. M., Hirata, T. M., Chandran, A. S., & Robinson, J. D. (1994). Television promotion of gender equality in societies. In P. S. Kalbfleisch & M. J. Cody (Eds.), *Gender, power, and communication in human relationships* (pp. 277–304). Hillsdale, NJ: Lawrence Erlbaum Associates.

Rogers, E. M., & Singhal, A. (1989). Estrategias de educacion entretenimiento. *Chasqui, 31,* 9–22.

Rogers, E. M., & Singhal, A. (1990). Mass communication and public health: The academic perspective. In C. Atkins & E. Arkin (Eds.), *Mass communication and public health* (pp. 176–181). Newbury Park, CA: Sage.

Rogers, E. M., & Steinfatt, T. M. (1999). *Intercultural communication.* Prospect Heights, IL: Waveland Press.

Rogers, E. M., & Storey, D. (1987). Communication campaigns. In C. Berger and S. Chafee (Eds.), *Handbook of Communication Sciences* (pp. 817–846). Newbury Park, CA, Sage.

Rogers, E. M., Vaughan, P. W., Swalehe, R. M. A., Rao, N., Svenkerud, P., Sood, S., & Alford, K. L. (1997). *Effects of an entertainment-education radio soap opera on family planning and HIV/AIDS prevention behavior in Tanzania.* Albuquerque, NM: University of New Mexico, Department of Communication and Journalism.

Rogers, E. M., Vaughan, P. W., Swalehe, R. M. A., Rao, N., Svenkerud, P., Sood, S., & Alford, K. L. (1998). *Effects of an entertainment-education radio soap opera on family planning in Tanzania.* Unpublished paper, University of New Mexico, Department of Communication and Journalism, Albuquerque.

Rosero-Bixby, L., & Casterline, J. B. (1993). Modeling diffusion effects in fertility transition. *Population Studies, 47,* 147–167.

Rosero-Bixby, L., & Casterline, J. B. (1994). Interaction diffusion and fertility transition in Costa Rica. *Social Forces, 73 (2):* 435–462.

Rota, J., & Tremmel, D. (1989, October). *The relationship between television use and national/cultural identity among urban children in Yucatan.* Paper presented to Culture and Communication Conference, Institute of Culture and Communication, Temple University, Philadelphia.

Rubin, A. M., & Perse, E. M. (1987). Audience activity and soap opera involvement: A uses and effects investigation. *Human Communication Research, 14,* 246–268.

Rubin, A. M., Perse, E. M., & Powell, R. A. (1985). Loneliness, parasocial interaction, and local television news viewing. *Human Communication Research, 12,* 155–180.

Rubin, A. M., & Rubin, R. C. (1985). Interface of personal and mediated communication: A research agenda. *Critical Studies in Mass Communication, 2,* 36–53.

Rubin, R. C., & McHugh, M. P. (1987). Development of parasocial interaction relationships. *Journal of Broadcasting & Electronic Media, 31,* 279–292.

Rushton, J. P. (1975). Generosity in children: Immediate and long-term effects of modeling, preaching, and moral judgment. *Journal of Personality and Social Psychology, 31,* 459–466.

Rushton, J. P. (1976). Socialization and the altruistic behavior of children. *Psychological Bulletin, 83,* 898–913.

Rushton, J. P. (1982). Television and prosocial behavior. In D. Pearl, L. Bouthilet, & J. Lazar (Eds.), *Television and behavior: Ten years of scientific progress and implications for the eighties* (Volume 2, pp. 248–258). Bethesda, MD: National Institute of Mental Health.

Rutenberg, N., & Watkins, S. C. (1997). The buzz outside the clinics: Conversations and contraception in Nyanza Province, Kenya. *Studies in Family Planning, 28*(4), 290–307.

Ryder, A. W. (1949). *The Panchtantra.* Translated from Sanskrit. New Delhi: Jaico Publishing House.

Sabido, M. (1989, March–April). *Soap operas in Mexico.* Paper presented at the Entertainment for Social Change Conference, Los Angeles, University of Southern California, Annenberg School for Communication.

Salmon, C. (Ed.). (1989). *Information campaigns: Balancing social values and social change.* Newbury Park, CA: Sage.

Schramm, W. (1977). *Big media little media.* Paris: UNESCO.

Schubert, J. (1988). Family planning uses traditional theater in Mali. *Development Communication Report, 2*(61), 1–16.

Schwarzer, R. (1992). Self-efficacy in the adoption and maintenance of health behaviors: Theoretical approaches and a new model. In R. Schwarzer (Ed.), *Self-efficacy: Thought control of action* (pp. 217–243). Washington, DC: Hemisphere.

Sera presentada en la TV Venezolana "Simplemente María," en versión local. (1970, January 10). *El Comercio,* p. 1.

Shannon, C. E., & Weaver, W. (1949). *The mathematical theory of communication.* Urbana, IL: University of Illinois Press.

Shefner-Rogers, C. L., Rao, N., Rogers, E. M., & Wayangankar, A. (1998). The empowerment of women dairy farmers in India. *Journal of Applied Communication Research, 26*(3), 319–337.

Shefner-Rogers, C. L., & Rogers, E. M. (1997, May). *Evolution of the entertainment-education strategy.* Paper presented at the Second International Conference on Entertainment-Education and Social Change, Athens, Ohio.

Shefner-Rogers, C. L., Rogers, E. M., & Singhal, A. (1998). Parasocial interaction with the television soap operas '*Simplemente María*' and '*Oshin.*' *Keio Communication Review, 20,* 3–18.

Shefner, C. L., Valente, T. W., & Bardini, T. (1993, May). *Fakube Jarra says entertainment-education works: Using radio drama to promote family planning in the Gambia.* Paper presented at the International Communication Association, Washington, DC.

Sherry, J. (1997). Prosocial soap operas for development: A review of research and theory. *Journal of International Communication, 4*(2), 75–101.

Silayan-Go, A. (1990). Entertainment for change and development: Will it work? In P. L. Coleman & R. C. Meyer (Eds.), *The enter-educate conference: Entertainment for social change* (p. 24). Baltimore: Johns Hopkins University, Center for Communication Programs.

Simplemente absurdo. (1970, February 22). *El Comercio,* p. 1.

"*Simplemente María*" se acabo. (1971, January 9). *Comercio Grafico,* p. 1.

Simplemente María promote tener gran exito en el pais. (1969, April 2). *El Comercio,* p. 1.

Singh, S., & Virtti, M. (1986, January). We'll miss you '*Hum Log*'. *The Sun,* pp. 5–8.

Singhal, A. (1988). *Pro-social observational learning from television soap opera models.* Unpublished manuscript, University of Southern California, Annenberg School for Communication, Los Angeles.

Singhal, A. (1990). *Entertainment-educational communication strategies for development.* Unpublished doctoral dissertation, University of Southern California, Los Angeles.

Singhal, A., & Brown, W. J. (1996). The entertainment-education communication strategy: Past struggles, present status, future agenda. *Jurnal Komunikasi, 12,* 19–36.

Singhal, A., Doshi, J. K., Rogers, E. M., & Rahman, S. A. (1988). The diffusion of television in India. *Media Asia, 15*(4), 222–229.

Singhal, A., Obregon, R., & Rogers, E. M. (1994). Reconstructing the story of "*Simplemente María*," the most popular telenovela in Latin America of all time. *Gazette, 54*(1), 1–15.

Singhal, A., & Rogers, E. M. (1988). Television soap operas for development in India. *Gazette, 41,* 109–126.

Singhal, A., & Rogers, E. M. (1989a). *India's information revolution.* New Delhi: Sage.

Singhal, A., & Rogers, E. M. (1989b). Educating through television. *Populi, 16*(2), 39–47.

Singhal, A., & Rogers, E. M. (1989c). Pro-social television for development in India. In R. E. Rice & C. Atkin (Eds.), *Public communication campaigns* (2nd ed., pp. 331–350). Newbury Park, CA: Sage.

Singhal, A., & Rogers, E. M. (1994). *Persuasion and planned social change.* In E. Bettinghaus & M. J. Cody (Eds.), *Persuasive communication* (5th ed., pp. 379–397). New York: Harcourt Brace.

Singhal, A., Rogers, E. M., & Brown, W. J. (1993). Harnessing the potential of entertainment-education *telenovelas. Gazette, 51,* 1–18.

Singhal, A., Rogers, E. M., & Cozzens, M. (1989, May). *The entertainment-education strategy for development: Effects of 'Hum Log,' a television soap opera in India.* Paper presented at the International Communication Association, San Francisco.

Singhal, A., Sood, S., Vaughan, P. W., Law, S., Rogers, E. M., Papa, M., & Pant, S. (1999). *Effects of an entertainment-education radio soap opera on status of women and family planning in India.* Athens, OH: Ohio University, School of Interpersonal Communication.

Singhal, A., & Svenkerud, P. (1994). Pro-socially shareable entertainment television programs: A programming alternative in developing countries. *Journal of Development Communication, 5*(2), 17–30.

Singhal, A., & Udornpim, K. (1997). Cultural shareability, archetypes, and television soaps: '*Oshindrome*' in Thailand. *Gazette, 59*(3), 171–188.

Smith, F. A. (1972). Health information during a week in television. *New England Journal of Medicine, 286,* 516–529.

Smith, M. L. (1975). The female domestic servant and social change: Lima, Peru. In R. Rohrlich-Leavitt (Ed.), *Women cross-culturally: Change and challenge* (pp. 163–179). Chicago: Mouton.

Smith, S. (1989). A film about teenage pregnancy. *World Health Forum, 10,* 350–354.

Sood, S., Law, S., & Singhal, A. (1998, April). *Audience effects of "Tinka Tinka Sukh," a radio soap opera in India.* Paper presented at a Workshop on the Social Use of Soap Operas, Mexico City, Mexico.

Sood, S., & Rogers, E. M. (1996, November). *Parasocial interaction by letter-writers to an entertainment-education soap opera in India.* Paper presented at the Speech Communication Association. San Diego, CA.

Sood, S., Singhal, A., & Law, S. (1997, May). *Analysis of educational themes and listeners' feedback to "Tinka Tinka Sukh," an entertainment-education radio soap opera in India.* Paper presented at the Second International Conference on Entertainment-Education and Social Change, Athens, Ohio.

Sprafkin, J. N., & Silverman, L. T. (1981). Update: Physically intimate and sexual behavior on prime-time television, 1978–79. *Journal of Communication, 31,* 45–59.

Stanley, A. (1994, March 20). Russians find their heroes in Mexican soap operas. *The New York Times,* pp. 1, 8.

Stephenson, W. (1967). *The play theory of mass communication.* Chicago: University of Chicago Press.

Stephenson, W. (1988). *The play theory of mass communication.* New Brunswick, NJ: Transaction Books.

Sthapitanonda-Sarabol, P., & Singhal, A. (1998). "Glocalizing" media products: Investigating the cultural shareability of the "Karate Kids" entertainment-education film in Thailand. *Media Asia, 25,* 170–175.

Stone, C. (1986). *First national survey on 'Naseberry Street' programme.* Unpublished manuscript, University of West Indies, Kingston, Jamaica.

Stone, C. (1988). *Second national survey on 'Naseberry Street' programme.* Unpublished manuscript, University of West Indies, Kingston, Jamaica.

Storey, D. (1995, May). *Entertainment-education, popular culture, and the sustainability of health communications: Lessons from Indonesia and Pakistan.* Paper presented at the International Communication Association Conference, Albuquerque, NM.

Storey, D. (1998). Discourse, popular culture and entertainment-education for sustainable health communication: Lessons learned from Pakistan and Indonesia. In T. Jacobson & J. Servaes (Eds.), *Theoretical approaches to participatory communication.* Cresskill, NJ: Hampton Press.

Straubhaar, J. (1991). Beyond media imperialism: Assymetrical interdependence and cultural proximity. *Critical Studies in Mass Communication, 8,* 39–59.

Sujan, D. K. (1993). Traditional folk media in rural development. In K. S. Nair & S. A. White (Eds.), *Perspectives on Development Communication* (pp. 172–176). New Delhi: Sage.

Sutherland, J. C., & Siniawsky, S. J. (1982). The treatment and resolution of moral violations on soap operas. *Journal of Communication, 32*(2), 67–74.

Svenkerud, P., Rahoi, R., & Singhal, A. (1995). Incorporating ambiguity and archetypes in entertainment-education programming: Lessons learned from "Oshin." *Gazette, 55,* 147–168.

Swalehe, R. M. A., Rogers, E. M., Gillboard, M. J., Alford, K., & Montoya, R. (1995). *A content analysis of the entertainment-education radio soap opera, "Twende na Wakati" (Let's Go with the Times) in Tanzania.* Albuquerque, NM: University of New Mexico, Department of Communication and Journalism.

Tan, A. (1985). *Mass communication theories and research.* New York: Macmillan.

Tan, A. S., & Tan, G. K. (1986). Television use and mental health. *Journalism Quarterly, 63*(1), 107–113.

Tannenbaum, P. H. (Ed.). (1980). *The entertainment functions of television.* Hillsdale, NJ: Lawrence Erlbaum Associates.

Tannenbaum, P. H., & Zillmann, D. (1975). Emotional arousal in the facilitation of aggression through communication. In L. Berkowitz (Ed.), *Advances in experimental social psychology* (pp. 149–192). New York: Free Press.

Tate, E., & Surlin, S. (1976). Agreement with opinionated TV characters across cultures. *Journalism Quarterly,* 199–203.

Televisa's Institute for Communication Research (1981a). *Toward the social use of soap operas.* Paper presented at the International Institute of Communication, Strasbourg, France.

Televisa's Institute for Communication Research (1981b). *Handbook for reinforcing social values through day-time T.V. serials.* Paper presented at the International Institute of Communication, Strasbourg, France.

Téllez, Rubén (1994). La radio y los procesos de integratíon de los migrantes a la cuidad. In R. M. Alfaro (Ed.), *Cultura de masa y cultura popular en la radio Peruana.* Lima: Tarea.

Thank you so much for your letters. Now shut up and listen. (1998, April 9). *The Guardian,* p. 23.

Thoman, E. (1989). Media education: Agenda for the 90s. *Media Ethics Update, 2*(1), 8–9.

Thomas, P. N. (1993). Alternative communications: Problems and prospects. *Media Asia, 20*(2), 63–65.

Tichenor, P. J., Donohue, G. A., & Olien, C. N. (1970). Mass media flow and the differential growth in knowledge. *Public Opinion Quarterly, 34,* 159–170.

Tuchman, G., Daniels, A. K., & Benet, J. (Eds.). (1978). *Hearth and home: Images of women in the mass media.* New York: Oxford University Press.

Turner, J. R. (1992). Parasocial interaction and *The Cosby Show:* A critical analysis. In C. Scodari & J. Thorpe (Eds.), *Media criticism: Journeys in interpretation* (pp. 126–132). Dubuque, IA: Kendall-Hunt.

Turner, J. R. (1993). Interpersonal and psychological predictors of parasocial interaction with different television performers. *Communication Quarterly, 41,* 443–453.

TV y no TV. (1970, January 2). *El Comercio,* p. 1.

Udornpim, K., & Singhal, A. (in press). Oshin, a pro-social media role model, in Thailand. *Keio Communication Review, 21.*

Ugboajah, F. O. (1980). *Communication policies in Nigeria.* Paris: UNESCO.

Ume-Nwagbo, Ebele N. E. (1986). 'Cock Crow at Dawn.' A Nigerian experiment with television drama in development-communication. *Gazette, 37,* 155–167.

Una novia radiante. (1970, January 25). *El Expreso,* p. 1.

United Nations (1987). *The prospects of world urbanization.* New York: United Nations.

Valente, T. W. (1997). On evaluating mass media impact. *Studies in Family Planning, 28*(2), 170–171.

Valente, T. W., & Bharath, U. (in press). An evaluation of the use of drama to communicate HIV/AIDS information. *AIDS Education and Prevention.*

Valente, T. W., Kim, Y. M., Lettenmaier, C., Glass, W., & Dibba, Y. (1994). Radio promotion of family planning in the Gambia. *International Family Planning Perspectives, 20,* 96–100.

Valente, T. W., Paredes, P., & Poppe, P. P. (1998). Matching the message to the process: The relative ordering of knowledge, attitudes, and practices in behavior change research. *Human Communication Research, 24*(3), 366–385.

Valente, T. W., Poppe, P. R., Alva, M. E., Briceño, R. V. de, & Cases, D. (1995). Street theater as a tool to reduce family planning misinformation. *International Quarterly of Community Health Education, 15*(3), 279–289.

Valente, T. W., Poppe, P. R., & Merritt, A. P. (1996). Mass-media-generated interpersonal communication as sources of information about family planning. *Journal of Health Communication, 1,* 247–265.

Valente, T. W., & Saba, W. P. (1998). Mass media and interpersonal influence in a reproductive health communication campaign in Bolivia. *Communication Research, 25,* 96–124.

Valente, T. W., Watkins, S. C., Jato, M. N., van der Straten, A., & Tsitol, L. P. M. (1997). Social network associations with contraceptive use among Cameroonian women in voluntary associations. *Social Science and Medicine, 45,* 677–687.

Van Erwen, E. (1987). Theater of liberation in action: The People's Theater Network of the Philippines. *New Theater Quarterly, 3*(10), 131–149.

Van Erwen, E. (1989). Plays, applause, and bullets. *The Drama Review,* Winter, 32–47.

Vasquez, J. (1970, February 15). *Un mar humano fue a la "Boda de María". El Expreso,* p. 1.

Vaughan, P. W. (1997). *'Apwe Plezi'*: Memo. Albuquerque, NM: University of New Mexico, Department of Communication and Journalism.

Vaughan, P. W. (1998, March). *Apwe Plezi: An entertainment-education radio soap opera to promote family planning and HIV/AIDS prevention in St. Lucia.* Paper presented at the International Conference on the Social Use of Commercial Television, Mexico City, Mexico.

Vaughan, P. W., & Rogers, E. M. (1996). *A communication model for the effects of an entertainment-education soap opera on the stages of family planning adoption.* Unpublished manuscript, University of New Mexico, Department of Communication and Journalism, Albuquerque.

Vaughan, P. W., & Rogers, E. M. (1997a, May), *A model of media effects on the adoption of family planning.* Paper presented at the Second International Conference on Entertainment-Education and Social Change, Athens, Ohio.

Vaughan, P. W., & Rogers, E. M. (1997b). *A communication model for the effects of an entertainment-education soap opera on the stages of family planning adoption.* Unpublished manuscript, University of New Mexico, Department of Communication and Journalism, Albuquerque.

Vidmar, N., & Rokeach, M. (1974). Archie Bunker's bigotry: A study in selective perception and exposure. *Journal of Communication, 24*(1), 36–47.

Vink, N. (1988). *The telenovela and emancipation: A study on television and social change in Brazil.* Amsterdam: Royal Tropical Institute.

Wallace, S. (1993). Evaluation of the BBC/HEA Health Show. *Health Education Journal, 52*(4), 221–226.

Wallack, L. (1990). Two approaches to health promotion in the mass media. *World Health Forum, 11,* 143–155.

Wander, P. (1977). On the meaning of 'Roots'. *Journal of Communication, 27*(4), 64–69.

Wang, B. (1935). Folksongs as regulators of politics. In A. Dundes (Ed.), *The study of folklore* (pp. 308–313). Englewood Cliffs, NJ: Prentice-Hall.

Wang, M., & Singhal, A. (1992), *Ke Wang,* a Chinese television soap opera with a message. *Gazette, 49*(3), 177–192.

Warburg, Philip (1988, July 21). Israel TV develops comedy about Arab–Jewish relations. *Los Angeles Times,* p. 11.

Weick, K. (1979). *The social psychology of organizing* (2nd ed.). Reading, MA: Addison-Wesley.

Whetmore, E. J., & Kielwasser, A. P. (1983). Soap opera audience speaks: A preliminary report. *Journal of American Culture, 6,* 110–115.

Wiebe, G. D. (1952). Merchandising commodities and citizenship on television. *Public Opinion Quarterly, 15,* 679–691.

Williams, F., Rice, R. E., & Rogers, E. M. (1988). *Research methods and the new media.* Newbury Park, CA: Sage.

Winsten, J. A. (1990). *The designated driver campaign.* Cambridge, MA: Harvard School of Public Health, Harvard University.

Wittink, R. D., & Hagenzieker, M. P. (1991). *Evaluation of three years 'Familie Oudenrijn' and the associated information policy.* Report No. R-91-11. Leidschendam, The Neteherlands: Institute for Road Safety Research.

World Radio & Television Receivers (1989). London: International Broadcasting and Audience Research Library, BBC.

WPBT (1978). Que Pasa, U.S.A.? Miami: WPBT2 Public Television.

Wray, R. (1991). *Taking stock of 'Consequences.'* Unpublished master's thesis, Cornell University, Department of Communication, Ithaca, NY.

Wright, L. (1991, May 20). King Lear's comeback. *Newsweek*, pp. 58–59.

Ximena, B., & Chaney, E. M. (1985). *Sellers and servants: Working women in Lima, Peru.* New York: Praeger.

Yin, R. K. (1984). *Case study research.* Newbury Park, CA: Sage.

Yoder, P. S., Hornik, R., & Chirwa, B. C. (1996). Evaluating the program effects of a radio drama about AIDS in Zambia. *Studies in Family Planning, 27,* 188–203.

Yount, J. W. (1996). *Differences in fertility goals within couples: Evidence from a family planning serial drama in Tanzania.* Unpublished master's thesis, University of Georgia, Athens.

Zillmann, D., & Bryant, J. (1982). Pornography, sexual callousness, and the trivialization of rape. *Journal of Communication, 32*(4), 10–21.

Name Index

Subject Index